EXCEL® BASICS
Foundations · Formulas · Graphs

Jeffrey Hsu, Ph.D.
Silberman College of Business
Fairleigh Dickinson University

Gary Bronson, Ph.D.
Silberman College of Business
Fairleigh Dickinson University

MERCURY LEARNING AND INFORMATION
Dulles, Virginia
Boston, Massachusetts
New Delhi

Publisher: David Pallai
MERCURY LEARNING AND INFORMATION
22841 Quicksilver Drive
Dulles, VA 20166
info@merclearning.com
www.merclearning.com
1-800-232-0223

J. Hsu and G. Bronson. *Excel® Basics.*
ISBN: 978-1-68392-772-3

Excel® is a registered trademark of Microsoft Corporation.

The publisher recognizes and respects all marks used by companies, manufacturers, and developers as a means to distinguish their products. All brand names and product names mentioned in this book are trademarks or service marks of their respective companies. Any omission or misuse (of any kind) of service marks or trademarks, etc. is not an attempt to infringe on the property of others.

Library of Congress Control Number: 2021944921

212223321   Printed on acid-free paper in the United States of America.

Our titles are available for adoption, license, or bulk purchase by institutions, corporations, etc. For additional information, please contact the Customer Service Dept. at 800-232-0223(toll free).

All of our titles are available in digital format at *academiccourseware.com* and other digital vendors. The sole obligation of MERCURY LEARNING AND INFORMATION to the purchaser is to replace the book, based on defective materials or faulty workmanship, but not based on the operation or functionality of the product.

To Lottie, who represents the future
for those who love science and technology!
— Jeffrey Hsu

To Serafina, Emerson, and Isaiah
— Gary Bronson

CONTENTS

PART 2   PRESENTATIONS

PREFACE

This book is designed to meet the needs of multiple audiences, including that of professionals and individuals who are interested in becoming well versed in the basics of using Excel spreadsheets, and also for courses of various levels where the primary focus is on learning and using Microsoft Excel.

Whether in the fields of business, science, statistics, mathematics, or data analytics, there are countless practical uses for Microsoft Excel, and this book will help to get you started in a friendly, non-technical, and approachable manner. It is suitable for those who prefer to learn Excel through self-study and learning, in order to further one's skills in analytical problem solving and decision-making using Excel as an analysis tool.

This book is also designed to be used as a textbook or supplemental reference resource for various levels and audiences, including secondary, higher education, seminars, and specialized training courses. With the recent and increased interest in STEM education, this book is an ideal choice for a broad range of audiences and courses.

This book was written to provide a firm foundation in Excel for beginning learners and students. Its intent is to present, in a clear and accessible manner, the key capabilities needed for spreadsheet applications. These capabilities include knowing the basic data types and when they should be used, how to format cells, how to print spreadsheets in landscape or fit-to-page modes, how to create formulas, how to use absolute and relative addresses appropriately in copying formulas, and the basic Excel functions. This text presents topics in a clear, unambiguous, and accessible manner for beginning learners and students of Excel.

A major consideration was to give readers and students an understanding of the what and how that goes into creating spreadsheets properly, so that they avoid the mistakes commonly made by beginners. One example is in clearly and fully understanding the basic data types and when they should be used. For example, some novice users, without this understanding, would enter zip codes as numeric data, and then not understand why leading zeros were not printed. Additionally, knowing how to format a cell or how to copy a cell formula down through a column or across a row is essential. Without a clear and focused understanding, many would simply retype the same general formula, over and over, using new cell references. As an understanding of these basics is essential for creating a solid foundation for beginning learners, they form the core of this book.

Interestingly, we always encountered many novice learners who claimed to have a good knowledge and experience with Excel. Many of them could actually produce acceptable and sometimes even professional-looking spreadsheets, but under closer examination were found to have noticeable gaps in their understanding. For example, when asked to present the formulas behind their spreadsheet, it was frequently discovered that many cells included manual calculator-determined results. As such, the power and versatility of Excel is not being properly utilized. To forestall the development of such habits from even starting, a central element of this text is to give readers and students a real understanding of how spreadsheets are constructed so that they develop practices that use Excel with maximum effectiveness.

To facilitate this learning process, this together with a separate *Excel 2019 Project Book* (Mercury Learning: Bronson and Hsu, 2021) require the student to properly create actual, practical spreadsheets. Each spreadsheet application requires either using a newly introduced capability, or reinforces one or more previously learned capabilities. This is done in incrementally and increasingly more involved and demanding ways, so that the reader gets to really understand the skill being presented. Both texts can be used independently or together.

Part One (Chapters 1-4) form the central core of this text. It is here that the basic structure of Excel is explained and the elementary but necessary features of entering data into a cell, the three types of data permitted by Excel, and saving, retrieving, and printing a spreadsheet are presented.

Additionally, formulas, functions, and formatting are explained, together with conditional formatting, specific categories of functions (statistical, financial, information, date and time, text) and a basic professional template that separates a spreadsheet into the input and result areas is presented. Specialized formulas and functions including the =IF, vertical and horizontal table lookups, and conditional expressions are covered. The applications discussed include car and mortgage loans calculations, repayment schedules, and text and character manipulation techniques. Finally, each chapter in this section contains a list of commonly made implementation errors and a chapter appendix providing information on less used but important concepts that users typically encounter.

Part Two (Chapters 5-6) presents Excel's chart and graph tools (column, pie, line graphs, etc.) and the concepts and process behind creating "summary table reports" using PivotTables. Included in the charts and graphs chapter is coverage of the benefits and steps involved in creating trend lines, using correlations, and developing histograms. Varying approaches, structures and applications are presented in the chapter on PivotTables.

Part Three (Chapters 7-8) contains more intermediate to advanced features that include sorting and filtering (searching) Excel lists, employing database functions, created subtotaled lists, setting up drop-down lists, using array functions, and developing user-created conditional-formatting formulas.

DISTINCTIVE FEATURES OF THIS BOOK

Writing Style. The goal of this book is to present the essentials and basics of an Excel spreadsheet, in a clear and easy to understand way. The discussion is supplemented by illustrations, examples, and helpful tips.

Application Testing. Every spreadsheet in this text has been successfully developed and tested using Excel on Windows-based computers, by novice learners and students who have used both these and Apple® Mac computers. This ensures that readers and students can both experiment and extend the existing spreadsheets and more easily modify them as required by a number of end-of-section exercises.

UNIQUE FEATURES

To facilitate the goal of making Excel accessible to beginners, the following unique features have been incorporated into the text:

Application Notes.   These shaded boxes in each chapter highlight important concepts, useful technical points, and developer tips and techniques used by professional spreadsheet developers.

End-of-Section Exercises.   Most sections of the book contain diverse skill builder and spreadsheet exercises.

Common Excel Errors.   Each chapter contains a section on common implementation errors typically encountered by beginning and novice users.

Chapter Appendices.   Each chapter ends with an appendix presenting more detail about specific topics, such as the Excel Development Screen, working with rows and columns, how to transfer data between sheets, how to locate and fix incorrectly copied formulas, and how to use a spreadsheet as a database.

Instructor Resources.   Instructor resources include PowerPoint slides for each chapter, video tutorials, sample syllabi, and sample tests and quizzes.

Jeffrey Hsu, Ph.D.
Gary Bronson, Ph.D.
September 2021

ACKNOWLEDGMENTS

We would like to express our thanks to the hard-working and dedicated staff at Mercury Learning and Information. To David Pallai, Publisher, for expressing confidence in and publishing this book, and for tirelessly working with us closely on all aspects of the publication process, from beginning to end. It is rare that authors can receive the "personal touch" from such a dedicated and experienced publishing professional, who guided us through the various intricacies and challenges of the process. To Jennifer Blaney, for her professionalism, production expertise, and in doing a great job keeping the book on schedule.

In particular, we would like to recognize the commitment to quality that has been shown by these individuals, in terms of the care shown during copyediting, resolving issues, requesting multiple rounds of page proofs, and providing us the opportunity to provide input into just about every aspect of our book and its production, marketing, and promotions. For this, we are grateful.

Jeffrey Hsu would like to express thanks to my friend, colleague, and co-author, Gary Bronson for the wonderful experience in working together. It was always stimulating and insightful, and I find that I always learn something new working with Gary. We often say to each other that "we make a good team" and indeed it is true!

Jeffrey Hsu would like to express thanks to my friend and colleague Mel Stern, who encouraged me to explore further and fully appreciate all that Excel has to offer.

Jeffrey Hsu would also like to express thanks to my niece, Lottie, who helped me select the cover design, and also to whom this book is dedicated.

Finally, to both our families, for being understanding with us during the many hours we spent working on the book, and for being ever more patient when they hear from us over and over that "we still have more work to do on the book."

ABOUT THE AUTHORS

Jeffrey Hsu, Ph.D., is a professor of information systems at the Silberman College of Business, Fairleigh Dickinson University. He is the author of numerous papers, chapters, and books, and has previous business experience in the software, telecommunications, and financial industries. His research interests include human-computer interaction, e-commerce, IS education, and mobile/ubiquitous computing. He is the editor in chief of the *International Journal of e-Business Research* (IJEBR). Dr. Hsu also serves as the managing editor of the *International Journal of Data Analysis and Information Systems* (IJDAIS), and is on the editorial board of several other journals. Dr. Hsu received his Ph.D. in information systems from Rutgers University, his M.S. in computer science from the New Jersey Institute of Technology, and an M.B.A. from the Rutgers Graduate School of Management.

Gary Bronson, Ph.D., is a professor of information systems at the Silberman College of Business, Fairleigh Dickinson University, where he was twice voted Teacher of the Year of the college and received the Distinguished Faculty Award for Research and Scholarship, of the university. He has worked as a senior engineer at Lockheed Electronics, an invited lecturer and consultant to Bell Laboratories, and a software consultant to a number of Wall Street financial firms. He is the author of the highly acclaimed *A First Book of C* and has authored several other successful programming textbooks on C++, Java, and Visual Basic. He is a co-author of the *Excel 2019 Project Book* with Jeffrey Hsu and the co-author of *Mathematics for Business* with Richard Bronson, and Maureen Kieff. Additionally, he is the author of a number of journal articles in the fixed-income financial and programming areas. Dr. Bronson received his Ph.D. from Stevens Institute of Technology.

Part **1**

BASIC SKILLS

CHAPTER 1

GETTING STARTED

This Chapter Contains

1.1   INTRODUCTION TO EXCEL SPREADSHEETS

At its most basic level, an Excel spreadsheet is simply a file containing sheets of individual storage locations, as shown in Figure 1.1. In general, a spreadsheet file is called a *workbook*, while the individual sheets are known as worksheets. By convention, the terms *worksheet* and *spreadsheet* are used synonymously, and both of these terms are used interchangeably throughout this text. Initially, and for many of your early applications, you will only need one spreadsheet. However, for more advanced applications, it is common to employ multiple worksheets within the same workbook.

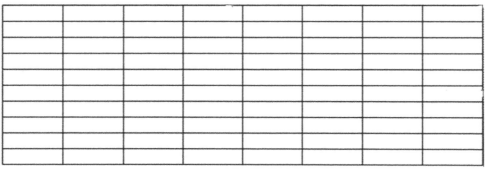

Figure 1.1 An example of an empty spreadsheet

Each individual location within a spreadsheet is referred to as a *cell*. To clearly locate a cell in a spreadsheet, each cell has a column and row designation. Columns are marked with a letter, starting with the letter A, and each row is marked with a number, starting with the number 1, as shown in Figure 1.2. There are many cells available on

---

Application Note
Relative, Absolute, and Mixed Cell Addresses

A cell address that consists of a column and row designation, such as A1, B24, or M256, without any other notations or symbols included, is known as a *relative cell address* (or *relative cell reference*). The vast majority of cell addresses you would encounter are of this type, and they are the type you typically would use most often, especially when you first start working with Excel.

There are times, however, when a different type of address, known as an *absolute cell address* (or *absolute cell reference*), such as ($A$1 or $B$24) or a *mixed cell address* (or *mixed cell reference*) , such as ($A1 or B$24) is needed. The reason for these other kinds of cell addresses is explained in Section 2.5. In general, relative cell addresses allow both the column and row to change when copied, absolute cell addresses allow neither to change, and mixed allow either the row or column to change (but not both). For now, simply be aware that the cell addresses you are currently using are one of three types of addresses available in Excel, and that each one serves a different purpose when copying cells.

---

an Excel worksheet. Excel 2019 supports over a million rows, over 16,000 columns, for a total of more than 17 billion cells on a single worksheet.

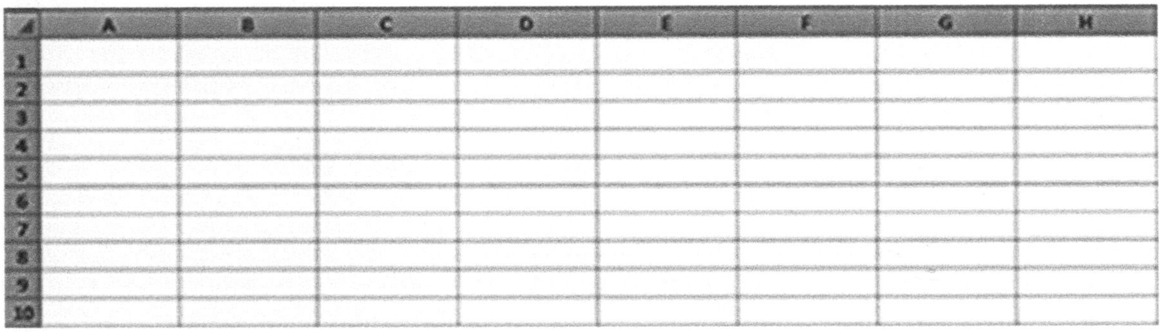

Figure 1.2 A spreadsheet with the rows and columns labeled

Every Excel spreadsheet has these same column and row markings. This permits a cell in a spreadsheet to be uniquely located and identified by giving its column and row designation, which together constitute the cell's *address*. For example, the address A1 refers to a spreadsheet's leftmost and topmost cell, while the address C4 refers to the cell located in column C and row 4. For convenience, these two cells have been highlighted in Figure 1.3.

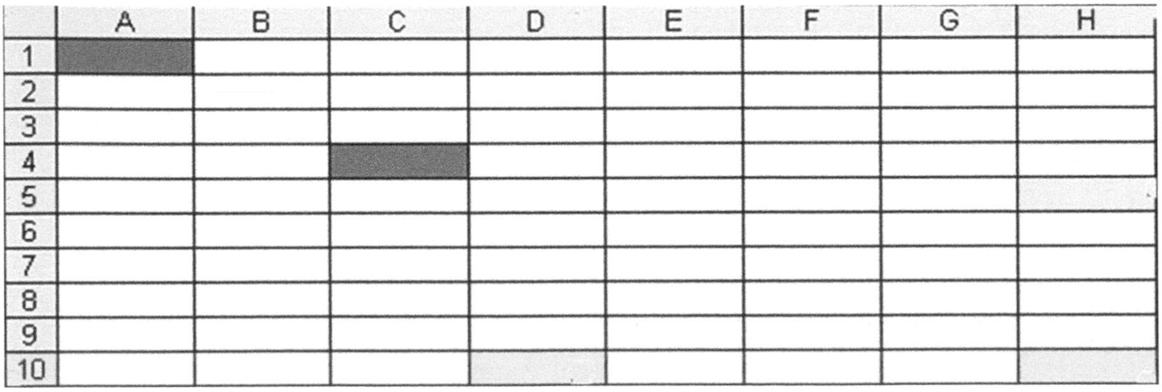

Figure 1.3 The cell addresses A1 and C4 are highlighted

In addition to providing the basic worksheet shown in Figure 1.3, what makes Excel so useful and more than just a sheet of storage locations are its following capabilities:

- The ability to enter, change, and delete data from individual cells and print parts of complete spreadsheets
- The ability to perform basic mathematical operations (such as addition or multiplication) on numerical data within two or more cells
- The availability of functions that can be used to determine square roots, payments on loans, averages, standard deviations, and many other statistical operations
- The ability to change the appearance of numbers and text (style, font, size, and color), and format numbers to appear in different ways (such as the number of decimal values to be displayed, dollar signs, and date)
- The ability to create and print graphs and summary tables
- The ability to change the width of individual columns and the height of individual rows
- The ability to use one or more worksheets that can be linked together (that is, data in one worksheet can be accessed by another worksheet)

In fact, most of this text is focused on showing you how to use these capabilities. Your expertise in using Excel will depend on your skill in learning and applying these capabilities to your own individual projects.

Cell Contents

It is particularly important to understand that each and every spreadsheet cell can contain only one main data entry (which may consist of various data sub-elements) at a time. The vast majority of data elements you will enter, and the only ones that are directly supported in Excel, must be one of the following:

1. Numbers
2. Text (sometimes referred to as *labels*)
3. Formulas

Excel identifies and stores each of these data types in its own internal manner as code by recognizing the following characteristics of the data:

A number is data that includes only the following characters:

- Numeric digits (0 through 9)
- Special symbols (such as -, $, and .)

Thus, a number, at a minimum, must contain one or more of the numeric digits 0 through 9. Additionally, a decimal point, commas, a leading dollar sign, and a leading + or – sign can, but need not, be included. By default, the content of a cell is interpreted as a number whenever these, and only these, symbols are present, and the cell has not been designated as holding a different type of data, which is accomplished using formatting (described in Section 2.4). By default, a number is displayed toward the right side of a cell, which is referred to as *right-alignment*. Each individual number is stored using a numerical code format.

Text is any data containing a letter or character, except data recognized as a formula or a function. Typically, text is used to create headings and labels. Thus, any cell that contains at least one letter or non-numeric symbol (!, #, &), begins with a double-quote ("), or the cell itself has been designated as a text cell (which is accomplished using formatting), is considered text and stored by Excel in a character-by-character code. Attempting to perform a mathematical operation using a cell containing text results in an error, or no result, since text does not have any numeric value.

A *formula* always begins with an equal (=) sign. Thus, a cell's contents that begin with an equal sign are considered to be a formula, as well as if the cell contains both operands and operators. One exception is when formatting has been used to change the formula into text. In this latter case, the formula will not compute anything but will display the formula as a text string.

Formulas can be user-created, such as =3*A1, which multiplies the value in A1 by 3, or =B1+B2+B3+B4, which adds the contents of cells B1, B2, B3, and B4. Typically, however, an Excel supplied function, such as SUM( ), is used within a formula.

A formula can contain a function, such as =SUM( ). A function is a self-contained "program" that can be used to do computations and perform operations. The ability to use formulas and functions to create new information from existing data and keep a spreadsheet current whenever data is changed forms the essence of what makes spreadsheets valuable.

For example, the functions =SUM(B1:B4) and =AVERAGE(B1:B4) calculate the sum and average, respectively, of the values in cells B1 through B4. Notice that the notation B1:B4 used in each of these functions indicates that a range of cells, from B1 through B4, inclusive, are used in the calculation of the sum and average, respectively. Instead of explicitly specifying operators and operands (as in an Excel formula), it is like a "black box" to which arguments (inputs) are fed, and the resulting output displayed. The result of each calculation appears in the cell containing the formula.

Example 1

Figure 1.4 shows a section of a spreadsheet that was created using all three data types: (numbers, text, formulas), and functions.

Application Note
The Importance of Formulas

Formulas form the backbone of all spreadsheet applications and are what distinguish an Excel spreadsheet from a table of values prepared using a word processing program. There are two main reasons for this.

First, when you create a spreadsheet application that has more than two or three columns and/or rows, which is the norm for most commercial applications, typically only a single formula needs be entered in the first cell of each column or row. This one formula is then simply copied, as needed, to the remaining cells in the column or row. (Because of relative cell addresses, Excel automatically adjusts cell references in the copied formula, described further in Section 2.2).

Second, when you use a spreadsheet and change any of the values used in a formula, the formula will automatically recalculate and display the correct value for the new data. This is extremely important in keeping a spreadsheet up-to-date and accurate for all displayed values.

	A	B
1		**Grades**
2		85
3		92
4		76
5	**Sum:**	253
6	**Average:**	84.33
7	**Sum:**	253
8	**Average:**	84.33

Figure 1.4 A spreadsheet that uses all three data types: (numbers, text, formulas) and functions

Figure 1.5 shows what was actually typed into each cell.

	A	B
1		**Grades**
2		85
3		92
4		76
5	**Sum:**	=B2+B3+B4
6	**Average:**	=B5/3
7	**Sum:**	=SUM(B2:B4)
8	**Average:**	=AVERAGE(B2:B4)

Figure 1.5 The input for Figure 1.4

As shown in Figure 1.5, cells B2 through B4 contain numbers, while cells B5 through B8 contain formulas and functions. In cell B5, the sum is found with a formula that uses the addition operator (+), while cell B7 uses Excel's SUM( ) function, both of which are explained in more detail in Chapter 2. Similarly, the average of the grades is determined in cell B6 using the division operator (/), while cell B8 uses Excel's AVERAGE( ) function. In all four cases, however, Excel knows these formulas and functions are to be calculated because they begin with an equal (=) sign. Although not shown, a function can be included within other functions and mathematical expressions as in =10 * SUM(B2:B4)/3.

Notice that in Figure 1.5, cells B1 and A5 through A8 all contain text. The text in cell B1 is referred to as a *heading*, as it is located at the top, or head, of a column and identifies what the column contains. The text in cells A5 through A8 is referred to as *labels*. Labels, like headings, are always text.

For the data entered in Figure 1.5, fill in the data types that you think Excel assigns to each entered item using Figure 1.6 below.

NOTE *Remember that there are three data types (number, text, formula) and functions.*

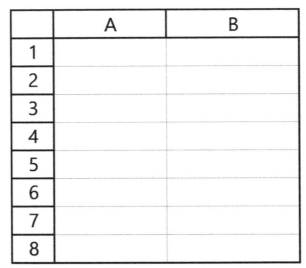

Figure 1.6 Fill in the spreadsheet with the correct data types for the data in Figure 1.5

Dates and Boolean Data

In addition to the three basic data types (numbers, text, and formulas) and functions, there are two other data items that can be entered into a cell: dates and Boolean data. Dates on or after 1/1/1900 are stored as consecutive integers, with the number 1 representing January 1, 1900 (i.e., 1/1/1900), the number January 2, 1900, and so on.[1] Dates prior to 1/1/1900 are stored as text, and can be changed to numbers. In all cases, dates prior to and after 1/1/1900 can always be displayed and stored as text.

Boolean data consist of the two values, TRUE and FALSE. These are described in detail in Section 3.3. Boolean data form the basis for comparison operations, such as "is the value in cell A5 greater than the value in cell B5." Internally, the Boolean TRUE and FALSE values are stored as the numbers 1 and 0, respectively.

---

[1] The integer numbers used to store dates on and after 1/1/1900 are referred to as *Serial Numbers* in Excel.

Figure 1.7 shows the appearances of dates in three of formats provided by Excel. How these formats are selected is presented in Section 2.3.

As Typed	2-Digit Format	Descriptive Format
5/3/2001	05/03/01	Thursday, May 3, 2001
6/20/2001	06/20/01	Wednesday, June 20, 2001
10/2/2001	10/02/01	Tuesday, October 2, 2001
12/28/2001	12/28/01	Friday, December 28, 2001

Figure 1.7 Different date appearances

Entering Data into a Cell

To enter data into a cell, first use either the mouse or the cursor arrow keys to go to the desired location. If you use the mouse, click when you are at the designated cell. When you do so, the cell border will appear as shown in Figure 1.8, indicating, in this case, that cell D4 is the currently selected (*active*) cell. Note that the currently selected cell location also appears in the *name box* (this provides another way of selecting a cell: simply type the cell location in the *name box*, which is also useful when creating named ranges for more advanced needs).

When the desired cell has been selected, type the number, text, formula, or function that you want stored in the cell. As you type, the data will appear in both the cell and in the Formula Bar. When either the enter key or one of the cursor arrow keys is pressed, the data is stored in the cell and becomes the cell's contents. (The shortcut key F5 can also be used on both the PC and the Mac.)

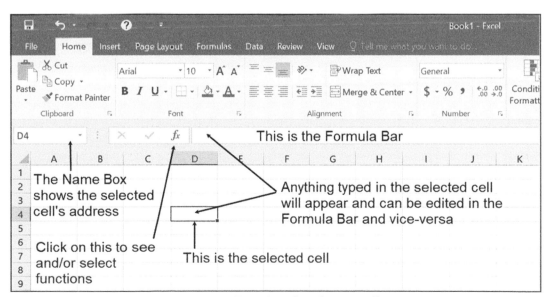

Figure 1.8 Entering data into a cell

EXERCISES 1.1

1. Answer the following questions.

   a. How is the location of an individual cell indicated?

   b. What is the term used for the cell addresses in the form A1, G5, and M26?

2. List the three basic types of data that can be entered into a cell and how Excel determines the data type of each item that is entered. What is a function?

3. How is a range of contiguous cells indicated in a formula?

4. Determine the data type of each of the following:

   a. 121.135

   b. =A1*B1

   c. =M5/N5

   d. ABOVE AVERAGE

   e. $89.47

   f. =AVERAGE(A1:A10).

5. For the data and formulas shown in the spreadsheet below, determine and fill in the values that will be calculated and displayed in cells A5, B5, and C1 through C4.

	A	B	C
1	3	14.2	=A1*B1
2	6	10.8	=A2*B2
3	10	6.43	=A3*B3
4	12	9.7	=A4*B4
5	=SUM(A1:A4)	=AVERAGE(B1:B4)	

	A	B	C
1	3	14.2	
2	6	10.8	
3	10	6.43	
4	12	9.7	
5			

6. For the data and formulas shown in the spreadsheet below, determine and fill in the values that will be calculated and displayed, using the spreadsheet to the right.

	A	B
1		Grades
2		92
3		67
4		88
5		75
6		95
7	Sum:	=(B2+B3+B4+B5+B6)
8	Sum:	=SUM(B2:B6)
9	Average:	=(B2+B3+B4+B5+B6)/5
10	Average:	=AVERAGE(B2:B6)

	A	B
1		Grades
2		92
3		67
4		88
5		75
6		95
7	Sum:	
8	Sum:	
9	Average:	
10	Average:	

7. Follow the directions for the spreadsheets.

a. Enter the text and numbers shown in the following spreadsheet:

	A	B	C	D
1	Designation	Cost per Hour	Hours	Cost
2	RN	$400.00	6	
3	LPN	$310.00	5	
4	Aide	$200.00	12	
5			Total Cost:	

b. Enter the appropriate formulas in cells D2 through D5 and other modifcations so that your completed spreadsheet looks as follows:

	A	B	C	D
1	Designation	Cost per Hour	Hours	Cost
2	RN	$400	4	$1,600
3	LPN	$310	5	$1,550
4	Aide	$200	12	$2,400
5			Total Cost:	$5,550

1.2 TWO ESSENTIAL SKILLS – HIGHLIGHTING AND COPYING

Once data is entered into a cell, the processing of the data can begin. In fact, most of this text is concerned with the Excel skills needed for this processing, such as finding the sum and/or average of the data within a range of cells, preparing the data so that it appears correctly when displayed or printed, or calculating profit and loss statements. These two skills are (1) highlighting a range of cells, such as a column of data whose sum is needed, and (2) copying one or more cells. How these are accomplished is described in this section.

Selecting Cells by Highlighting

A large portion of spreadsheet processing typically requires using a group of related cells. For example, the sum of a column of data may be needed, or perhaps the average of grades in a row, where each row corresponding to a student's test grades may be required to determine a final grade. A commonly used technique for specifying a range of cells is to highlight the cells within the range.[2] While the cells are highlighted, they form a unit that can then be processed by a formula or configured so that all individual cell values in the group have the same format when displayed.

Note that we are not referring to highlighting a cell's contents by changing the color of the cell's data. What is being highlighted is a set of one or more adjacent (that is, touching) cells that designates them as a single unit while they are highlighted. In Excel, a set of adjacent cells is referred to as a *range of cells*, or *cell range*, for short.

---

[2] A second method is to list the top left-most cell address in the range, followed by a colon, followed by the lowest right-most cell address.

Figure 1.9 shows a number of highlighted cell ranges. The underlying criterion for each range is that every cell in the range is adjacent to, that is, touches, at least one other cell in the range. Also shown under each range is how the range is designated using cell addresses. You will note that cell ranges can be horizontal, vertical, or square/rectangular in shape.

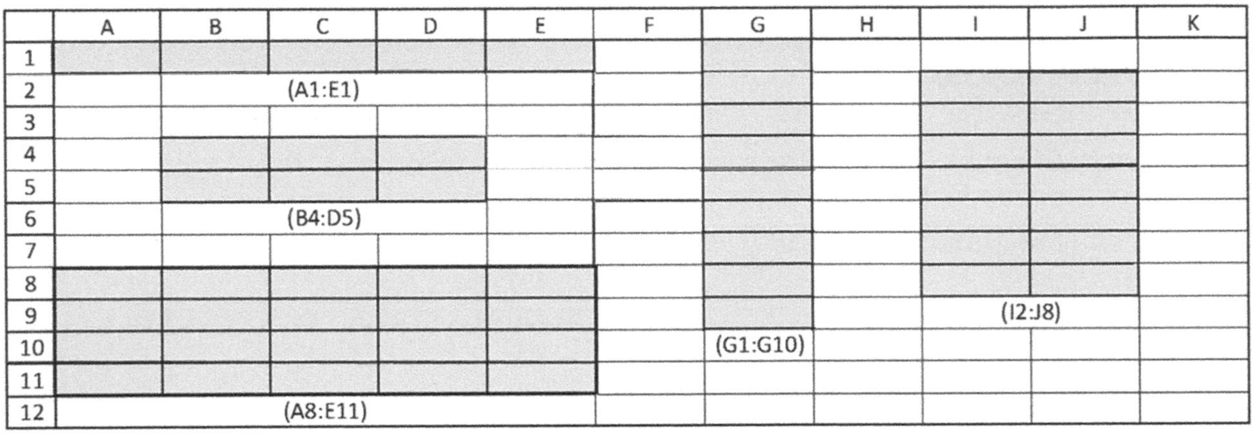

	A	B	C	D	E	F	G	H	I	J	K
1											
2			(A1:E1)								
3											
4											
5			(B4:D5)								
6											
7											
8											
9										(I2:J8)	
10							(G1:G10)				
11											
12			(A8:E11)								

Figure 1.9 Examples of cell ranges

To highlight a range of cells, you must first select a single cell at the top or bottom or corner cell in the desired range. For example, in Figure 1.10, the cursor has been moved to a selected starting cell, which in this case is B4. Notice the shape of the cursor in the cell.

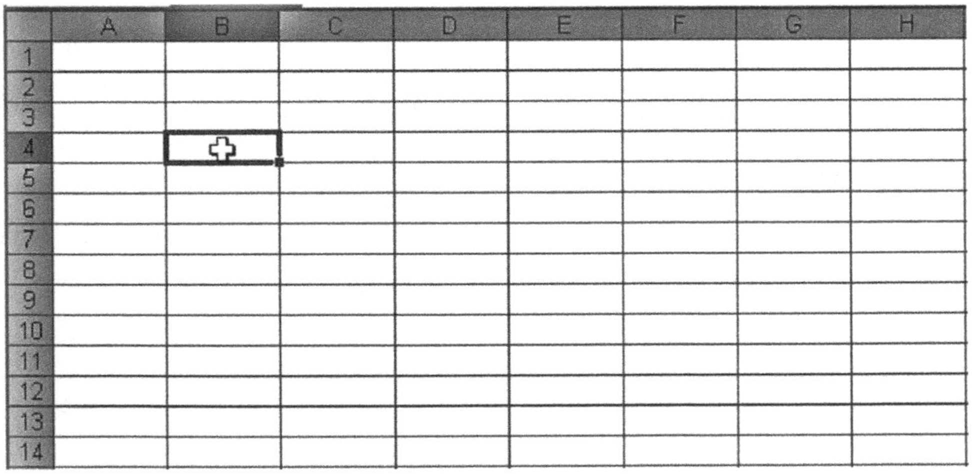

Figure 1.10 Selecting the first cell in a range of cells

Once you have selected the first cell in the desired range, you can now define the desired group of cells by doing one of the following:

1. Press and hold the left mouse button down, starting from the first cell, and move the mouse so that the cursor points to the desired last cell in the range. Then release the left mouse button.

2. Click and then release the left mouse button on the first cell in the desired range. Then hold the Shift key down and click and release the left mouse button on the last cell in the desired range.

3. Click and release the left mouse button on the first cell in the desired range. Then hold the Shift key down and use the keyboard arrow keys (← ↑ ↓ →) to go to the last cell in the desired range, and then release the Shift key.

Figure 1.11 shows how the selected cells look using the first method, where the left mouse button has been pressed and held down as the mouse cursor is moved from its initial position in cell B4 to cell B11, and then the left mouse button is released. The cells, as shown in Figure 1.11, become highlighted as they are included in the range. This same highlighting would occur if any of the other two methods are used.

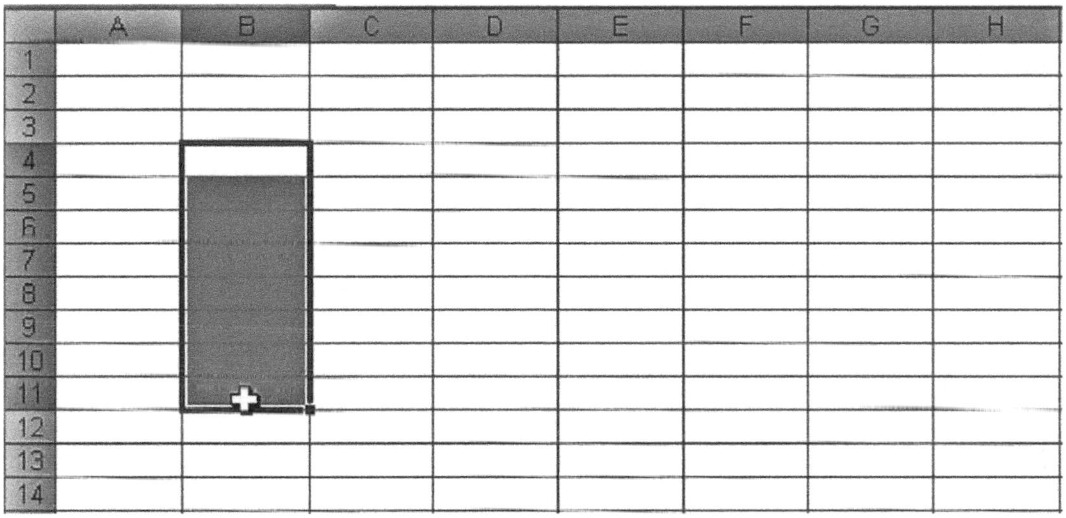

Figure 1.11 Completing the range selection

Copying Cell Contents

The contents of a single cell are copied by first moving the cursor to the lower right-hand corner of the selected cell, as shown in Figure 1.12.

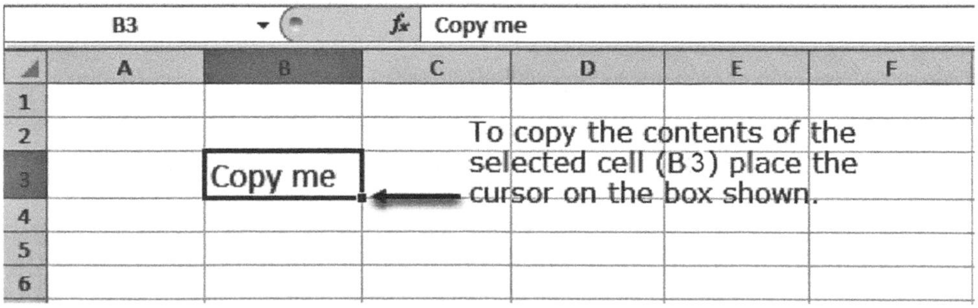

Figure 1.12 Locating the copy rectangle

When the cursor appears as a cross-hair (+), as shown in Figure 1.13, the selected cell is ready to be copied. This is known as the *fill handle*.

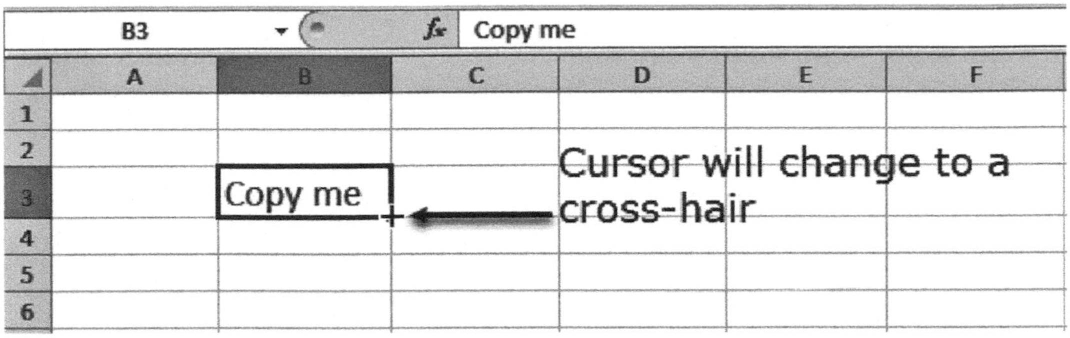

Figure 1.13 Placing the cursor on the fill handle (the cursor changes to a cross-hair)

Once the cursor has changed to a cross-hair (fill handle), press and hold the left mouse button while you drag the cursor over the cells where you want the copy to occur. As you do so, each cell where the copy will take place becomes highlighted, as shown in Figure 1.14. Here, the contents of cell B3 are being copied to cells C3 through E3. *The copy takes place when the left mouse button is released.*

Note that the copy could just as easily been made up or down column B, rather than across the third row (row 3). The only restriction on this method is that the copy is always made to adjacent (touching cells), which is usually what is required. If a copy to non-adjacent cells is needed, standard cut-and-paste techniques should be used.

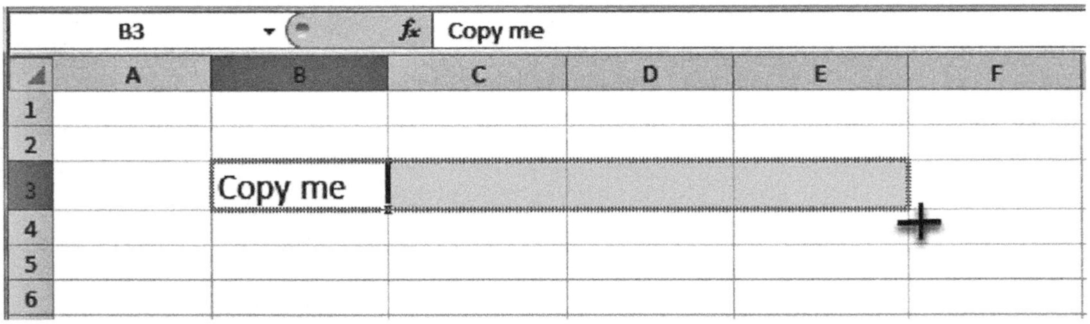

Figure 1.14 Copying cell B3 to cells C3, D3, and E3

Adaptive Pattern Matching

When copying dates, text, and numbers (and more importantly formulas, as described in Section 2.1), Excel tries to determine if a pattern exists. Based on any detected pattern, Excel places the next value in the pattern into the copied cell. This is sometimes referred to as *completing a series or sequence.*

Typically, for formulas and text, (and other commonly used sequences) such as days-of-the-week and months, Excel only requires one cell to determine the pattern; for dates and numbers (and less frequently used sequences), two adjacent cells are typically needed. For example, consider the spreadsheet segment shown in Figure 1.15a.

	A	B	C	D	E	F
1	January					

Figure 1.15a The original cell contents

Now, if cell A1 is copied to cells B1 through cell F1, the spreadsheet segment will appear as shown in Figure 1.15b. Note, as the contents of cell A1 were formatted to be centered in the cell, the copied cells retain this format. The reason is that the Copy feature normally brings over not just the data, but also the cell format from the source to the destination.

	A	B	C	D	E	F
1	January	February	March	April	May	June

Figure 1.15b The cell contents after cell A1 is copied

Give It a Try

In Figure 1.16, write in the contents that you think Excel will display when cell A1 is copied from cell B1 through F1. If you can, check your answer by using an actual Excel spreadsheet.

	A	B	C	D	E	F
1	Jan					

Figure 1.16 Write the contents that will be displayed when cell A1 is copied from cell B1 through F1

To detect a pattern in numbers and dates, Excel requires that two adjacent cells be highlighted and then copied. For example, consider Figure 1.17a, where a number pattern appears in cells A2 and A3. If these two cells are highlighted and then copied, this spreadsheet segment will appear as shown in Figure 1.17b.

	A
1	Payments
2	1
3	2
4	
5	
6	
7	
8	
9	
10	
11	

Figure 1.17a Original data

	A
1	Payments
2	1
3	2
4	3
5	4
6	5
7	6
8	7
9	8
10	9
11	10

Figure 1.17b Copied cell results

EXERCISES 1.2

1. For each of the following spreadsheets, determine and fill in the text that will displayed if the text in cell A1 is copied to the right.

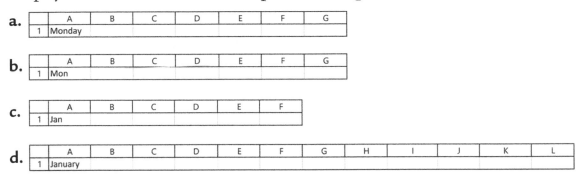

a.

	A	B	C	D	E	F	G
1	Monday						

b.

	A	B	C	D	E	F	G
1	Mon						

c.

	A	B	C	D	E	F
1	Jan					

d.

	A	B	C	D	E	F	G	H	I	J	K	L
1	January											

2. For each of the following spreadsheets, determine and fill in the text that will displayed if the text in cells A1 and A2 are first highlighted and then copied down.

a.

	A
1	2019
2	2020
3	
4	
5	
6	
7	
8	

b.

	A
1	2019
2	2021
3	
4	
5	
6	
7	
8	

c.

	A
1	10
2	11
3	
4	
5	
6	
7	
8	
9	
10	

d.

	A
1	10
2	14
3	
4	
5	
6	
7	
8	
9	
10	

3. In Figure 1.18, write in the contents that will be displayed when cells A1 through B1 are highlighted and then copied to cells C1 through H1.

	A	B	C	D	E	F	G	H
1	10.5	12.5						

Figure 1.18 Write your answer

4. In Figure 1.19, write in the contents that will be displayed when cells A1 through B1 are highlighted and then copied to cells C1 through H1.

	A	B	C	D	E	F	G	H
1	1/1/2018	1/1/2019						

Figure 1.19 Write your answer

1.3 OPENING, SAVING, RETRIEVING, AND PRINTING SPREADSHEETS

Opening, saving, and printing your spreadsheets is accomplished using the Quick Access Toolbar, which is located at the top of the Excel screen as shown in Figure 1.20, and provided in detail on Figure 1.21. These tasks can also be done using the commands located in the Excel ribbon under the File tab.

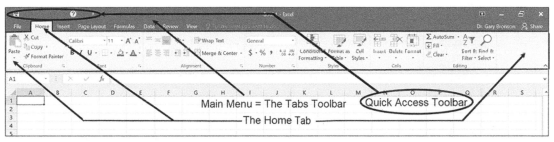

Figure 1.20 Locations of the Home tab, Tabs toolbar, and Quick Access Toolbar

The options on the Quick Access Toolbar, shown in Figure 1.21, are used to open either a new or existing spreadsheet, to save the spreadsheet you are currently working on, and to print parts or all of the current spreadsheet. Additionally, it provides an option for customizing the Quick Access Toolbar.

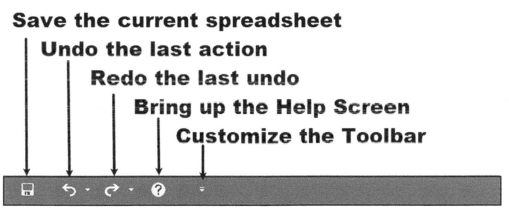

Figure 1.21 The Quick Access Toolbar

Opening a New or Existing Spreadsheet

As shown on Figure 1.22, to open a new, blank spreadsheet, select the New option from the File tab's submenu. This causes the window pane to the right of the menu to appear. Within this pane, you can select a new blank workbook to be displayed, select one of the pre-formatted spreadsheets, or search for an online spreadsheet template. It should be pointed out that while the main focus of this book is on creating your own spreadsheets, Excel does offer the means to help some users get started quickly by providing pre-formatted, partially completed templates for spreadsheets.

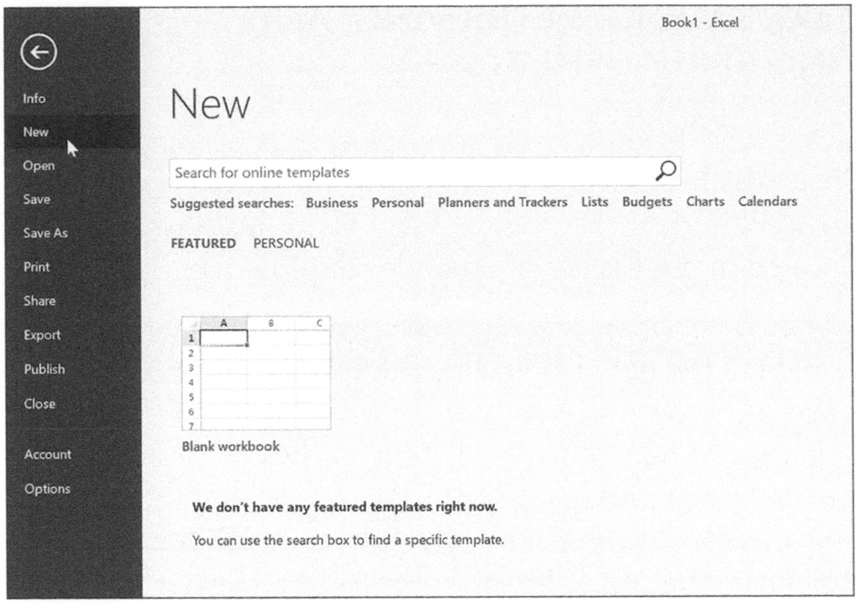

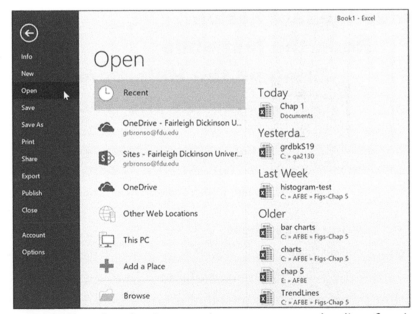

Figure 1.22 Opening a new spreadsheet

To open a previously saved spreadsheet, click on the File tab's Open option, as shown in Figure 1.23. Doing this automatically brings up the window pane shown to the right of the menu. Here, a list of recently saved spreadsheets is provided. You can either select one of the displayed spreadsheets or click on the Browse option at the bottom of the pane and enter the location and filename of the desired saved spreadsheet.

Figure 1.23 Choosing the Open option opens up another list of options

Saving a Spreadsheet

It is important to save your work and remember the location where it is saved. Frequently, Excel will provide you with a list of your most recently saved files; however, this is not always the case if you are using a public computer. Always make a note of the directory and name of your saved spreadsheets when you save them.

There are a number of methods to save a spreadsheet. The easiest method to resave a previously saved spreadsheet is to click on the Quick Access Toolbar's Save option, which is shown on Figure 1.21.

The first time you save a spreadsheet, however, you should use the File tab's Save As option shown in Figure 1.24 or the spreadsheet will be saved using a default name provided by Excel.[3] Clicking on this option automatically triggers the window pane shown to the right of the menu. Selecting the Browse option at the bottom of this window pane (see figure) permits you to enter a location and filename for your spreadsheet. Note that if you only provide a filename, the file is saved in the current directory. If you are using a public computer or classroom computer lab, the contents of the current public directory are typically erased at the end of the day, so make sure to save your spreadsheets, either on a directory dedicated for your use and/or a flash drive. You need to remember that the importance of saving your Excel workbook frequently is critical because at least part of your file may be residing in the computer's RAM, rather than on your hard disk, SSD, flash drive, or other storage device.

An interesting feature of the File menu's Save option, located above the Save As option shown in Figure 1.24, is that it this selection automatically activates the Save As option and the screen shown in Figure 1.24. In essence, it defaults to the Save As operation when you save your file for the first time.

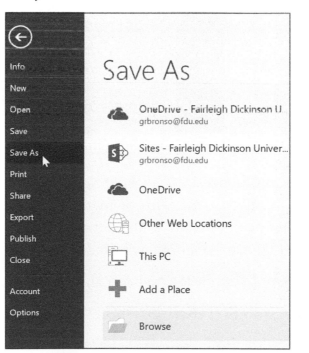

Figure 1.24 The Save As option

---

[3] The default name is Bookn, where n is a consecutive number, starting at 1, which keeps track of the number of default spreadsheet names you have accumulated.

Printing a Spreadsheet

Printing your spreadsheet requires first selecting the File tab, as shown in Figure 1.25.

Figure 1.25 Click on the File tab

Clicking on the File option shown in Figure 1.25 brings up the File menu, shown in the left-hand pane in Figure 1.26. From this menu, select the Print option, as indicated. This activates the Print menu, shown in the right-hand pane of Figure 1.26. Clicking on the Print button in this pane causes the worksheet to be printed from the top of the spreadsheet up to and including the last row and column in which data was entered.

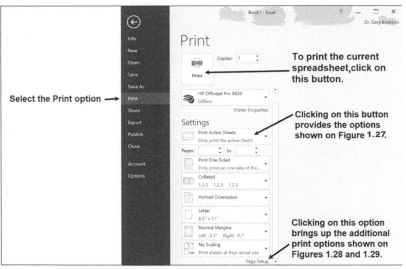

Figure 1.26 Print options

Additionally, as shown on Figure 1.26, clicking the Print Active Sheets button brings up the dialog shown in Figure 1.27. This dialog permits you to print any section of your worksheet that has been previously highlighted.

Extremely useful additional print options include the following:

1. Printing a worksheet in either Portrait or Landscape mode

2. Printing a worksheet to fit on a single page (using scaling or other features)

3. Printing a worksheet with gridlines that clearly delineate the rows and columns

4. Printing the worksheet with Excel's row (1, 2, 3…) and column (A, B, C…) headings.

These options are activated by selecting the Page Setup option shown at the bottom of Figures 1.26 and 1.27. When this Page Setup option is selected, four sub-tabs are displayed, which can be seen in Figures 1.28 and 1.29. The annotations on these two figures illustrate how to activate the landscape, fit-to-page, gridlines, and row and column headings. (These printing options are also available through the Excel ribbon's Page Layout Tab options).

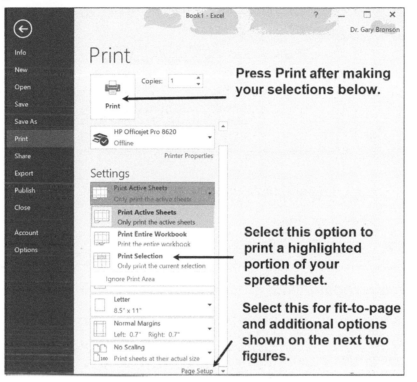

Figure 1.27 Selected print options

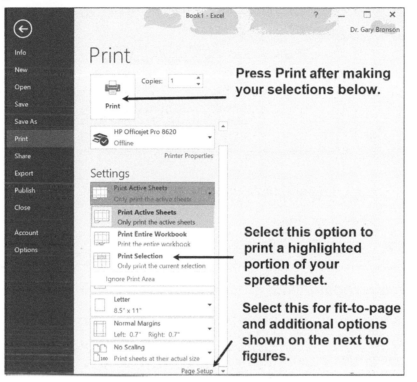

Figure 1.28 The orientation option and scaling option

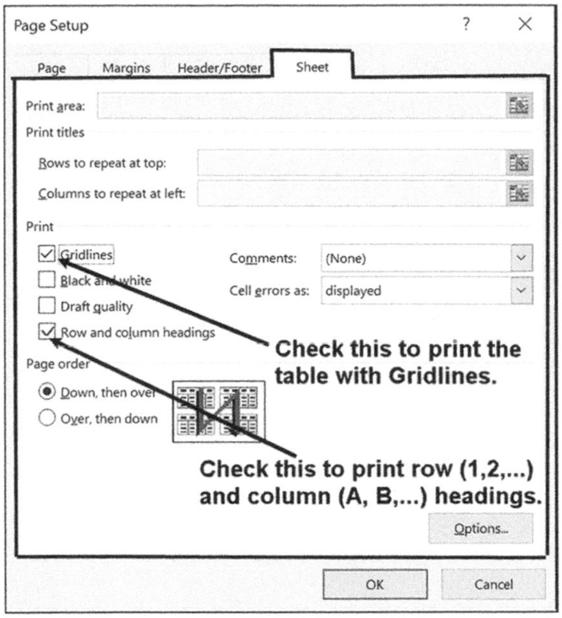

Figure 1.29 Gridline and heading options

EXERCISES 1.3

1. Follow the directions below.

a. Launch Excel, open up a blank worksheet, and create the following spreadsheet (Boldfacing can be achieved by selecting the desired cell and pressing the Ctrl and B keys at the same time or by pressing the Home tab's **Bold** icon. To convert the contents in cells C6, C7, and C8 to text, type them with a leading single quote, as in '/shift. Without the leading single quote, which forces the cell's contents to be text, the division symbol will be marked as an invalid division error).

	A	B	C	D	E	F	G	H	I
1									
2	**Profit:**	7%							
3									
4				**First Shift**		**Second Shift**		**Third Shift**	
5	**Designation**	**Nursing**	**Cost**	**Hired**	**Cost**	**Hired**	**Cost**	**Hired**	**Cost**
6	RN		$400 /shift	2		3		6	
7	LPN		$310 /shift	4		8		9	
8	Aide		$200 /shift	0		4		8	
9			Total Cost:						
10			Profit:						
11			Charge for Service:						

b. Print the spreadsheet you created in Exercise 1a.

c. Save the spreadsheet you created in Exercise 1a. Use the name of your choice for the saved spreadsheet. (***Hint:*** Use a name that is descriptive and one that you will remember later.)

d. Close the Excel program.

2. Follow the directions below.

   a. Launch Excel, open up a blank worksheet, and create the following spreadsheet (**Note:** Boldfacing can be achieved by selecting the desired cell and pressing the Ctrl and B keys at the same time or by pressing the Home tab's **Bold** icon.).

	A	B	C	D	E	F	G
1	**Tax Rate:**	18.50%					
2							
3	**Emp. No.**	**Name**	**Hourly Rate**	**Hrs. Worked**	**Gross Pay**	**Taxes**	**Net Pay**
4	32479	Abrams	$16.72	35			
5	03623	Bohm	19.55	30			
6	14145	Gwodz	18.72	20			
7	25987	Hanson	19.64	40			
8	07634	Robbins	18.55	36			
9	39567	Williams	17.75	39			
10							
11		**Average Rate:**					
12		**Average Hrs. Worked:**					

   b. Print the spreadsheet you created in Exercise 2a.

   c. Save the spreadsheet you created in Exercise 2a. Use the name of your choice for the saved spreadsheet. (**Hint:** Use a name that is descriptive and one that you will remember in the future.)

   d. Close the Excel program, then re-launch Excel and open the spreadsheet to view it before closing Excel again.

3. Follow the directions below.

   a. Launch Excel and create the following spreadsheet (**Note:** Boldfacing can be achieved by selecting the desired cell and pressing the Ctrl and B keys at the same time, or by pressing the Home tab's **Bold** icon.).

	A	B	C	D	E
1	**Loan Amount:**	$5,000.00			
2	**Interest Rate:**	6%			
3	**Years:**	3			
4	**Monthly Payment:**	$152.11			
5					
6	**Payment No.**	**Payment**	**Interest**	**Principal**	**Balance**
7	0				=B1
8	1				=E7-D8
9					
10					
11					

b. Copy the Payment Numbers 0 and 1 down through Cell A12 and verify that Excel enters the correct payment numbers.

c. Print the spreadsheet you created in Exercise 3a.

d. Save the spreadsheet you created in Exercise 3a. Use the name of your choice for the saved spreadsheet. (***Hint:*** Use a name that is descriptive and one that you will be able recall at a later date.)

e. Close the Excel program and then re-launch Excel and open the spreadsheet to view it before closing Excel again.

1.4 PROFESSIONAL SPREADSHEET GUIDELINES[4]

When completing the assignments in this book, it is useful to remember that you are acting in two distinct roles: the first is as the developer of a spreadsheet and the second is as its end-user. In many commercial applications, these two roles are separate. That is, one person will develop a spreadsheet for an application that will be used by one or more other people, the end-users. To ensure that the end-users correctly use the spreadsheet and cannot erroneously change cell values or formulas within it, two features are typically designed into the spreadsheet by the developer.

The first of these features is to format the spreadsheet to have one or more clearly defined input areas for data entry by the end-user. Here, cells are provided to permit the end-user to enter the data necessary for the spreadsheet to produce its desired calculations and results.

The second feature is to restrict the user so that they must use the designated input areas and cannot access any other areas of the spreadsheet. This second feature is accomplished by password protecting all of the cells except the designated input cells. In this section, we address the first feature, correctly formatting a spreadsheet to have a clearly defined input data entry area. The locking of cells by password is presented in Section 8.5.

Input and Results Sections

A professional spreadsheet layout separates the spreadsheet into two areas: an Input area and a Results area, as shown in Figure 1.30.

The purpose of the Input area (also known as the Assumptions area) is to enable a user to clearly see what data is needed, and then provide an area for entering the input data. If possible, this area should be placed at the top left-hand corner of the spreadsheet, as shown in Figure 1.30; when not possible, it is placed within columns along the top of the spreadsheet and/or in the left-hand rows of the spreadsheet.

---

[4] This topic can initially be omitted without loss of subject continuity.

The Results area, also illustrated in Figure 1.30, consists of two sections. One section, placed immediately after the Input area, provides single formula results, and example of this configuration is illustrated in Figure 1.31.

Rarely, however, does a specific application conform exactly to the configurations shown in Figures 1.30 and 1.31.

Although all professionally constructed spreadsheets have the basic Input and Result sections shown in Figure 1.30 as their objective, not all spreadsheets will conform to such precise separation of areas due to specific application requirements, nevertheless, the goal of separating your spreadsheets into clearly defined Input and Results sections is one that you should always keep in mind.

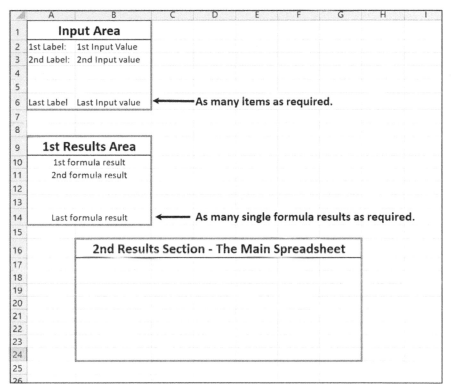

Figure 1.30 The Input area and Results area

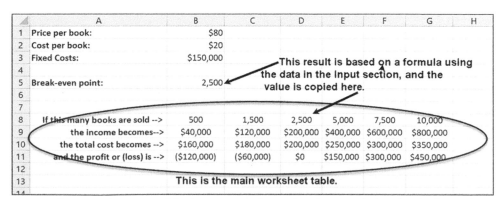

Figure 1.31 The Results area with the output from the data and the single formula results

An example of an application that does not fit directly into the preferred form of distinct Input and Results areas is the one shown in Figure 1.32. In this spreadsheet, some of the inputs are entered in the Results area. In this spreadsheet, all of the shaded cells contain input data. In keeping with the basic input format, however, the tax rate is at the top of the spreadsheet and the remaining input data is contained within the main Results area.

The type of spreadsheet illustrated in Figure 1.32 is typical of a majority of spreadsheets you will create in your college and professional careers. This type of spreadsheet lends itself extremely well to introducing such basic elements as entering and copying formulas, as well as formatting cells to distinguish between text and data values. As a result, it is highly useful to be able to structure worksheets based on the model of separate Input and Results areas shown in Figure 1.30.[5]

	A	B	C	D	E	F	G
1	Tax Rate:	18.50%					
2							
3	Employee Number	Employee Name	Hourly Rate	Hours Worked	Gross Pay	Taxes Withheld	Net Pay
4	32479	Abrams, B	$10.72	35.00	$375.20	$69.41	$305.79
5	03623	Bohm, P	9.54	30.00	286.20	52.95	233.25
6	14145	Gwodz, K	8.72	25.00	218.00	40.33	177.67
7	25987	Hanson, H	9.64	40.00	385.60	71.34	314.26
8	07634	Robbins, L	8.50	36.50	310.25	57.40	252.85
9	39567	Williams, B	7.30	39.00	284.70	52.67	232.03
10				Totals:	$1,859.95	$344.09	$1,515.86
11							
12	Average Hourly Rate:		$9.07				
13	Average Hours Worked:		34.3				

Figure 1.32 An example of a typical spreadsheet

1.5 COMMON EXCEL ERRORS

Part of learning any application software is making the elementary mistakes that beginners typically make. Each program has its own set of common implementation errors waiting for the unwary, and these mistakes can be quite frustrating. The most common errors associated with the material presented in this chapter are listed below.

You should review these errors now and then come back to them again after you have completed the first set of exercises. At that time, many of them will make much more sense to you.

[5] Note that this spreadsheet follows conventional accounting guidelines that stipulate that only the first currency value at the start of a column or after an underline, in addition to single currency items, receives a currency symbol, which in this case is the $ symbol.

Common Errors

1. Rushing to create a spreadsheet without spending enough time learning about what is really needed and the relationship between the inputs and outputs. In this regard, it is worthwhile to remember the saying, "It is impossible to construct a successful spreadsheet for an application that is not fully understood." A similar and equally valuable saying is "The sooner you start creating a spreadsheet, the longer it usually takes to complete."

2. Forgetting to save your spreadsheet in a file that will be available to you when you return the next day. This is especially true if you are working on a public computer in which the public storage area is cleared at the end of each day. The safest method is to save two copies of your work: the first copy on a dedicated section of the computer that is reserved for your personal backup files and the second copy on a removable USB flash drive.

3. Entering the same input piece of data more than once on your spreadsheet. If the same item is needed in more than one cell, the additional cells should reference the one cell into which the data was initially entered within the spreadsheet's Input area. This will prevent you from forgetting to change the value in the second cell when a change is made in the original cell.

4. Using a calculator to determine a value that you then enter into a cell. Rather, an Excel formula should always be used to make all calculations.

5. Forgetting to initially check a result, using a calculator, in the first cell where a formula is entered. Checking the result ensures that you are initially using the correct formula.

6. Assuming that all data containing only digits should be left as Excel's default numeric data type (such as General). For example, zip codes and identification numbers should never be considered as numeric data, as they are used for calculations or generating numeric results. One of the issues that results is that leading zeroes will not be displayed, either in the spreadsheet or when the spreadsheet is printed. As a result, it is usually best to format these kinds of data as text or some other alternative format.

1.6   CHAPTER APPENDIX: THE EXCEL DEVELOPMENT SYSTEM

As noted in Section 1.1, Excel provides both a set of worksheets (within a file called a workbook) and a set of capabilities for organizing and maintaining these worksheets. Figure 1.33 shows the display you will see when you first launch Excel. As shown, the central and greater part of the display is a worksheet consisting of rows and columns, which is the worksheet described and used in the previous two sections.

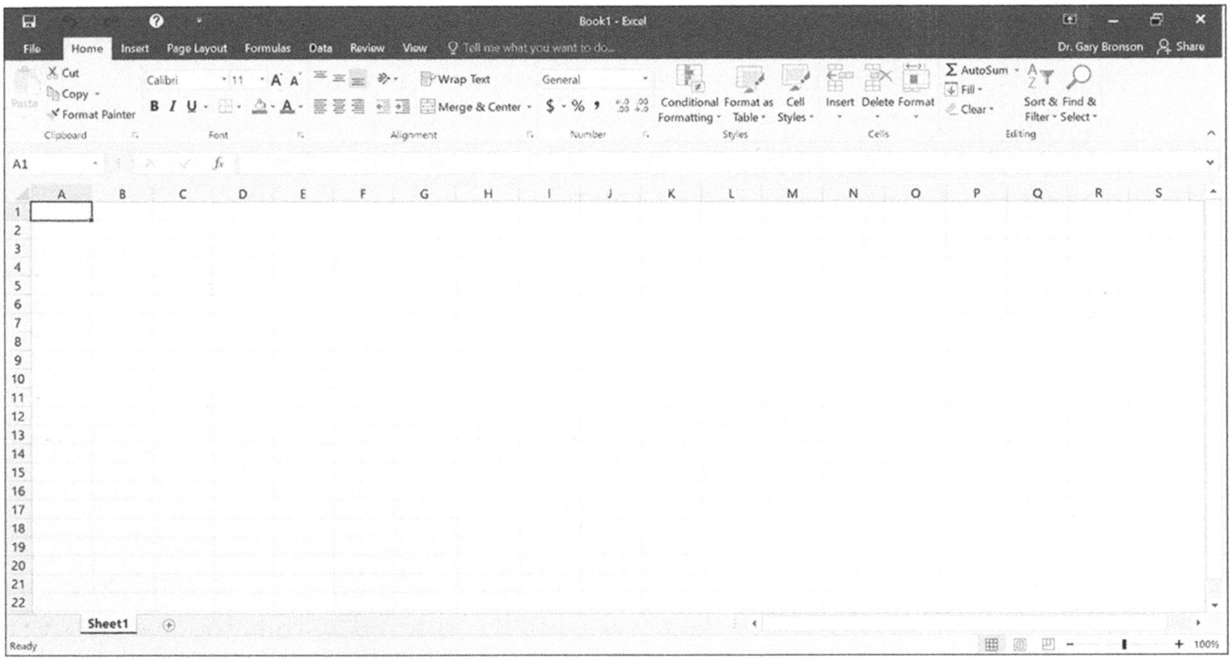

Figure 1.33 Excel's Initial Development Screen

To make it easier to understand and use these worksheets (or *sheets*, for short) and their capabilities effectively, the four key functional sections of the initial screen shown in Figure 1.33 are highlighted in Figure 1.34. The use of these four sections, both individually and together to achieve specific results, is the purpose of this chapter.

Figure 1.35 illustrates just the spreadsheet section shown in Figure 1.34, with additional details of this section highlighted. As seen, the main area is the spreadsheet presented in the previous section.

At any given time, and in the absence of using multi-window or split screen features, Excel will display only one sheet, and even then, only a small number of the worksheet's rows and columns will be visible on the screen. The worksheet you see actually can have over 16,384 columns and 1,048,576 rows, yielding over 17 billion cells possible on a single sheet. Few users will ever use that many cells, and there are also constraints based on the hardware of the computer you are using, the amount of memory you have, and numerous other factors. However, the potential for a large worksheet certainly exists. To see these other parts of the worksheet, again, in smaller sections, you can either use the vertical row and horizontal column scroll bars (labelled in the right-hand bottom corner of Figure 1.35), or the keyboard cursor control (arrow) keys.

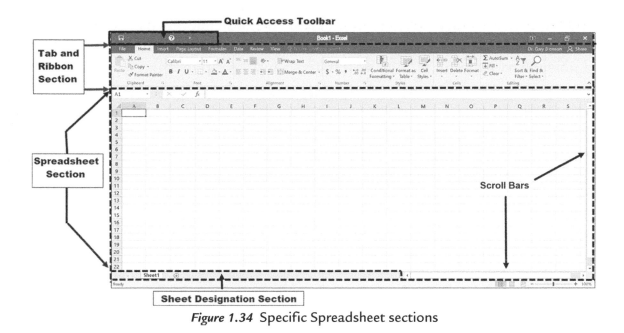

Figure 1.34 Specific Spreadsheet sections

To go directly to an individual cell, you can either click on the desired cell (use the cursor arrows or the scroll bars shown in Figure 1.35 to move to other sections of the spreadsheet, if needed) or enter the cell's row and column designation at the top of the worksheet into the *name box* shown in the figure. (There is also a shortcut key to do this, F5 on the PC and Mac). To enter data into the selected cell, you can either type directly into the selected cell or position the cursor in the area shown at the top of the worksheet in Figure 1.35, and then type or copy the desired data.

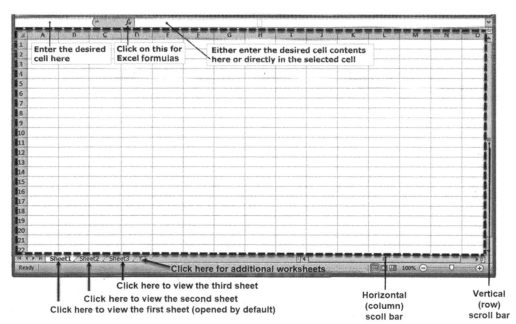

Figure 1.35 Spreadsheet features

As noted in the Section 1.1, the column and row designations permit every cell in a spreadsheet to be uniquely located and identified, and only one item can be stored in an individual cell at a time. The stored item must be either a number, text, formula, or function.

In addition to the currently active displayed worksheet, Excel also allows many additional worksheets to be created, limited only by your computer's memory. Each worksheet initially is assigned a designated sheet number, but that can be changed on the sheet tab to a more descriptive name. Clicking on one of the sheet numbers shown at the bottom of Figure 1.35 causes the associated worksheet to be displayed, so you can easily move between worksheets. By default, when Excel is first launched, Sheet 1 is activated. Thereafter, whenever Excel is launched, the last actively displayed worksheet is initially displayed. To add sheets to your spreadsheet, click on the + icon in the sheet designation section.

Using Excel's Options

In general, there are three main methods of accessing Excel's options for maintaining both individual worksheet cells and groups of cells. These are:

1. Using the Excel ribbon tabs shown in Figure 1.34 and then selecting one of the options that appears in one of the tab's groups when a tab is selected. In Figure 1.34, the Home tab is shown as having been selected.

2. Clicking on one of the options in the Quick Access Toolbar, also shown in Figure 1.34.

3. Right–clicking on the mouse when a cell or group of cells has first been highlighted, as presented in Section 1.2.

Using the Excel Ribbon Tabs Toolbar

Figure 1.36 illustrates the main groups of Excel options provided by the Excel ribbon tab and its associated groups of options (command icons). All of the tabs together collectively are known as the Excel *ribbon*. As illustrated, there are eight option groups, with each group identified by a unique tab. When one of these eight tabs is selected, a subset of options (sometime known as icons or buttons) associated with that tab is displayed immediately under the tab. The one exception in terms of structure to this tab and ribbon structure is provided by the File tab, which is presented in the next section.

In Figure 1.36, both the Home tab and its associated groups and commands have been outlined by a dotted line. As shown in the figure, the Home tab starts with the Paste option at the left-end and ends with the Editing options at the right. Initially, this is the tab that you will most often be using. At any time, however, you can click on a different tab and see that tab's available Groups and Options. As you will also be using the File tab for saving, retrieving and printing your work, a pointer to this tab is also shown.

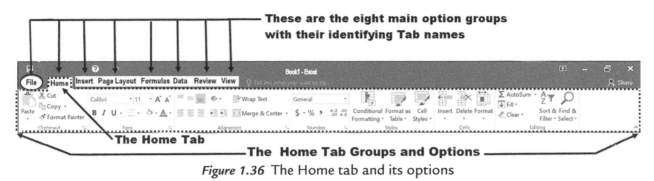

Figure 1.36 The Home tab and its options

The File tab and its use were described in Section 1.3. Each of the other tabs and their associated groups and command icons are presented in detail in the remaining chapters.

In addition to the Excel tabs, a second method of activating Excel options is to use the Quick Access Toolbar. This toolbar provides a quick way of selecting frequently used options without the need of first selecting a tab and then working your way through the various ribbon choices to activate the desired option.

Figure 1.37, previously shown as Figure 1.21, shows the Quick Access Toolbar that is illustrated in the top left had corner of Figure 1.34, with the purpose of each icon listed on the figure. This toolbar can be customized by adding and deleting your own personal selection of options. This is accomplished by clicking on the last option, the down-facing arrow, shown on the figure. This same customization can also be accomplished using the File tab's options menu.

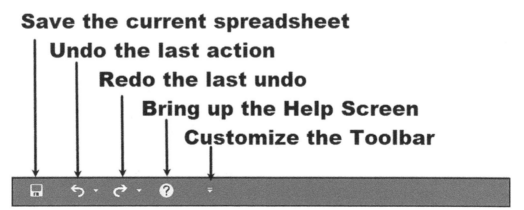

Figure 1.37 The Quick Access Toolbar

Appendix Exercises

1. List the main features that are provided by the Excel spreadsheet program

2. How many columns and rows are available in a worksheet that is displayed when Excel is launched?

3. How many worksheets are available when Excel is launched?

4. List the four main areas provided in an Excel spreadsheet.

5. Launch the Excel program on your computer and identify the four main areas of the displayed spreadsheet.

6. Create the following spreadsheet on your computer after you have launched the Excel program and opened up a new blank worksheet. (**Note:** Boldfacing is achieved by selecting the desired cell and pressing the Ctrl and B keys at the same time or by pressing the Home tab's B icon. To convert the contents in cells C6, C7, and C8 to text, type them with a leading quote, as in '/hr. Without the leading single quote, ', which converts the cell's contents to text, the division symbol will be marked as an invalid division error).

	A	B	C	D	E	F	G	H	I
1	Your Name								Project 2
2									
3	18%	Profit:	18%						
4				CLEAN-UP		FERTILIZE		LAWN	CARE
5	Item	Unit	Cost	Units	Cost	Units	Cost	Units	Cost
6	Labor	22.00	/hr	3	$66.00	1	$22.00	4.5	$99.00
7	Fertillize	6.00	/lb	0	0.00	5	30.00	0	0.00
8	Disposal	3.75	/cu. Yd.	7.5	28.13	0	0.00	4	15.00
9			Total Cost		$94.13		$52.00		$114.00
10			Profit		16.94		9.36		20.52
11			Charge for Service		$111.07		$61.36		$134.52

7. List the first four tabs located on the Excel ribbon.

8. What do each of the tab's ribbons consist of?

9. Answer the following.

    a. What is the purpose of the Quick Access Toolbar?

    b. List three of the options provided by the Quick Access Toolbar.

CHAPTER 2

FORMULAS AND FORMATTING

2.1   FORMULAS

Formulas form the backbone of all Excel spreadsheets. They are one of the key elements that make Excel the essential tool it has become and what separates a spreadsheet from a word processing program's data table. Using a formula, the data in one or more cells can be used to calculate new values or examined to make decisions. For example, consider the following spreadsheet segment in Figure 2.1a, paying particular attention to the formula in cell C2.

	A	B	C
1	Length	Width	Area
2	22.5	11.8	=A2*B2

Figure 2.1a Sample spreadsheet with the original input

The display produced by this spreadsheet is shown in Figure 2.1b.

	A	B	C
1	Length	Width	Area
2	22.5	11.8	265.5

Figure 2.1b Sample spreadsheet with the results of the calculation

In the spreadsheet shown in Figure 2.1b, if either the length value in cell A2 or the width value in cell B2 were changed, the formula in cell C2 would automatically be recalculated and a correct new value displayed in C2. The formula entered into cell C2 follows the basic structure of all Excel formulas, and has the general form

$$= \textbf{\textit{expression}}$$

Here, the *expression* is any combination of one or more operands, connected with mathematical *operators* that can be evaluated to yield a result. An *operand* is a number, cell address, or Excel function. Examples of Excel expressions are as follows:

A1 + B1

A2 * B2

0.06 * C3

E2 /D2

(E3 – F3) / (D2 – C2)

Each of these expressions uses the primary mathematical operators ^, +, -, *, and /. The only criterion in creating an expression is that an arithmetic symbol (+, -, *, /) **must be** used between two operands, be they cell addresses and/or numeric values and/or Excel functions, which are presented in the next section. Additionally, the multiplication symbol, *, **must be** used for multiplication. Thus, while A1*B2 is valid, both A2B2 and(A2)(B2) are invalid.

The available mathematical operators in Excel are listed Table 2.1.

Table 2.1 Summary of arithmetic operators

Operation	Operator
Exponentiation	^
Addition	+
Subtraction	–
Multiplication	*
Division	/

Expressions are calculated using standard arithmetic computational rules. These rules are presented in detail at the end of this section, and summarized below:

1. Parentheses can be used to form groupings.

2. When parentheses are present, operations within parentheses are calculated first, starting from the innermost set of parentheses to the outermost set.

3. An arithmetic symbol (^, +, -, *, /) **must be** used between two operands. Thus, =A1*B1 is valid, while =A1B1 is invalid.

4. The multiplication symbol must be used for multiplication (not parentheses). Thus, A1*B2 is valid and (A2)(B2) is invalid.

5. Multiplication and division are performed before addition and subtraction, and calculations are performed from left to right.

From Expressions to Formulas

Placing an equal sign (=) in front of an expression turns it into a formula. The formula can then be entered into an individual cell. Thus, the following are valid Excel formulas:

$$= A1 + B1$$
$$= A2*B2$$
$$= 0.06 *C3$$
$$= E2/D2$$
$$= (E3 - F3) / (D2 - C2)$$
$$= C5 *(D5 + E5)$$
$$= C1 + D1 +(E1*F1)$$

The spaces around the arithmetic operators in these examples are inserted strictly for clarity and may be omitted without affecting the value of the expression. The equal sign causes the expression to be evaluated and then stored and displayed in the cell containing the formula. Any cell referenced in a formula that does not contain a number is assigned a value of 0.

Example 1

Determine what each of the formulas does in the following cells:

	C
1	=A1+B1

	D
1	=A1+B1-12

Solution: The formula in cell C1 adds the values displayed in cells A1 and B1 and displays the sum in cell C1. It is important to note that the formula in cell D1 is a valid entry for this cell, whether or not cells A1 and B1 have any values in them. The formula will display a correct sum only when values actually reside in cells A1 and B1, otherwise it displays 0.

The formula in cell D1 adds the values located in cells A1 and B1, subtracts 12 from this sum, and displays the result in cell D1. Here, the formula in D1 could also have been entered as =C1–12.

Example 2

Determine what the formulas do.

	E
2	=C5*D4

	F
3	=0.005*C3/D3

Application Note
Displaying Formulas

The Excel default is to calculate and display the result in the cell wherever a formula is entered. You can, or course, always see the formula by clicking on the cell and looking at the formula bar directly above the spreadsheet. There is also the F2 shortcut key (or Ctrl- U on the Mac) which allows you to do the same thing.

Another way to see all of the formulas entered into a spreadsheet is to press the Ctrl and ~ keys together (the ~ key is at the top left-hand corner of the keyboard, directly below the Esc key). Doing so will change the display to reveal all entered formulas.

The Ctrl ~ combination is a toggle switch; this means pressing them again will toggle the spreadsheet back to its normal default display.

Solution: The formula in cell E2 multiplies the values in cells C5 and D4 and displays the result in cell E2.

NOTE — *A correct result is displayed in F2 only when cells C5 and D4 contain valid values; otherwise, cell F2 displays a 0.*

The formula in cell F3 multiplies the value in cell C3 by 0.005, divides this result by the value in cell D3, and displays the result in cell C3. A correct result is displayed in F3 only when cells C3 and D3 contain valid values; otherwise, a value of 0 is displayed.

Give It a Try

For the spreadsheet illustrated in Figure 2.2a, determine the values displayed in the cells containing each formula. Use Figure 2.2b to record your answers.

	A	B	C	D
1	4	8	=A1+B1	=B1-A1
2	10	20	=A2*B2	=B2/A1
3	=A1+A2	=B1+B2/2	=C1+C2	
4		=(B1+B2)/2		

Figure 2.2a Original input for the spreadsheet

	A	B	C	D
1	4	8		
2	10	20		
3				
4				

Figure 2.2b Calculate the results of the input in Figure 2.2a

Graphically Selecting Cells

Excel provides multiple ways for achieving almost anything you will need to accomplish. One of these alternative methods provides an extremely useful way of entering cell addresses into a formula. Using this method, you can point to and click on a desired cell rather than typing the cell's address. This is advantageous in that it visually shows you the referenced cells, avoids the necessity of determining the cell's address and, perhaps, mistyping the address in the formula.

The general procedure for selecting cells using this point and click method is as follows:

Step 1: Type an = sign in the cell where you want the formula located.

Step 2: If the next operand is a number, type it in; otherwise, if it is a cell, move the cursor to the desired cell and left-click the mouse.

Step 3: Type in a mathematical operator.

Step 4: If the next operand is a number, type it in; otherwise, if it is a cell, move the cursor to the desired cell and left-click the mouse.

Step 5: Repeat Steps 3 and 4 until the formula is complete; then press the Enter key.

To see how this procedure works in practice, consider that the formula =A1+B1 is entered in cell C1 using this point and click method.

Figure 2.3a shows how cell C1 appears after the initial = sign is entered (Step 1). Figure 2.3b shows how the cursor looks when it is moved to cell A1, while Figure 2.3c shows how cells A1 and C1 appear after the mouse is clicked on cell A1. Notice in Figure 2.3c that the formula now includes cell A1.

Figure 2.3a Beginning the formula in cell C1

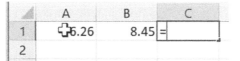

Figure 2.3b The cursor over cell A1

Once cell A1 has been included in the formula, as shown in Figure 2.3c, the multiplication operator (*) is typed (Step 3, shown in Figure 2.3d).

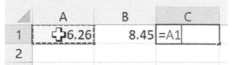

Figure 2.3c After clicking on cell A1

Application Note
Formulas as Cell Contents

A formula is a valid and acceptable cell entry, whether or not the cells used in the formula contain valid data values. However, the formula will calculate and display a correct result only when the referenced cells contain and display valid data.

   Clearly, it is more satisfying and easier to understand when an entered formula references cells that have data in them. In that case, you can immediately check that the formula is working as you expect. However, there will be times you will have to enter formulas before the referenced data is available.

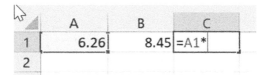

Figure 2.3d Typing the desired mathematical symbol

The selection of the second cell reference, in this case B1, is now made (Step 4, shown in, Figures 2.3e and 2.3f). This selection follows the same procedure used in selecting the first operand, cell A1. Notice in Figure 2.3f that the desired formula now is located in cell C1 and the cells referenced in this formula are highlighted.

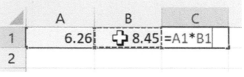

Figure 2.3e The cursor over cell B1

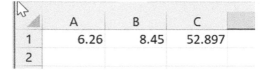

Figure 2.3f After clicking on cell B1

Once the desired formula is complete, as shown in Figure 2.3f, pressing the Enter key (Step 5) ends the formula, which is then computed, resulting in the value shown in Figure 2.3g. As always, because a formula is a valid cell entry, the data in any cell referenced by the formula need not be entered prior to entering the formula.

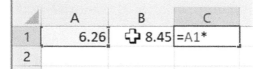

Figure 2.3g The result computed by the entered formula

Copying Formulas

The contents of a range of cells can be copied using standard Windows cut and paste techniques. In addition, Excel provides a unique technique for copying the contents of one or more cells to other cells with one mouse movement. This technique is extremely useful and one that will save you a tremendous amount of time in preparing your spreadsheet.

To understand why copying a formula from a single cell to one or more cells is such a powerful and frequently used technique, consider the spreadsheet shown in Figure 2.4a. This spreadsheet is intended to keep track of living expenses for the first six months of the year.

Now look at cell B7, which is the selected cell in Figure 2.4a. Notice that the *value* in the cell is 0, but that the cell's *formula*, seen in the Formula Bar at the top of the spreadsheet, is =B4+B5+B6. As expenses for January are entered into the spreadsheet, the value in cell B7 will change to reflect the total of the entered expenses. This leads to a very important concept, namely, that ***a formula may be entered into a cell before any data is entered into the cells that are referenced in the formula***.

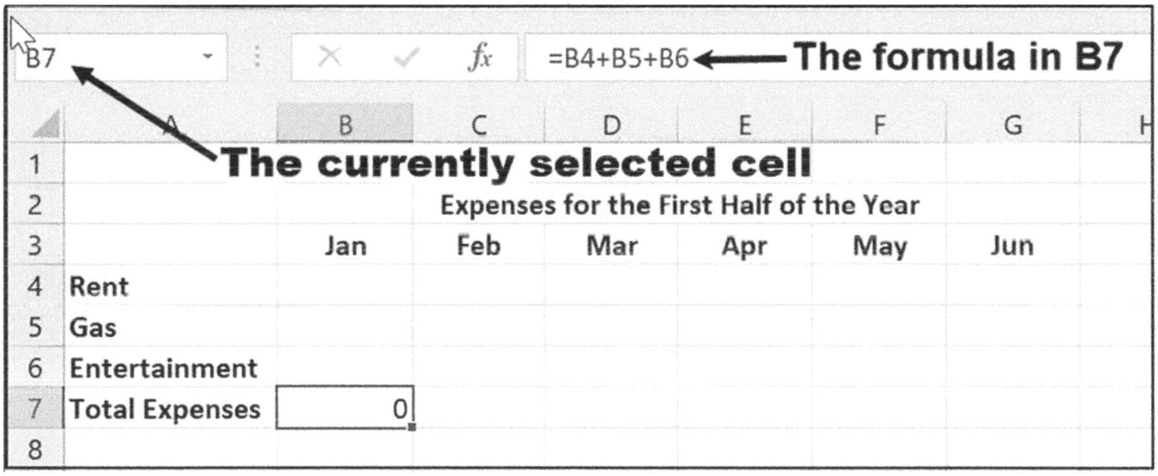

Figure 2.4a Keeping track of expenses

Now let us see how we can easily enter the formulas for cells C7 through G7, which represent the totals for each of the months, February through June. (Again, these formulas may be entered before or after any actual data for these months is entered.) The correct formulas for the months February through June can be entered simply by copying the contents of cell B7 to cells C7 through G7, using the fill handle, as shown in Figure 2.4b.

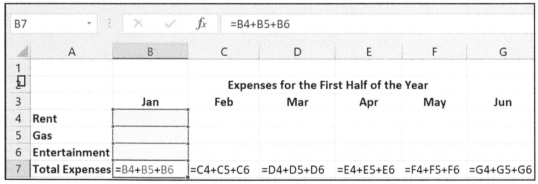

Figure 2.4b Copying the formula in cell B7

What makes this copy feature so powerful is that Excel will alter the references to the cells in a formula as it is copied from column to column or row to row, unless explicitly instructed not to do so. That is, it is assumed by the spreadsheet that, in this case, if you are using cell B7 to add the contents of column B cells, that you intend to add the equivalent C cells when the formula in B7 is copied to cell C7, and so on, for the sums in cells D7 through G7. This result comes about when the cell references in question have been written as relative cell references, which allows for the automatic altering of cell references when copied to other cells. The described result can be verified by pressing the Ctrl and ~ keys after the copy has been made, which causes all spreadsheet formulas to be displayed. This is shown in Figure 2.4c.

B7			×	✓	*fx*	=B4+B5+B6		
	A	B		C	D	E	F	G
1								
2				Expenses for the First Half of the Year				
3		Jan		Feb	Mar	Apr	May	Jun
4	Rent							
5	Gas							
6	Entertainment							
7	Total Expenses	=B4+B5+B6		=C4+C5+C6	=D4+D5+D6	=E4+E5+E6	=F4+F5+F6	=G4+G5+G6

Figure 2.4c The copied formulas

Notice that as the formula was copied from column to column, the spreadsheet changed the column designation in each cell address used in the formula. That is, the copy does not produce an exact copy of the formula but adjusts the column designation as the formula is copied from column to column. This same adjustment is made in row designations when a formula is copied up or down from row to row. This is known as *relative cell referencing* (or *addressing*). It should be noted that for certain situations, the automatic adjustment characteristic is not desired, and that is the reason why there are other cell referencing methods which can be used, including absolute and mixed.

Expression Construction Rules[1]

The formulas required for the vast majority of spreadsheet applications, such as budgeting, accounting, inventory, and sales, generally consist of expressions using only a few of the most commonly used arithmetic operations. When writing more complex formulas, however, you will need to be aware of the following rules, which apply equally to all expressions, be they simple or complex:

1. Two binary operator symbols must never be placed side by side. For example, 5 */ 6 is invalid because the two operators, * and /, are placed next to each other.

2. Parentheses may be used to form groupings, and all expressions enclosed within parentheses are evaluated first. For example, in the expression (6 + 4) / (2 + 3), the 6 + 4 and 2 +3 are evaluated first to yield 10 / 5. The 10 / 5 is then evaluated to yield 2.

3. Sets of parentheses may also be enclosed by other parentheses. For example, the expression (2 * (3 + 7)) / 5 is valid and evaluates to 4. When parentheses are included within parentheses, the expressions in the innermost parentheses are always evaluated first. The evaluation continues from innermost to outermost parentheses until the expressions in all parentheses have been evaluated. The number of closing parentheses must always equal the number of opening parentheses so that there are no unpaired sets.

4. Parentheses cannot be used to indicate multiplication. The multiplication operator, *, must explicitly be used. For example, the expression (3 + 4) (5 + 1) is invalid. The correct expression is (3 + 4) * (5 + 1).

As a general rule, parentheses should be used to specify logical groupings of operands and to indicate clearly the intended order of arithmetic operations. In the absence of parentheses, expressions containing multiple operators are evaluated by the priority, or *precedence*, of each operator. Table 2.2 lists both the precedence and associativity of the operands considered in this section.

Table 2.2 Operator precedence and associativity

Operator	Associativity
^	Left to Right
* /	Left to Right
+ −	Left to Right

---

[1] This topic may be omitted on first reading without loss of subject continuity.

The precedence of an operator establishes its priority relative to all other operators. The operators at the top of Table 2.2 have a higher priority than the operators at the bottom of the table. Thus, in expressions with multiple operators, the operator with the higher precedence is used before an operator with a lower precedence. For example, in the expression 6 + 4 / 2 + 3, the division is done before the addition, yielding an intermediate result of 6 + 2 + 3. The additions are then performed to yield a final result of 11.

Expressions containing operators with the same precedence are evaluated according to their *associativity*. This means that evaluation is either from left to right or from right to left as each operator is encountered. For example, in the expression 8 + 5 * 7 / 2 * 4, the multiplication and division operators are of higher precedence than the addition operator, and are evaluated first. Both of these operators, however, are of equal priority. Therefore, these operators are evaluated left-to-right, yielding

$$8 + 5 * 6 / 2 * 4 =$$
$$8 + 30 / 2 * 4 =$$
$$8 + 15 * 4 =$$
$$8 + 60 = 68$$

EXERCISES 2.1

1. Use the spreadsheet shown in Figure 2.5a for the following exercises.

	A	B	C
1			=A1+B1
2			=A2*B2
3	=A2-A1	=B2/B1	=C1+C2

Figure 2.5a Input for the exercise in Exercise 1

a. Determine and write in the values that will be displayed in cells C1, C2, C3, A3, and B3 for the values shown in Figure 2.5b.

	A	B	C
1	4	10	
2	8	20	
3			

Figure 2.5b Compute and enter the answers for Exercise 1a

b. Determine and write in the values that will be displayed in cells C1, C2, C3, A3, and B3 for the values shown in Figure 2.5c.

	A	B	C
1	4	10	
2	-8	20	
3			

Figure 2.5c Compute and enter the answers for Exercise 1b

2. Use the spreadsheet in Figure 2.6a for the following exercises.

	A	B	C	D	E
1	Month	Balance	Income	Expenses	Net Income
2	January				=C2-D2
3	February	=B2-E2			

Figure 2.6a Spreadsheet for Exercise 2

a. Using the formulas shown in Figure 2.6a, determine the dollar values that will be displayed in cells E2 and B3 for the values shown in Figure 2.6b. Assume all values have been formatted as currency, with a leading $ sign.

	A	B	C	D	E
1	**Month**	**Balance**	**Income**	**Expenses**	**Net Income**
2	January	$258.27	$400.00	$320.75	
3	February				

Figure 2.6b Compute and enter the answers for Exercise 2a

b. Using the formulas shown in Figure 2.6a, determine the dollar values that will be displayed in cells E2 and B3 for the values shown in Figure 2.6c. Assume all values have been formatted as currency, with a leading $ sign.

	A	B	C	D	E
1	**Month**	**Balance**	**Income**	**Expenses**	**Net Income**
2	January	$258.27	$300.00	$320.75	
3	February				

Figure 2.6c Spreadsheet to compute and enter Exercise 2b answers

3. Figure 2.7a shows how the first two payments for a 4-year loan (48 monthly payments) at 5% annual interest would be calculated and displayed in a spreadsheet. Use the formulas shown in the figure for the following problems.

	A	B	C	D	E	F
1	Payment No.	Balance	Payment	Interest	Net Payment	New Balance
2	1			=0.05/12*B2	=C2-D2	=B2-E2
3	2	=F2				

Figure 2.7a Original spreadsheet input

a. Assuming that all values have been formatted as currency with a leading $ sign, determine the dollar values that will be displayed in cells D2, E2, F2, and B3 for the values shown in Figure 2.7b. In Section 2.4, you will see how to format numbers as currency.

	A	B	C	D	E	F
1	Payment No.	Balance	Payment	Interest	Net Payment	New Balance
2	1	$15,000.00	$353.00			
3	2					

Figure 2.7b Compute and enter the answers for Exercise 3a

4. Determine the formula for cell B2 in Figure 2.8 that calculates the circumference of a circle whose radius is entered into cell A2. The equation for determining the circumference, c, of a circle is $c = 2\pi \, radius$ and π equals 3.1416.

	A	B
1	Radius	Circumference
2	2.5	

Figure 2.8 Spreadsheet for Exercise 4

5. Determine the formula for cell B2 in Figure 2.9 that calculates the area of circle whose radius is entered into cell A2. The equation for determining the area, a, of a circle is $a = \pi r^2$, where r is the radius and π equals 3.1416.

	A	B
1	Radius	Area
2	2.5	

Figure 2.9 Compute and enter the answer for Exercise 5

6. Determine the formula for cell B2 in Figure 2.10 that converts the Fahrenheit temperature in cell A2 to degrees Celsius. The equation for this conversion is *Celsius = 5/9 (A2 − 32)*.

	A	B
1	Fahrenheit	Celsius
2	75	

Figure 2.10 Compute and enter the answer for Exercise 6

7. Determine the formula for cell B2 in Figure 2.11 that calculates the round trip distance of a trip whose one-way distance is in cell A2.

	A	B
1	One-way Dist	Round-trip Dist.
2	124.8	

Figure 2.11 Compute and enter the answer for Exercise 7

8. Determine the formula for cell C2 in Figure 2.12 to calculate the elapsed time, in minutes, that it takes to make a trip. The equation for computing elapsed time is *elapsed time = total distance / average speed*. Assume that the distance, in miles, is in cell A2 and the average speed, in miles/hour, is in cell B2. Make sure to convert your answer to minutes.

	A	B	C
1	Distance (miles)	Avg. speed (miles/hour)	Time (minutes)
2	170	52	

Figure 2.12 Compute and enter the answers for Exercise 8

9. Listed below are algebraic expressions and the incorrect Excel formulas corresponding to them. Find the errors and write the corrected Excel formulas.

Algebra	**Excel Formula**
a. $(2)(3) + (4)(5)$	$= (2)(3) + (4)(5$
b. $\dfrac{6+18}{2}$	$= 6 + 18 / 2$
c. $\dfrac{4.5}{12.2-3.1}$	$= 4.5 / 12.2 - 3.1$
d. $4.6(3.0 + 14.9)$	$= 4.6(3.0 + 14.9)$
e. $(12.1 + 18.9)(15.3 - 3.8)$	$= (12.1 + 18.9)(15.3 - 3.8)$

10. If cell A1 contains the number 12, cell B1 contains the number 3, cell D4 contains the number 2, and cell M5 holds the number 45, determine the value of the following formulas:

a. =A1 / B1 + 3

b. =M5 / B1 + A1 − 10 * D4

c. =M5 - 3 * A1 + 4 * D4

d. =D4 / 5

e. =18 / B1

f. =−B1 * A1

g. −M5 / 20

h. (M5 + A1) / (B1 + D4)

i. M5 + A1 / B1 + D4

11. Determine the value of the following expressions, paying attention to the precedence and associativity of all arithmetic operators as listed in Table 2.2.

a. $3 + 4 * 6$

b. $3 * 4 / 6 + 6$

c. $2 * 3 / 12 * 8 / 4$

d. $10 * (1 + 7 * 3)$

e. $20 - 2 / 6 + 3$

f. $20 - 2 / (6 + 3)$

g. $(20 - 2) / 6 + 3$

h. $(20 - 2) / (6 + 3)$

i. $2 * 3 / 12 * 8 / 4$

j. $10 * (1 + 7 * 3)$

k. $20 - 2 / 6 + 3$

l. $20 - 2 / (6 + 3)$

m. $(20 - 2) / 6 + 3$

n. $(20 - 2) / (6 + 3)$

2.2 INTRODUCTION TO EXCEL FUNCTIONS

As we have seen, formulas are used to perform calculations and change the contents of the cell containing the formula. For example, the formula

$$= A1 * B1$$

multiplies the value in cell A1 times the value in cell B1 and assigns the resulting value to the cell containing the formula. Although addition, subtraction, multiplication, exponentiation, and division are easily accomplished using Excel's arithmetic operators, no such operators exist for finding the square root of a number, determining certain statistical values, and other more complex, but commonly employed, calculations. To facilitate such calculations, Excel provides standard preprogrammed functions that you can incorporate into your formulas.

An Excel function has the general form

$$\boxed{= \textbf{\textit{Function-name(arguments)}}}$$

As with all functions, the equal sign indicates to Excel that a formula is to follow. The *function-name* indicates the desired function; it is followed by the required parentheses, which contain the data that is sent to the function. This data sent is formally referred to as the function's *arguments*. Examples of Excel formulas using functions are as follows:

= SUM(B2:B15) ← This sums the values in cells B2 through B15

= SUM(A1:B4) ← This sums the values in cells A1 through B4

= SUM(A1,A5,B3,C4) ← This is the same as =A1+A5+B3+C4

= AVERAGE(C2:C20) ← This calculates the average of the values in cells C2 through C20

= MAX(A1:A52) ← This finds the maximum (largest) value in cells A1 through A52

A complete list of Excel functions is found by clicking on the f_x Insert Function icon shown on Figure 2.13. Clicking this icon brings up the dialog box shown in Figure 2.14.

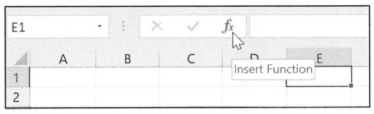

Figure 2.13 The Insert Function icon

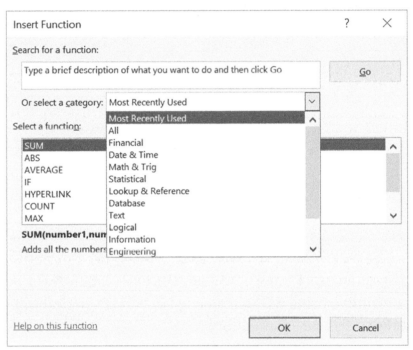

Figure 2.14 Insert Function dialog box

It is also possible to bring up the Insert Function dialog box from the Excel ribbon Formulas tab). As seen in Figure 2.14, Excel's preprogrammed functions can be displayed by application type, such as Financial, Date, and Time, or all together in alphabetical order, or by most recently used. Clicking on the desired function within a group allows the user to enter the arguments using a menu-based dialog, followed by the completed function being inserted in the currently active cell.

The functions that you will initially use most often in your work (except for the PRODUCT( ) function, which is included for completeness; see the Application Note on page 52) are listed in Table 2.1. By definition, a function calculates and displays the value(s) obtained after processing by the function, using the arguments provided. It should be noted that using the incorrect type, number, or data types of arguments may bring about uncertain results, or result in the display of an error message.

The examples shown in Table 2.3 illustrate that some functions, such as SQRT( ), require a single argument, while other functions, such as SUM( ), take multiple arguments, and some require no arguments at all, such as TODAY(). In addition, each argument can be a cell reference, another function, or in some cases, a range of cell addresses. Additionally, an expression that can be computed to yield a value of the required data type is also valid. Thus, for example, the formula =SQRT(C2–C1) is valid.

Table 2.3 Commonly Used Mathematical Functions

Function Name	Description	Example
ABS( )	Absolute value	=ABS(D5)
AVERAGE( )	Average	=AVERAGE(A2:A25)
COUNT( )	Number of items	=COUNT(C7:C33)
MAX( )	Maximum value	=MAX(A1:A10)
MIN( )	Minimum value	=MIN(A1:A10)
PMT( )	Loan payment	=PMT(.05,48,15000)
POWER( )	Raise a value to a power	=POWER(C2,3)
PRODUCT( )	Product of two or more values	=PRODUCT(A1:C1)
SUM( )	Sum of one or more values	=SUM(B2:B20) =SUM(A1:A5,B2,C1)
SQRT( )	Square root of its argument	=SQRT(D2)

Example 1

The spreadsheet shown in Figure 2.15a contains sales data for a six-month period. Determine the formula, using SUM( ), needed in cell H1 to determine the six-month total of these sales.

	A	B	C	D	E	F	G	H
1		Jan	Feb	Mar	Apr	May	Jun	Total
2	Sales	$124,800	$165,250	$143,070	$138,960	$155,540	$148,910	

Figure 2.15a Spreadsheet data for Example 1

Solution: The formula that should be entered in cell H1 is =SUM(B2:G2).

*Although this produces the same result as =B2+C2+D2+E2+F2+G2, this latter formula **generally should not** be used. Using the longer formula both indicates a truly inexperienced developer and someone not able to use one of the most basic and commonly used Excel functions, which is SUM( ).*

Once the correct sum formula is entered into cell H1, the spreadsheet will appear as shown in Figure 2.15b.

	A	B	C	D	E	F	G	H
1		Jan	Feb	Mar	Apr	May	Jun	Total
2	Sales	$124,800	$165,250	$143,070	$138,960	$155,540	$148,910	$876,530

Figure 2.15b Results for Example 1

Example 2

The spreadsheet shown in Figure 2.16a contains the hourly rate and hours worked for the employees of a local company. Determine the formula needed in cells D2 through D7 to compute each employee's net pay, where *Net Pay = (Hourly Rate)* * (Hours Worked)*. Provide the formula in cell D8 that will sum all of values in cells D2 through D7.

	A	B	C	D
1	**Name**	**Hourly Rate ($/Hr)**	**Hrs. Worked**	**Net Pay**
2	Bill Biggins	$20.00	40	
3	Jane Cousins	22.50	40	
4	Laura Demaio	16.80	35	
5	John Farnsworth	16.80	35	
6	Rachel Smith	35.00	38	
7	Douglas Timinsky	22.70	38	
8			Total Paid:	

Figure 2.16a Data for Example 2

Solution: The required formulas are shown in Figure 2.16b.

	A	B	C	D
1	**Name**	**Hourly Rate ($/Hr)**	**Hrs. Worked**	**Net Pay**
2	Bill Biggins	20	40	=B2*C2
3	Jane Cousins	22.5	40	=B3*C3
4	Laura Demaio	16.8	35	=B4*C4
5	John Farnsworth	16.8	35	=B5*C5
6	Rachel Smith	25	38	=B6*C6
7	Douglas Timinsky	22.7	38	=B7*C7
8			Total Paid:	=SUM(D2:D7)

Figure 2.16b Formulas for Example 2

Once the formulas shown in Figure 2.16b are entered into the spreadsheet, it will appear as shown in Figure 2.16c.

	A	B	C	D
1	**Name**	**Hourly Rate ($/Hr)**	**Hrs. Worked**	**Net Pay**
2	Bill Biggins	$20.00	40	$800.00
3	Jane Cousins	22.50	40	900.00
4	Laura Demaio	16.80	35	588.00
5	John Farnsworth	16.80	35	588.00
6	Rachel Smith	25.00	38	950.00
7	Douglas Timinsky	22.70	38	862.60
8			Total Paid:	$4,688.60

Figure 2.16c Results for Example 2

Functions may also be included as part of larger expressions. Thus, the formula

$$= 4 * SQRT(4.5 * B5) - 2.0$$

is valid. Additionally, a function's calculated value may be included within a larger expression, or even used as an argument to another function. For example, the nested function

$$=SQRT(POWER(ABS(A1),B1)$$

is also valid. Because parentheses are present, the computation proceeds from the inner to the outer pairs of parentheses. Thus, the absolute value of cell A1 is computed first and used as an argument to the POWER( ) function. The square root of value calculated by this function is then computed and displayed in the cell containing the complete formula. This is called a *nested function*, since it actually contains no fewer than three functions, which are wrapped or "nested" within each other. The ABS( ) function is contained within the POWER( ) function, and the entire expression is contained within the SQRT( ) function.

Formulas containing functions are copied in the identical way as the arithmetic formulas described in the prior section. As each formula is copied, cell references are automatically adjusted unless absolute cell addresses are used, as shown in Section 2.6.

As a specific example of copying a formula containing an Excel function, consider Figure 2.17a. As shown in this formula, the correct formula has been entered into cell B10.

Once this initial formula is entered in cell B10, the formulas for cells C10 through G10, which represent the totals for February through June can be entered simply by copying the contents of cell B10 to cells C10 through G10, as shown in Figure 2.17b.

(Note, if you are unsure of how this copy is done, review **Copying Formulas** and Figures 2.4a through 2.4c in the previous section.)

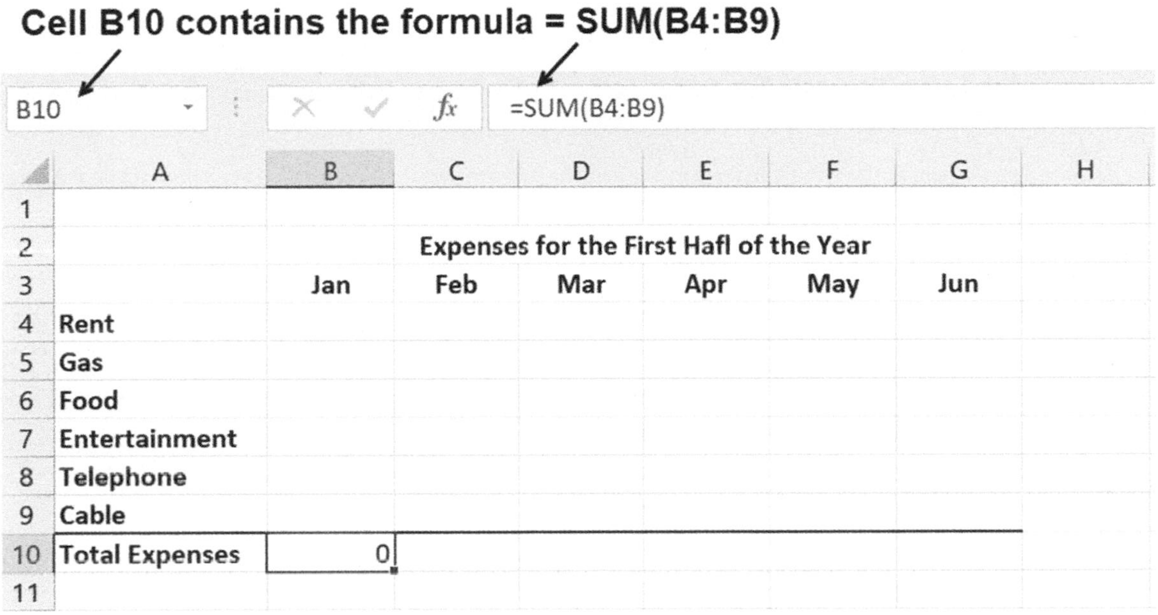

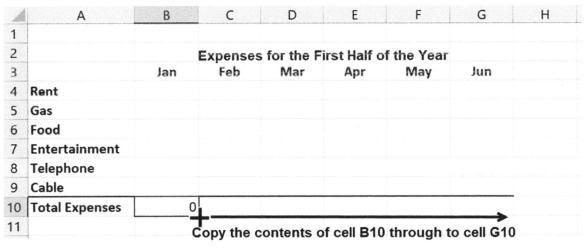

Cell B10 contains the formula = SUM(B4:B9)

Figure 2.17a Keeping track of expenses

Figure 2.17b Copying the formula in cell B10

Again, as noted in Section 2.1, what makes this copy so powerful is that Excel will alter the references to the cells in a formula as it is copied from column to column or row to row (relative cell referencing), unless explicitly instructed not to do so. In this case, Excel assumes that if you are using cell B10 to add the contents of column B cells, that you intend to add the equivalent C cells when the formula in B10 is copied to cell C10,

---

Application Note
Most and Least Commonly Used Functions

The most and least commonly used functions in Table 2.3 for basic spreadsheets are the SUM( ) and PRODUCT( ) functions, respectively. The reason for this is the same for both functions; a function should only be used to simplify development, not complicate it. In this regard, the general development rule is to only use a function when it replaces a more complicated or longer mathematical expression, or there is no other way to calculate the desired result.

As this applies to the SUM( ) and PRODUCT( ) functions, it means that if there are only two values that have to be added or multiplied, an arithmetic expression can be used just as easily as a function. For example, the formula =A1+A2 is equally useful as =SUM(A1:A2); similarly, =A1*B1 can be used in lieu of =PRODUCT(A1:B1). If the number of data items to be summed or multiplied is 3 or more, it may make more sense to use the function.

The same can hold true for the POWER( ) function, for which the exponentiation operator can do the exact same thing as =5^2 could be substituted for =POWER(5,2).

Again, for three or more arguments the respective functions are preferable (for exactly three arguments, some developers will use SUM( ) and some will not). Certainly, the formula =SUM(A1:A10) is more concise and requires less typing than the equivalent =A1+A2+A3+A4+A5+A6+A7+A8+A9+A10. In summary, for a small number of arguments, there is no hard and fast rule as to whether it is better to use a function or a formula. It is a judgment call. For larger numbers or arguments, use of a function if available is generally recommended.

---

and so on for the sums in cells D10 through G10. This is verified by pressing the Ctrl and ~ keys after the copy has been made, which causes all spreadsheet formulas to be displayed, as shown in Figure 2.17c.

B10		f_x	=SUM(B4:B9)			
	A	B	C	D	E	F	G
1							
2		Expenses for the First Half of the Year					
3		Jan	Feb	Mar	Apr	May	Jun
4	Rent						
5	Gas						
6	Food						
7	Entertainment						
8	Telephone						
9	Cable						
10	Total Expenses	=SUM(B4:B9)	=SUM(C4:C9)	=SUM(D4:D9)	=SUM(E4:E9)	=SUM(F4:F9)	=SUM(G4:G9)

Figure 2.17c The copied formulas

Note that if an absolute address is used for a cell's referencing (see Section 2.6), the cell so designated will not be altered in any way when the formula is copied. If mixed references are used, it will restrict how the cell references will be copied, whether to change by row or column, but not both. Absolute and mixed cell referencing and the situations that require their use are described in Section 2.5.

Highlighting Selected Arguments

As always, Excel provides multiple ways of accomplishing almost anything you want to do, including selecting function arguments. The SUM( ) function, in particular, is so frequently used in both introductory and advanced applications that most practitioners typically type in its name and then select its arguments by highlighting, as presented in Section 1.2, rather than typing in the arguments' addresses. For example, consider Figure 2.15a, which is reproduced below as Figure 2.18a.

	A	B	C	D	E	F	G	H
1		Jan	Feb	Mar	Apr	May	Jun	Total
2	Sales	$124,800	$165,250	$143,070	$138,960	$155,540	$148,910	

Figure 2.18a A copy of the spreadsheet in Figure 2.15a

To calculate the desired total in cell H1, the formula =SUM(B2:G2) should be used. However, rather than typing the complete function into the cell, you can begin by entering "=SUM(" and then highlighting cells B2 through G2. Doing this produces the spreadsheet shown in Figure 2.18b.

	A	B	C	D	E	F	G	H	I
1		Jan	Feb	Mar	Apr	May	Jun	Total	
2	Sales	$124,800	$165,250	$143,070	$138,960	$155,540	$148,910	-SUM(B2:G2	

Figure 2.18b Highlighting the range after typing =SUM(

Notice that the highlighted range has automatically been provided as arguments to the SUM( ) function in cell H2. At this point, you can type in a comma and add additional arguments to the function or press the *Enter* key to complete the function. When you press the *Enter* key, Excel will provide the closing parenthesis, enter and calculate the formula, and produce the result shown in Figure 2.18c.

	A	B	C	D	E	F	G	H
1		Jan	Feb	Mar	Apr	May	Jun	Total
2	Sales	$124,800	$165,250	$143,070	$138,960	$155,540	$148,910	$876,530

Figure 2.18c Results of highlighting after typing =SUM( )

EXERCISES 2.2

1. Write Excel functions or formulas to determine the following:

a. the square root of the contents of cell A1

b. the square root of the contents of cell A2

c. the absolute value of the contents of cell B1

d. the absolute value of the contents of cell B2

e. the value of cell D5 raised to the 4th power.

2. Use this spreadsheet for Exercise 2.

	A	B	C
1	25	5.2	=A1*B1
2	22.5	11.8	=A2/B2
3	18	24	=SQRT(A1)
4	=A1+10	57	=POWER(A2,3)
5	=A1+A2	=B1*B2	=(B3-A3)/(B4-A4)

Write the values, in the following spreadsheet, that will appear in cells C1 through C5, A5, and B5.

	A	B	C
1			
2			
3			
4			
5			

3. Using the SUM( ) function, write functions that determine the following:

a. the sum of cells A1, B5, C3, and D3.

b. the sum of cells B2, C2, D4, and E5

c. the sum of cells A3 through A10

d. the sum of cells A3 through D3

e. the sum of cells H2 through H30

f. the sum of cells B2 through B8 and D5.

4. Using the AVERAGE( ) function, write functions that determine the following:

  a. the average of cells A3 through A10

  b. the average of cells A3 through D3

  c. the average of cells H2 through H30.

5. Enter the data shown in the first spreadsheet, including the necessary function or formula in cell H2, to verify that it produces the correct totals shown in the second spreadsheet that follows.

	A	B	C	D	E	F	G	H
1		Jan	Feb	Mar	Apr	May	Jun	Total
2	Sales	$124,800	$165,250	$143,070	$138,960	$155,540	$148,910	$876,530

	A	B	C	D	E	F	G	H
1		Jan	Feb	Mar	Apr	May	Jun	Total
2	Sales	$124,800	$165,250	$143,070	$138,960	$155,540	$148,910	$876,530

6. Use the data shown in the first spreadsheet to produce the results given in the spreadsheet that follows it.

	A	B	C	D
1	Name	Hourly Rate ($/Hr)	Hrs. Worked	Net Pay
2	Bill Biggins	$20.00	40	
3	Jane Cousins	22.50	40	
4	Laura Demaio	16.80	35	
5	John Farnsworth	16.80	35	
6	Rachel Smith	35.00	38	
7	Douglas Timinsky	22.70	38	
8			Total Paid:	

	A	B	C	D
1	Name	Hourly Rate ($/Hr)	Hrs. Worked	Net Pay
2	Bill Biggins	$20.00	40	$800.00
3	Jane Cousins	22.50	40	900.00
4	Laura Demaio	16.80	35	588.00
5	John Farnsworth	16.80	35	588.00
6	Rachel Smith	25.00	38	950.00
7	Douglas Timinsky	22.70	38	862.60
8			Total Paid:	$4,688.60

7. The spreadsheet shown in Figure 2.19 contains labels, income, and expense data for a six-month period. In the four highlighted cells, write in the functions or formulas needed to calculate the indicated totals. Because the remaining totals are easily obtained by copying the functions or formulas in the highlighted cells, only the four highlighted formulas need to be entered by hand.

	A	B	C	D	E	F	G	H
1		**Jan**	**Feb**	**Mar**	**Apr**	**May**	**Jun**	**Six-Month Totals**
2	**Income:**							
3	**Seminars**	$4,000	$5,000	$2,000	$6,000	$5,000	$3,000	
4	**Books**	$250	$270	$140	$720	$200	$220	
5	**Consulting**	$2,000	$1,000	$3,000	$2,000	$1,000	$3,000	
6	**Totals**							
7								
8	**Expenses**							
9	**Rent**	$500	$500	$500	$500	$500	$500	
10	**Utilities**	$150	$175	$75	$200	$175	$120	
11	**Phone**	$250	$250	$250	$300	$275	$230	
12	**Equipment**	$300	$350	$175	$410	$350	$280	
13	**Totals**							
14	**Monthy Profit:**							

Figure 2.19 Spreadsheet data for Exercise 7

a. The spreadsheet shown in Figure 2.20 contains labels, income, and expense data for a six-month period. Determine the functions or formulas needed to calculate the Totals indicated in column H and rows 6 and 14.

	A	B	C	D	E	F	G	H
1		**Jan**	**Feb**	**Mar**	**Apr**	**May**	**Jun**	**Six Month Totals**
2	**Income:**							
3	**Seminars**	$4,000	$5,000	$2,000	$6,000	$5,000	$3,000	
4	**Books**	$250	$270	$140	$720	$200	$220	
5	**Consulting**	$2,000	$1,000	$3,000	$2,000	$1,000	$3,000	
6	**Totals**							
7								
8								
9	**Expenses**							
10	**Rent**	$500	$500	$500	$500	$500	$500	
11	**Utilities**	$150	$175	$75	$200	$175	$120	
12	**Phone**	$250	$250	$250	$300	$275	$230	
13	**Equipment**	$300	$350	$175	$410	$350	$280	
14	**Totals**							
15								
16	**Monthly Profit:**							

Figure 2.20 Spreadsheet for Exercise 7a

b. Using your computer, enter the spreadsheet shown in Figure 2.20 above, along with all the required functions or formulas. Using a calculator, verify the displayed totals. Note that you are verifying that you entered the correct function or formula, not that Excel is miscalculating the formula that you did enter.

c. Print out the spreadsheet you entered in Part b.

d. In place of typing the arguments into the SUM( ) functions in cell H3, which cells could be highlighted to provide the same result?

e. In place of typing the arguments into the SUM( ) functions in cell B6, which cells could be highlighted to provide the same result?

2.3 FORMATTING

Besides producing correct results, it is extremely important for a spreadsheet to display its results attractively. Most spreadsheets are judged on their perceived ease of use, style, and presentation. Formally, a cell's appearance and the shape and style of its contents is referred to as its *format*. Formatting a cell means setting how a cell looks (such as the border style, font color, and cell shading) and setting the appearance of its contents, including its data type (such as number, currency, or accounting).

For example, consider the two spreadsheets shown in Figure 2.21, both of which present the same information. Figure 2.21a shows how the spreadsheet appears using the default formats in effect when the information was entered; Figure 2.21b shows the results after explicit formatting has been applied.

Yearly Summary	
Items Sold:	54
Price per item:	485.8
Total Sales:	26233.2
Total Cost:	12395
Net Profit:	13838.2

Figure 2.21a Default format

Yearly Summary	
Items Sold:	54
Price per item:	$485.80
Total Sales:	$26,233.20
Total Cost:	$12,395.00
Net Profit:	$13,838.20

Figure 2.21b With explicit formatting

Clearly, the presentation in Figure 2.21b is preferable. This spreadsheet presents its information in a manner that is easier to read and understand than that in Figure 2.21a.

Once a single cell or range of cells has been selected, either by clicking on a single cell or highlighting a range of cells, formatting can be applied using one of the following methods:

Method 1: Use the formatting tools available on the Home tab of the Excel ribbon.

Method 2: Activate the complete set of format tools by either

a. Activating the Dialog box launchers on the Home Ribbon by right clicking on the small arrow, ▣ at the lower right of the three groups of icons (Font, Alignment, Number), or

b. Right clicking the mouse within the selected cells and selecting the Format Cells option located toward the bottom of the dropdown menu.

Method 1

This method provides quick access to the most commonly used formatting tasks. Figure 2.22 shows the three most used formatting groups.

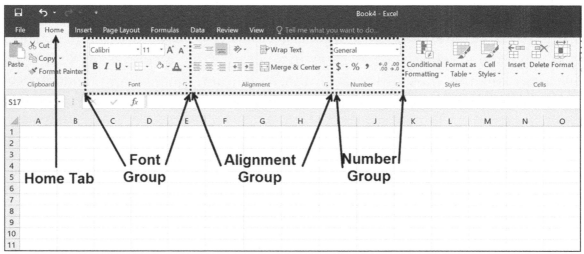

Figure 2.22 Formatting groups in the Home tab

Each group shown in Figure 2.22 specifically provides frequently needed formatting tasks as follows:

- **Font Group** – used to set font attributes, such as type, size, color, bold, italic, underline, background, and cell borders.
- **Alignment Group** – used to set both horizontal data alignment (left, right, center), vertical alignment (top, center, bottom), merging and unmerging cells, and text wrapping within a cell or cells.
- **Number Group** – used to both set the data type within a cell and the display of numbers as currency, percent, and number of decimal values.

The quick formatting icons within each group that you will be using most often are shown in Figure 2.23. As always, a range of one or more cells must be selected before one of these options is selected.

Application Note
What is Formatting?

Formatting allows you to change the appearance of a cell's value – that is, how numbers, and text in a cell are displayed. Formatting can also be used to change the data types of values (for example, a number can be changed into text), but it is more generally used to simply change a displayed item's appearance.

For example, the number 12.45 can be displayed in currency format as $12.45 or in percentage format as 1245%. When a number is either entered or calculated, it is given the default general format, which displays as many decimal places as in the entered or calculated value. In this format, when the cell width is too small to show all of the number's decimal values, the number is rounded to fit the cell. Should the cell be too small to fit the integer part of a number, scientific notation is displayed; when the cell is too small even for this notation, it is filled with pound symbols, ####, which is in actuality, one of Excel's error messages). For text, the general format displays only those characters, starting from the left, that fit in the cell.

A date value, such as 1/1/2019, is actually stored as the number 43466 (the number of days elapsed since 1/1/1900, also known as a *serial number*). However, using Excel's number to date algorithm and formatting, this date can be changed to appear as 01/01/19 or Friday, November 1, 2019, or other date display presentations.

Once a format is set for a cell, this format remains in effect for all values subsequently entered into the cell, until the format is changed or removed. While in effect, the format resides within the cell and will control the appearance of all data entered into it, even if the data changes.

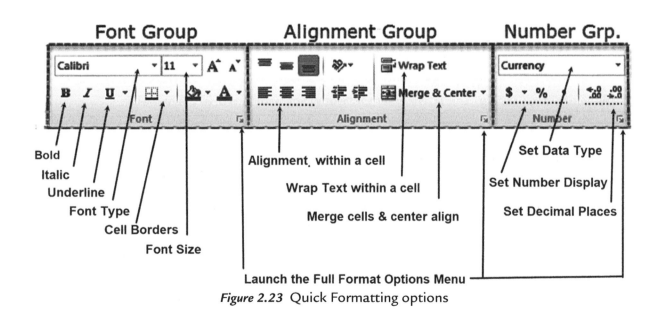

Figure 2.23 Quick Formatting options

Method 2

This method provides access to the complete set of formatting options. These options can either be activated by clicking on the Launch icons illustrated in Figure 2.23 or right clicking on a selected cell or cell range, as shown in Figure 2.24.

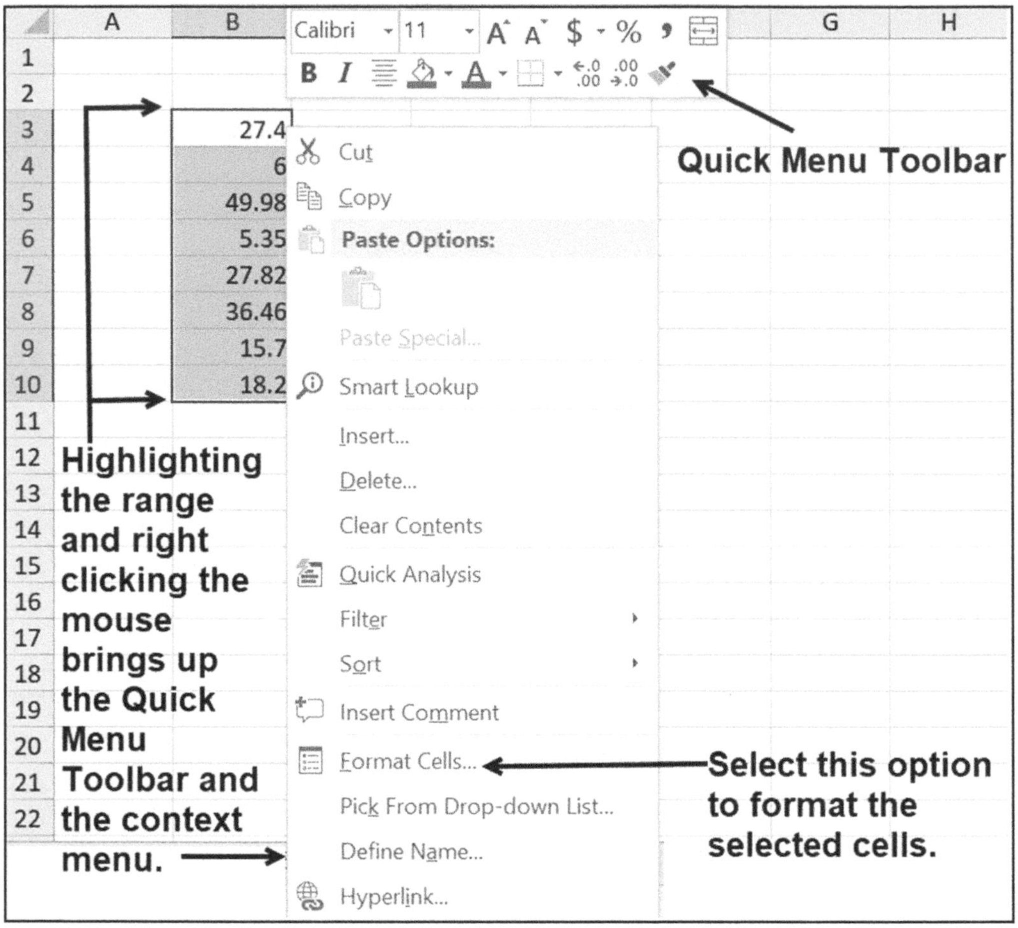

Figure 2.24 Right-clicking the mouse on a selected range

In both methods, the complete format window, as shown in Figure 2.25, appears. This window enables the choosing of the data type of the selected cells and how they will appear. This includes setting the number of decimal places to display for numbers, whether to include a comma for numbers larger than 999, or whether to display the number as currency, using a dollar ($) sign. If Text is selected, it permits aligning the text within the cell(s) and whether the text should be wrapped around multiple lines (word wrap) when the text does not fit within the specified width for the cell. Additionally, provision is made for formatting text designated as date and time data.

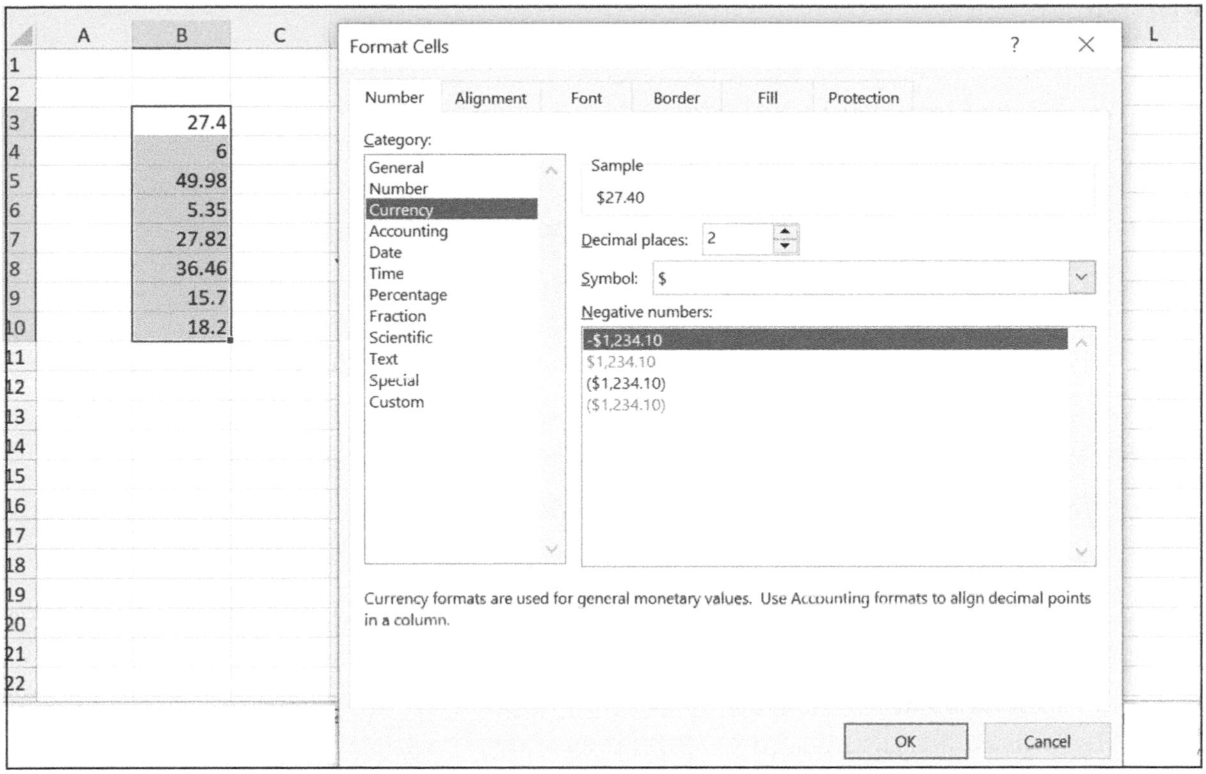

Figure 2.25 The Format Cells window (formatting numbers)

As shown in Figure 2.25, a currency format has been selected that will use the dollar ($) symbol and two decimal places. Making this selection produces the display shown in Figure 2.26 for the selected range.

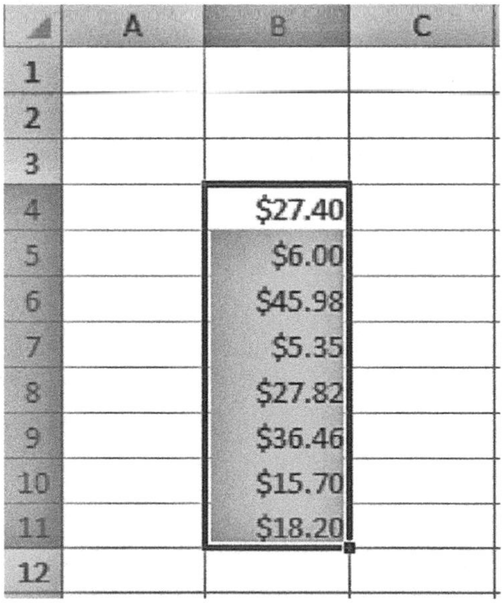

Figure 2.26 The selected cells formatted as currency

EXERCISES 2.3

1. What is cell formatting and why is it important?

2. List the following:

   a. the three main formatting groups in the Excel ribbon Home tab

   b. the format categories available in the Number Group. Do this by clicking on the arrow in the input box at the top of the Number Group.

3. Do parts a and b.

   a. Enter the spreadsheet shown below on the left side, using the formulas

   *Total Sales = Items Sold * Price per item*

   Net Profit = Total sales – Total Cost

   The Items Sold, Price per Item, and Total Cost are user-input values, and must be entered individually. Once you have entered the required inputs and calculated the Total Sales and Net Profit, make sure that the spreadsheet cells have been formatted so that they appear as shown on the right side.

Yearly Summary			Yearly Summary	
Items Sold:	54		Items Sold:	54
Price per item:	485.8		Price per item:	$485.80
Total Sales:	26233.2		Total Sales:	$26,233.20
Total Cost:	12395		Total Cost:	$12,395.00
Net Profit:	13838.2		Net Profit:	$13,838.20

   b. Could spreadsheet cells have been formatted before any data or formulas were entered?

4. Do parts a and b.

   a. Create a spreadsheet using the formula

   *Net Pay = Hourly Rate * Hours Worked*

   Use the SUM() function to determine the total amount paid in cell D8.

   Once you have entered the required inputs and calculated the Total Paid, format the spreadsheet cells so that they appear as shown in the spreadsheet that follows the incomplete spreadsheet.

	A	B	C	D
1	**Name**	**Hourly Rate ($/Hr)**	**Hrs. Worked**	**Net Pay**
2	Bill Biggins	$20.00	40	
3	Jane Cousins	22.50	40	
4	Laura Demaio	16.80	35	
5	John Farnsworth	16.80	35	
6	Rachel Smith	35.00	38	
7	Douglas Timinsky	22.70	38	
8			Total Paid:	

	A	B	C	D
1	**Name**	**Hourly Rate ($/Hr)**	**Hrs. Worked**	**Net Pay**
2	Bill Biggins	$20.00	40	$800.00
3	Jane Cousins	22.50	40	900.00
4	Laura Demaio	16.80	35	588.00
5	John Farnsworth	16.80	35	588.00
6	Rachel Smith	25.00	38	950.00
7	Douglas Timinsky	22.70	38	862.60
8			Total Paid:	$4,688.60

b. Could you have specified the required formats for the spreadsheet before you entered any data or formulas?

5. Do parts a and b.

a. Create a spreadsheet as follows, using the formulas

*Gross Pay = Hourly Rate * Hours Worked*

*Taxes Withheld = Tax Rate * Gross Pay*

Net Pay = Gross Pay – Net Pay

	A	B	C	D	E	F	G
1	**Tax Rate:**	**18.50%**					
2							
3	**Employee Number**	**Employee Name**	**Hourly Rate**	**Hours Worked**	**Gross Pay**	**Taxes Withheld**	**Net Pay**
4	32479	Abrams, B	$10.72	35.00	$375.20	$69.41	$305.79
5	03623	Bohm, P	9.54	30.00	286.20	52.95	233.25
6	14145	Gwodz, K	8.72	25.00	218.00	40.33	177.67
7	25987	Hanson, H	9.64	40.00	385.60	71.34	314.26
8	07634	Robbins, L	8.50	36.50	310.25	57.40	252.85
9	39567	Williams, B	7.30	39.00	284.70	52.67	232.03
10				Totals:	$1,859.95	$344.09	$1,515.86
11							
12		Average Hourly Rate:	$9.07				
13	Average Hours Worked:		34.3				

Use the SUM() and AVERAGE( ) functions to determine the displayed totals and averages. Once you have entered the required inputs and calculated the required totals and averages, format the cells so that they appear as shown in the spreadsheet.

b. Could you have specified the required formats for the spreadsheet before you entered any data or formulas?

2.4 CASH-FLOW AND CASH-BALANCE SPREADSHEETS

One of the most common applications for Excel spreadsheets is the construction of cash-flow and cash-balance spreadsheets. These types of spreadsheets form the basis of many accounting applications, and they were the original driving force for computer generated spreadsheets.[2]

A cash-flow spreadsheet is a list of the cash coming into a business, organization, seminar, or event and the cash paid out. Such lists, typically constructed for one-time, weekly, monthly, or yearly applications, form the basis for many Excel accounting applications. Figures 2.16, 2.19, and 2.20 are all examples of this type of spreadsheet.

Cash-flow spreadsheets are easily constructed using the Excel skills you already have. As an example, and to familiarize yourself with the essential elements of a cash-flow spreadsheet, consider Figure 2.27, which presents a cash-flow spreadsheet for a student who will be working during the summer recess.

	A	B	C	D	E	F
1		May	June	July	August	Totals
2						
3	Cash Inflows:					
4	Work:	$500	$950	$875	$1,000	$3,325
5	Gifts:	0	50	100	500	650
6	Odd Jobs:	250	375	375	375	1,375
7	Net Cash In:	$750	$1,375	$1,350	$1,875	$5,350
8						
9						
10	Cash Outflows:					
11	Gas:	$125	$200	$180	$250	$755
12	Lunch:	80	160	130	150	520
13	Car Insurance:			1,000		1,000
14	Net Cash Out:	$205	$360	$1,310	$400	$2,275
15						
16	Net Cash Flow:	$545	$1,015	$40	$1,475	$3,075
17						

Figure 2.27 A cash-flow spreadsheet

---

[2] Spreadsheets were in wide accounting usage prior to computer generated spreadsheets. The first computer programmed spreadsheet program, VisiCalc, introduced in 1979, originated as an accounting application.

The three main categories of a cash-flow statement, highlighted in Figure 2.27, are:

1. Net Cash In: This is the total of all the listed cash inflows.

2. Net Cash Out: This is the total of all the listed cash outflows.

3. Net Cash Flow: This is Net Cash (item 1) minus the Net Cash Out (item 2).

If Net Cash In (item 1) is greater than Net Cash Out (item 2), then Net Cash Flow (item 3) is positive. This indicates money is being accumulated; if it is negative, money is being lost. Clearly, a healthy operation will have more money coming in than is going out. Another way of saying this is that the Net Cash Flow is positive.

Interestingly enough, except for the individual cash inflow and cash outflow values that must be entered, the three cash flow categories (items 1, 2, and 3) require entering only three formulas or functions in the first cash-flow column. Once the correct three formulas or functions are entered, they can be copied to the right (using the Copy command or fill handle), for as many cash-flow columns that are contained in the spreadsheet. This is true for all cash balance spreadsheets, whether the columns are delimitated in weeks, months, or years. Similarly, as we have done before, any total formulas can also be copied. The highlighted cells in Figure 2.28 show the required three formulas for Figure 2.27's cash balance statement. These are the more heavily highlighted cells in column B in Figure 2.28. Also shown are the SUM( ) formulas that would be copied.

	A	B	C	D	E	F
1		May	June	July	August	Totals
2						
3	Cash Inflows:					
4	Work:	500	950	875	1000	=SUM(B4:E4)
5	Gifts:	0	50	100	500	
6	Odd Jobs:	250	375	375	375	
7	Net Cash In:	=SUM(B4:B6)		Copy through		
8						
9						
10	Cash Outflows:					
11	Gas:	125	200	180	250	=SUM(B11:E11)
12	Lunch:	80	160	130	150	
13	Car Insurance:			1000		
14	Net Cash Out:	=SUM(B11:B13)		Copy through		
15						
16	Net Cash Flow:	=B7-B14		Copy through		
17						

Figure 2.28 Example of a cash-flow spreadsheet

A Cash-Balance Spreadsheet

A cash-balance spreadsheet is one that shows, in addition to the cash flows, the cash balances of a business over a period of time. This type of spreadsheet is created by adding beginning and ending cash balances to each column of a cash-flow spreadsheet, as shown by the highlighted two rows in Figure 2.29.

	A	B	C	D	E	F
1		May	June	July	August	Totals
2	Beginning Balance:	$3,000	$3,545	$4,560	$4,600	
3	Cash Inflows:					
4	Work:	$500	$950	$875	$1,000	$3,325
5	Gifts:	0	50	100	500	650
6	Odd Jobs:	250	375	375	375	1,375
7	Net Cash In:	$750	$1,375	$1,350	$1,875	$5,350
8						
9						
10	Cash Outflows:					
11	Gas:	$125	$200	$180	$250	$755
12	Lunch:	80	160	130	150	520
13	Car Insurance:			1,000		1,000
14	Net Cash Out:	$205	$360	$1,310	$400	$2,275
15						
16	Net Cash Flow:	$545	$1,015	$40	$1,475	$3,075
17	Ending Balance:	$3,545	$4,560	$4,600	$6,075	

Figure 2.29 A cash-balance spreadsheet

For the first month, the Beginning Balance is a user-entered number representing the cash on hand at the start of the month (in this case May). In Figure 2.29, the Beginning Balance for May in cell B2 is $3,000. The Ending Balance is always the sum of the Beginning Balance plus the Net Cash Flow. For Figure 2.30, the correct formula in cell B17 is =B2 + B16. For all subsequent months, the Beginning Balance for the month is set equal to the prior month's Ending Balance.

As shown in Figure 2.30, the only three formulas or functions that need to be entered for the cash-balance rows have been circled. Once the correct three formulas or functions are entered, two of them can be copied to the right, as shown, for as many cash-flow columns as are contained in the spreadsheet. This is true for all cash-balance spreadsheets, whether the columns are delimitated in weeks, months, or years.

	A	B	C	D	E	F
1		May	June	July	August	Totals
2	Beginning Balance	3000	=B17	=C17	=D17	
3	Cash Inflows:					
4	Work:	500	950	875	1000	=SUM(B4:E4)
5	Gifts:	0	50	100	500	=SUM(B5:E5)
6	Odd Jobs:	250	375	375	375	=SUM(B6:E6)
7	Net Cash In:	=SUM(B4:B6)	=SUM(C4:C6)	=SUM(D4:D6)	=SUM(E4:E6)	=SUM(F4:F6)
8						
9						
10	Cash Outflows:					
11	Gas:	125	200	180	250	=SUM(B11:E11)
12	Lunch:	80	160	130	150	=SUM(B12:E12)
13	Car Insurance:			1000		=SUM(B13:E13)
14	Net Cash Out:	=SUM(B11:B13)	=SUM(C11:C13)	=SUM(D11:D13)	=SUM(E11:E13)	=SUM(F11:F13)
15						
16	Net Cash Flow:	=B7-B14	=C7-C14	=D7-D14	=E7-E14	=F7-F14
17	Ending Balance:	=B2+B16	=C2+C16	=D2+D16	=E2+E16	

Figure 2.30 The formulas and functions needed for the cash-balance spreadsheet

EXERCISES 2.4

1. For a cash-flow spreadsheet, how is a period's Net Cash In calculated?

2. For a cash-flow spreadsheet, how is a period's Net Cash Out calculated?

3. For a cash-flow spreadsheet, how is a period's Net Cash Flow calculated?

4. Create the cash-flow spreadsheet that follows; print it out.

	A	B	C	D	E	F
1		May	June	July	August	Totals
2						
3	Cash Inflows:					
4	Work:	$500	$950	$875	$1,000	$3,325
5	Gifts:	0	50	100	500	650
6	Odd Jobs:	250	375	375	375	1,375
7	Net Cash In:	$750	$1,375	$1,350	$1,875	$5,350
8						
9						
10	Cash Outflows:					
11	Gas:	$125	$200	$180	$250	$755
12	Lunch:	80	160	130	150	520
13	Car Insurance:			1,000		1,000
14	Net Cash Out:	$205	$360	$1,310	$400	$2,275
15						
16	Net Cash Flow:	$545	$1,015	$40	$1,475	$3,075
17						

5. What is the difference between cash-flow and cash-balance spreadsheets?

6. What is the relationship between each period's Beginning Balance and the period's Ending Balance?

7. Except for the first period's Beginning Balance, what is the relationship between each succeeding period's Beginning Balance and the prior period's Ending Balance?

8. Create and then complete the cash-flow spreadsheet that follows. Add the appropriate formulas/functions as needed.

	A	B	C	D	E	F
1		May	June	July	August	Totals
2	Beginning Balance:	$3,000	$3,545	$4,560	$4,600	
3	Cash Inflows:					
4	Work:	$500	$950	$875	$1,000	$3,325
5	Gifts:	0	50	100	500	650
6	Odd Jobs:	250	375	375	375	1,375
7	Net Cash In:	$750	$1,375	$1,350	$1,875	$5,350
8						
9						
10	Cash Outflows:					
11	Gas:	$125	$200	$180	$250	$755
12	Lunch:	80	160	130	150	520
13	Car Insurance:			1,000		1,000
14	Net Cash Out:	$205	$360	$1,310	$400	$2,275
15						
16	Net Cash Flow:	$545	$1,015	$40	$1,475	$3,075
17	Ending Balance:	$3,545	$4,560	$4,600	$6,075	

2.5   ABSOLUTE ADDRESSES

Copying formulas containing relative addresses produces the correct results for many of the applications you will be creating. There are cases, however, where this is not the case. One of these occurs in spreadsheets that have an input (or assumptions) section, and this situation is presented next; the second case is less frequent, but equally important, and is presented at the end of this section. Finally, the third case occurs in Conditional Formatting, and is presented in Section 3.4.

Case 1: Magic Numbers as Input Values

Frequently, the same number is required throughout a spreadsheet. For example, in spreadsheets used to determine bank interest charges, the interest rate would typically appear repeatedly throughout the spreadsheet. Similarly, in a spreadsheet used to calculate taxes, the tax rate might appear in many individual cell formulas. If either the interest rate or tax rate changes, and the actual number were placed throughout the spreadsheet, you would have the cumbersome task of changing the value everywhere it appears. Multiple changes, however, can lead to errors: If just one rate value is overlooked and not changed, the result displayed in one or more cells will be incorrect. Numbers that appear many times in the same spreadsheet are referred to by developers as *magic numbers*. By themselves, the numbers are quite ordinary, but in the context of a particular application they have a special ("magical") meaning.

To avoid the problem of having a magic number spread throughout a spreadsheet, developers provide the user with the capability to enter the value once, in the input section of the spreadsheet. Then, a special reference to the input cell, referred to as an *absolute cell reference address*, is used throughout the program. This special reference ensures that Excel will not alter or modify this address when it is copied. Should the number ever need to be changed, the change is made only once in the input cell. This ensures that both the original and any changed value is correctly used in any formula in which it is referenced.

To create a single value that is not changed when its cell address is copied within a formula requires the following two-step process:

1. The value should be clearly labeled in one cell and entered in an adjoining cell. This is typically done in a recognizable Input section.

2. Whenever the cell containing the desired value is referenced, it should use absolute addressing. This means placing a $ sign before the column cell reference and a $ sign before the row cell reference.[3] This can be accomplished by manually editing the cell reference(s), using the shortcut key F4 on the PC, or using the shortcut key ⌘ + T on Apple Mac computers.

---

[3] The $ sign in front of the column address locks the column reference, while the $ in front of the row address locks the row reference. Each of these can be locked separately, such as $B2 and C$3 (mixed cell referencing). One such case where this is used in presented in Section 3.5.

As an example of when absolute addressing is used, consider Figure 2.31a. In the figure, the monthly growth of $1,000, placed in a bank account that pays 5% interest is computed and displayed.

	A	B	C	D	E	F
1	Interest Rate	5%				
2	Beginning Balance	$1,000.00				
3						
4			Month	Beginning Balance	Interest	Ending Balance
5			1	$1,000.00	$4.17	$1,004.17
6			2	$1,004.17	$4.18	$1,008.35
7			3	$1,008.35	$4.20	$1,012.55
8			4	$1,012.55	$4.22	$1,016.77
9			5	$1,016.77	$4.24	$1,021.01
10			6	$1,021.01	$4.25	$1,025.26
11			7	$1,025.26	$4.27	$1,029.53
12			8	$1,029.53	$4.29	$1,033.82
13			9	$1,033.82	$4.31	$1,038.13
14			10	$1,038.13	$4.33	$1,042.46
15			11	$1,042.46	$4.34	$1,046.80
16			12	$1,046.80	$4.36	$1,051.16

Figure 2.31a An example of absolute cell addressing usage

Figure 2.31b shows the formulas that produced Figure 2.31a. Look at the formula in cell D5 that is used to calculate the monthly interest. This formula divides the interest rate contained in cell B1 by 12 and multiples this monthly interest rate times the beginning balance for the month. Notice that the formula in cell D5 uses the absolute address, $B$1, to reference the interest rate. Doing this permits this formula to be copied without changing the cell reference being changed to B2, B3, B4, and so forth as the formula is copied.

The four highlighted cells are, in fact, the only formulas that need to be entered, three of which can be copied as indicated by the arrows. The two dotted lines indicate input values that have been referenced using absolute addresses in the body of the spreadsheet. It should be noted that the absolute address used in cell C5 ($B$2) is not necessary in this case, because this value is only used once and is not copied. Absolute addresses must be used, however, wherever a single cell is referenced in a formula that will be copied to other cells. **As a general rule, however, you should use an absolute address in any formula that references a number from a spreadsheet's input section.**

◢	A	B	C	D	E
1	Interest Rate	0.05			
2	Beginning Balance	1000			
3					
4			Month	Beginning Balance	Interest	Ending Balance
5			1	=$B$2	=($B$1 / 12) * C5	=C5+D5
6			2	=E5	=($B$1 / 12) * C6	=C6+D6
7			3	=E6	=($B$1 / 12) * C7	=C7+D7
8			4	=E7	=($B$1 / 12) * C8	=C8+D8
9			5	=E8	=($B$1 / 12) * C9	=C9+D9
10			6	=E9	=($B$1 / 12) * C10	=C10+D10
11			7	=E10	=($B$1 / 12) * C11	=C11+D11
12			8	=E11	=($B$1 / 12) * C12	=C12+D12
13			9	=E12	=($B$1 / 12) * C13	=C13+D13
14			10	=E13	=($B$1 / 12) * C14	=C14+D14
15			11	=E14	=($B$1 / 12) * C15	=C15+D15
16			12	=E15	=($B$1 / 12) * C16	=C16+D16

Figure 2.31b The formulas that produced Figure 2.31a

Let's look at a slightly more complicated example. Figure 2.32a illustrates a spreadsheet displaying the monthly payments on a three-year, $7,000 car loan. Based on an interest rate of 3.75%, the monthly payment for this loan is $205.89 per month. Part of each payment goes to the loan company as interest, and the remainder to paying off the actual loan.

For example, at the start of the first month, the total balance due on the loan is $7,000. Out of the first payment of $205.89, $21.88 is an interest payment to the loan company, and the remaining $184.02 goes to paying off the loan (principal). Although only the first year's payments are displayed, continuing the spreadsheet to the 36th month would result in a zero loan balance.

The formulas for constructing Figure 2.32a's spreadsheet are relatively simple and are shown in Figure 2.32b. As illustrated, only five formulas need be entered. Four of these can be copied, either individually, or by highlighting them as a group and copying them together.

It should be noted that this area which holds the data being referenced numerous times in both examples is also sometimes known as the *input area* or *assumptions area*. The values themselves, whether known as "magic numbers," "inputs", or "assumptions," all basically refer to placing frequently-used data in a specific area to be referenced, rather than being re-written multiple times in formulas and functions throughout the worksheet.

Application Note
Debugging Incorrectly Copied Formulas

An incorrectly copied formula that references an invalid cell almost always reveals itself by displaying text such as #VALUE!, #REF! (two kinds of Excel error messages) or an obviously incorrect numerical result. To avoid or correct this error, there is a set protocols you should always use immediately after copying a cell's formula.

First, before copying a formula, use a calculator to verify that the function or formula produces a correct result in the original cell. Your purpose here is not merely to check that the formula is producing a correct value, but that you are using the correct formula. Clearly, if the correct formula is being used, it will most likely produce a correct result. An incorrect value indicates an incorrect formula, and copying an incorrect formula will simply produce more incorrect formulas.

Once you are sure the original formula works, visually look at the first copy of the formula. What you are looking for here is that cells referenced in the copied formula are correct. Many times, you will discover that one or more of the cell references, that *should not* have been changed, were changed. This is your signal that, most likely, absolute addressing should have been used in the original formula before it was copied. Note that frequently the offending formula is not located in the cell displaying the error, but in a preceding cell, so be sure to check prior formulas that created values used by the cell displaying the error. As you progress further on in learning Excel, you can employ the Formula Auditing features to help you with this, but at this point, it is beyond the scope of this book.

	A	B	C	D	E	F
3	Annual Interest Rate:	3.75%				
4	Monthly Payment:	$205.89				
5						
6		Payment Number	Payment Amount	Interest Paid	Principal Paid	Outstanding Balance
7		0				$7,000.00
8		1	$205.89	$21.88	$184.02	$6,815.99
9		2	$205.89	$21.30	$184.59	$6,631.39
10		3	$205.89	$20.72	$185.17	$6,446.23
11		4	$205.89	$20.14	$185.75	$6,260.48
12		5	$205.89	$19.56	$186.33	$6,074.16
13		6	$205.89	$18.98	$186.91	$5,887.25
14		7	$205.89	$18.40	$187.49	$5,699.76
15		8	$205.89	$17.81	$188.08	$5,511.68
16		9	$205.89	$17.22	$188.67	$5,323.01
17		10	$205.89	$16.63	$189.26	$5,133.76
18		11	$205.89	$16.04	$189.85	$4,943.91
19		12	$205.89	$15.45	$190.44	$4,753.47

Figure 2.32a The Loan payment example results

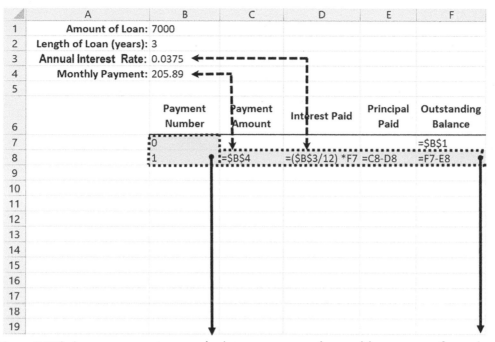

Figure 2.32b Loan payment example: interest rate and monthly payment formulas

Case 2: Running Sub-Totals

Although much less common, but equally necessary, is the use of absolute addresses in computing running sub-totals. The requirement here is that each sub-total must start at the same cell address. Because the formula calculating each total can be copied, and the copies should not have a different starting address, an absolute cell address is called for. As seen in Figure 2.33b, the range argument provided to the SUM( ) function in cell D2 is $C$2. This ensures that when the formula in this cell is copied, the starting address remains the same and only the ending address is correctly adjusted.

Item	Date	Sold For	Total
Junior Planetarium	3/14/2019	$67.00	$67.00
#1 Scrooge McDuck	3/28/2019	$230.00	$297.00
Epcot Poster	4/7/2019	$55.00	$352.00
Scrooge Piggy Bank	4/25/2019	$42.00	$394.00
Donald Duck Piggy Bank	5/10/2019	$36.00	$430.00

Figure 2.33a An example of running subtotals

	A	B	C	D
1	Item	Date	Sold For	Total
2	Junior Planetarium	43538	67	=SUM($C$2:C2)
3	#1 Scrooge McDuck	43552	230	=SUM($C$2:C3)
4	Epcot Poster	43562	55	=SUM($C$2:C4)
5	Scrooge Piggy Bank	43580	42	=SUM($C$2:C5)
6	Donald Duck Piggy Bank	43595	36	=SUM($C$2:C6)

Figure 2.33b Formulas for the running subtotals

EXERCISES 2.5

1. What is an absolute cell reference and how does it differ from a relative cell reference? What is a mixed cell reference?

2. What is the general rule for when an absolute cell reference should be used? When should a mixed reference be used?

3. Complete parts a-d.

   a. For the spreadsheet in Figure 2.34a, write in the formula that appears in each of the highlighted cells when the formula in cell A4 is copied to these cells.

	A	B	C
1	2	3	4
2	5	6	7
3	8	9	10
4	=3*$A$1		
5			
6			

   Figure 2.34a Spreadsheet for Exercise 3a

   b. For the spreadsheet in Figure 2.34b, write in the formula that appears in each of the highlighted cells when the formula in cell A4 is copied to these cells.

	A	B	C
1	2	3	4
2	5	6	7
3	8	9	10
4	=3*A1		
5			
6			

   Figure 2.34b Spreadsheet for Exercise 3b

   c. For the spreadsheet in Figure 2.34c, write in the formula that appears in each of the highlighted cells when the formula in cell A4 is copied to these cells.

	A	B	C
1	2	3	4
2	5	6	7
3	8	9	10
4	=3*$A1		
5			
6			

   Figure 2.34c Spreadsheet for Exercise 3c

d. For the spreadsheet in Figure 2.34d, write in the formula that appears in each of the highlighted cells when the formula in cell A4 is copied to these cells.

	A	B	C
1	2	3	4
2	5	6	7
3	8	9	10
4	=3*A$1		
5			
6			

Figure 2.34d Spreadsheet for Exercise 3d

4. The spreadsheets in Figures 2.31b and 2.32b contain the number 12 throughout their formulas. Would it be appropriate to place this number in a cell and use absolute addressing in all formulas using them?

5. Complete parts a-c.

a. Create the spreadsheet that follows on your computer.

	A	B	C	D	E	F
1	Interest Rate	5%				
2	Beginning Balance	$1,000.00				
3						
4			Month	Beginning Balance	Interest	Ending Balance
5			1	$1,000.00	$4.17	$1,004.17
6			2	$1,004.17	$4.18	$1,008.35
7			3	$1,008.35	$4.20	$1,012.55
8			4	$1,012.55	$4.22	$1,016.77
9			5	$1,016.77	$4.24	$1,021.01
10			6	$1,021.01	$4.25	$1,025.26
11			7	$1,025.26	$4.27	$1,029.53
12			8	$1,029.53	$4.29	$1,033.82
13			9	$1,033.82	$4.31	$1,038.13
14			10	$1,038.13	$4.33	$1,042.46
15			11	$1,042.46	$4.34	$1,046.80
16			12	$1,046.80	$4.36	$1,051.16

b. For the spreadsheet in Exercise 5a, change the absolute address $B$1 (interest rate 5%) in cell D5 to the relative address B1 and then copy the resulting formula down through cell D16. What errors appeared in your spreadsheet from this change?

   c. For the spreadsheet created in Exercise 5a, change the absolute address $B$2 (beginning balance $1000) in cell C7 to the relative address B2. Why did this change not result in any errors?

6. Expand the spreadsheet shown Exercise 5a so that it displays the balances for 36 months.

7. Figure 2.35a shows the first three years for a spreadsheet that determines how an initial bank deposit that pays 5% annual interest, paid monthly, grows at the end of each year. (Note that the ending balance for the first year is the same as that shown for month 12 in Figure 2.31a). The initial formulas for Figure 2.35a are shown in Figure 2.35b. Complete parts a-c.

   a. Complete the spreadsheet shown in Figure 2.35a to display the ending yearly balances for the first twenty years.

   b. Using the spreadsheet you developed for Exercise 6a, determine in what year the initial deposit has doubled. How close is this doubling year to the rule of 72, which states that a close approximation to when a deposit will double is obtained by dividing the interest rate into the number 72?

   c. Using the spreadsheet you developed for Exercise 6a, change the interest rate to 3%. Determine in what year the initial deposit has doubled. How close is this doubling year to that determined using the rule of 72 given in Exercise 6b? Does changing the initial deposit to $2000 change the time in which the initial deposit doubles?

Interest Rate	5%			
Beginning Balance	$1,000.00			
	Year	Beginning Balance	Ending Balance	Interest Earned
	1	$1,000.00	$1,051.16	$51.16
	2	$1,051.16	$1,104.94	$53.78
	3	$1,104.94	$1,161.47	$56.53

Figure 2.35a Spreadsheet for Exercise 7a

	A	B	C	D	E
1	Interest Rate	0.05			
2	Beginning Balance	1000			
3					
4		Year	Beginning Balance	Ending Balance	Interest Earned
5		1	=$B$2	=POWER((1 +$B$1 / 12),12) * C5	=D5-C5
6		2	=D5		

Figure 2.35b Spreadsheet with formulas and functions for Exercise 7a

8. Complete parts a-b.

    a. Create the following spreadsheet on your computer.

    b. Expand the spreadsheet created in Exercise 8a to include 36 payments and verify that the balance of the loan goes to zero after the last payment is made.

	A	B	C	D	E	F
3	**Annual Interest Rate:**	3.75%				
4	**Monthly Payment:**	$205.89				
5						
6		**Payment Number**	**Payment Amount**	**Interest Paid**	**Principal Paid**	**Outstanding Balance**
7		0				$7,000.00
8		1	$205.89	$21.88	$184.02	$6,815.99
9		2	$205.89	$21.30	$184.59	$6,631.39
10		3	$205.89	$20.72	$185.17	$6,446.23
11		4	$205.89	$20.14	$185.75	$6,260.48
12		5	$205.89	$19.56	$186.33	$6,074.16
13		6	$205.89	$18.98	$186.91	$5,887.25
14		7	$205.89	$18.40	$187.49	$5,699.76
15		8	$205.89	$17.81	$188.08	$5,511.68
16		9	$205.89	$17.22	$188.67	$5,323.01
17		10	$205.89	$16.63	$189.26	$5,133.76
18		11	$205.89	$16.04	$189.85	$4,943.91
19		12	$205.89	$15.45	$190.44	$4,753.47

9. For the spreadsheet created in Exercise 7b, change the absolute address $B$4 in cell C7 to the relative address B4 and then copy the resulting formula down through cell C18. What errors appeared in your spreadsheet from this change?

10. For the spreadsheet created in Exercise 8a, change the absolute address $B$3 in cell D8 to the relative address B3 and then copy the resulting formula down through D18. What errors appeared in your spreadsheet from this change?

2.6 COMMON EXCEL ERRORS

1. Entering the same input data item more than once. If the same item is needed in two or more cells, these additional values should reference the one cell into which the data was initially entered (usually using absolute addressing). The reason for this is that if the value needs to be changed later, it only has to be changed in the first input cell where the data was initially entered. This prevents an error from occurring when you forget to change the value in one of the additional cells requiring the same value.

2. Entering the same formula more than once in the same row or column. If you find that you are entering the same basic formula, either in the same row or the same column, except with changes in the cells referenced in the formula, you are almost always wasting time and making a common beginner's mistake. Formulas should be created using relative and absolute addressed operands so that they can be copied, either across a row or down a column.

3. Referencing Input Section data items using relative, rather than absolute addresses, unless there is a reason to do so. The reason for this is that if an absolute address for the input data cell is used in a formula, and the formula is copied, the correct input data item will still be referenced in the copied formula. Using a relative address almost always produces an error where the wrong cell is referenced in the copied formula.

4. Using a calculator to determine a value that you then enter into a cell. Rather, enter a formula into the cell so that Excel does the calculation. Then, use a calculator to verify that the formula is correct as presented in the next item.

5. Not checking that the first copy of a formula is correct. When using a formula, always check the result using a calculator, in the first cell where the formula is entered. The same is true when copying a formula; verify, using a calculator, that the first copied formula yields a correct value.

6. Not using the SUM( ) function when adding the contents of more than three cells. Although not actually an error, it is easier and more professional to use the SUM( ) function, such as =SUM(C1:C10) rather than the equivalent formula

$$=C1+C2+C3+C4+C5+C6+C7+C8+C9+C10.$$

However, both formulas will provide the same value.

7. Using an addition operator within a SUM( ) function. For example,

$$=SUM(A+A2+A3+A4).$$

This is simply taking the sum of a sum. Either use the SUM( )function or the addition operator, but not both together.

2.7   CHAPTER APPENDIX: WORKING WITH ROWS AND COLUMNS

There are three situations that will require you to widen a column or a row. In the first, shown in Figure 2.36a, a numerical result is too large to fit in its cell. In this case, the problem is indicated by a succession of displayed x's, such as xxxxxxx (the Excel error message).[4] Widening the cell permits the complete number to be displayed (Figure 2.36b).

Figure 2.36a Outsized result

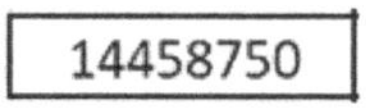

Figure 2.36b Correct fit

The second situation occurs when a text label is too small to fit within its cell margins. As shown in Figures 2.36c through 2.36e, depending on the cell alignment (left, right, or center) only a portion of the label is displayed.[5] By widening the cell (Figure 2.36f), the complete text is displayed.

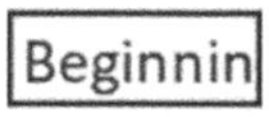

Figure 2.36c Left aligned

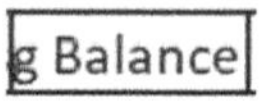

Figure 2.36d Right aligned

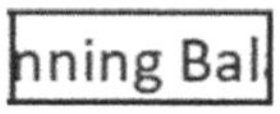

Figure 2.36e Center aligned

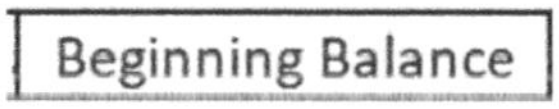

Figure 2.36f Widened

The third situation occurs when an attempt to word wrap text in a cell that is too narrow to accommodate more than one line of text. In case, the row must be widened.

Finally, you will occasionally have to either insert or delete a row or column within an existing spreadsheet. How a column or row's width is adjusted, and how columns and rows can be inserted or deleted within a spreadsheet are described in the following section.

Adjusting Column and Row Widths

Figure 2.37 shows the four steps required to either widen or narrow a column, in this case column C. As indicated, in the first step the cursor must be positioned to the right of the column being adjusted and moved until the cursor changes to the indicated cross-hairs (Step 1).

---

[4] This occurs only if the cell is formatted as a number. If a general format is used, the display will default to scientific notation.

[5] The one exception to this is when the cells to the right of the cell are empty. In this case, the complete text is displayed until data is entered into one of the empty cells displaying the original text..

Once the cross-hairs appear as shown, the left mouse is pressed and held (Step 2) and the mouse moved right or left (Step 3) to widen or narrow the column, respectively. Once the desired width is obtained, the mouse button is released (Step 4).

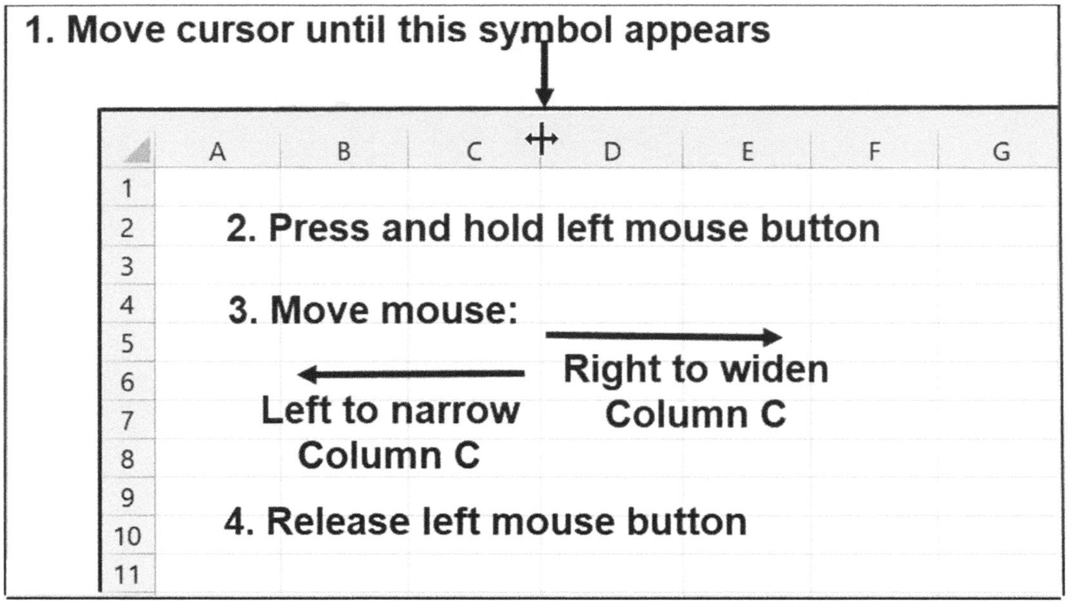

1. Move cursor until this symbol appears

2. Press and hold left mouse button

3. Move mouse:

Right to widen Column C

Left to narrow Column C

4. Release left mouse button

Figure 2.37 Adjusting a column's width

The same procedure for adjusting individual column widths is used to adjust individual row widths, as shown in Figure 2.38. The only difference is that the cross-hairs must appear below the row being adjusted, and the mouse is moved either down to widen, or up to narrow the selected row.

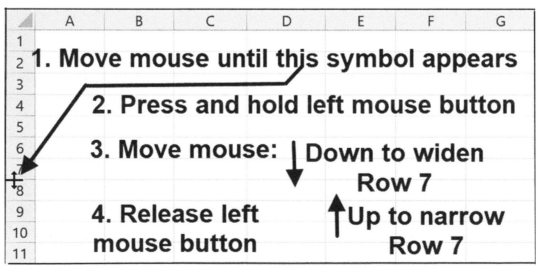

Figure 2.38 Adjusting a column's width

Adjusting Ranges of Rows and Multiple Columns

A group of adjacent rows or columns, respectively, can be widened or narrowed together using the Home tab's Format Cells menu option, as shown in Figure 2.39. This requires higlighting the desired group of rows or columns, using either the Row or Column headings.

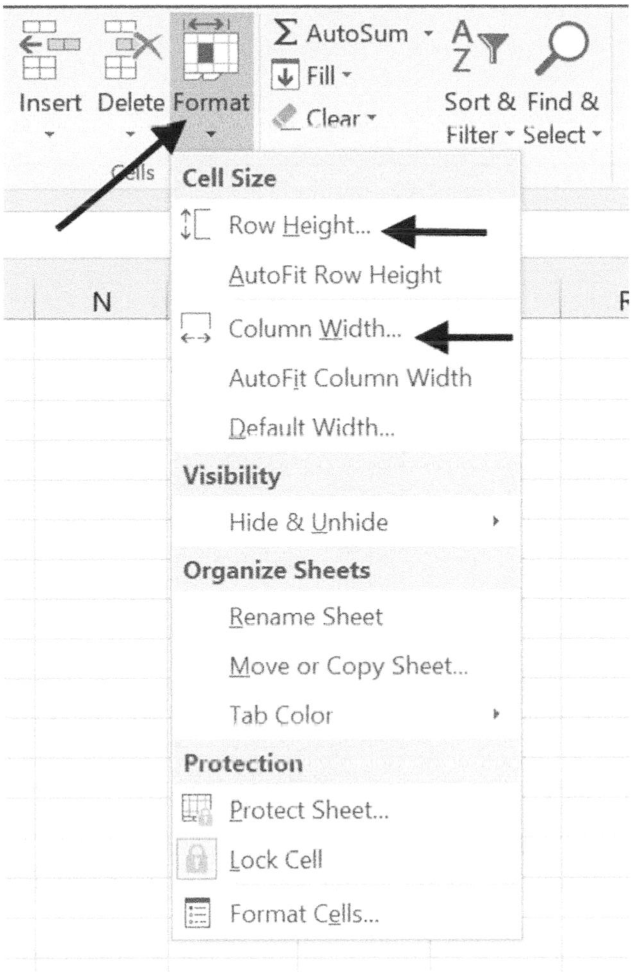

Figure 2.39 Adjusting a width or height

Inserting and Deleting Columns and Rows

A single column is inserted or deleted in front of an existing one by first positioning the cursor at the top of the column that will be either be deleted or moved right to make room for a newly inserted column. When positioned correctly, the cursor appears as shown in Figure 2.40.

At this point, right clicking the mouse will bring up the options menu shown in Figure 2.41. Selecting the Insert option results in a new column, as shown in Figure 2.42, while selecting the Delete option will delete the selected column.

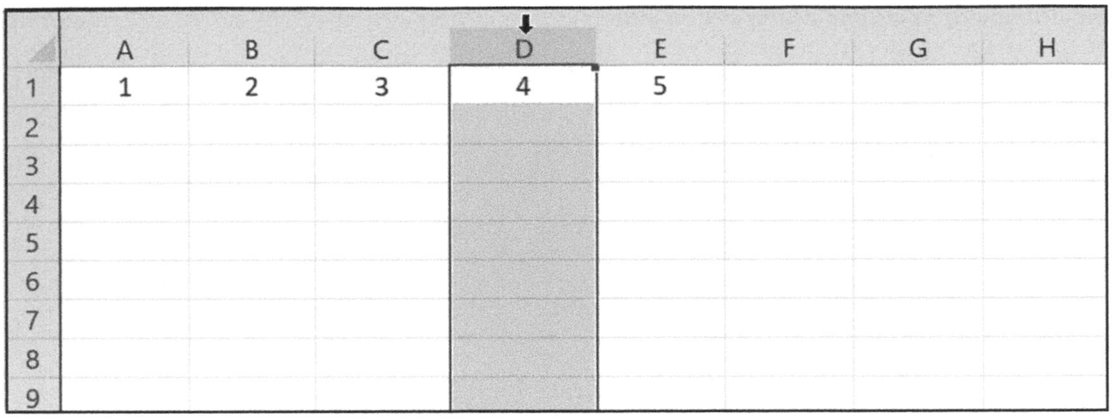

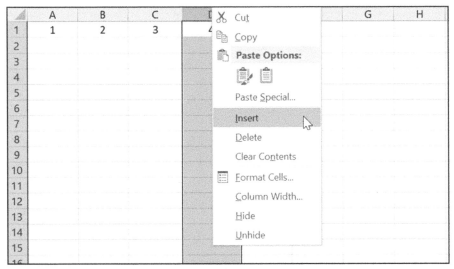

Figure 2.40 Highlighting a column

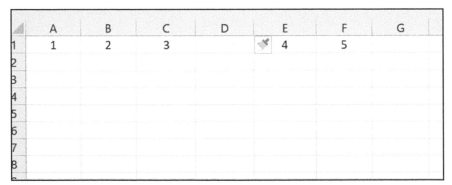

Figure 2.41 Choosing Insert

Figure 2.42 Inserted column using the previous column's label

As illustrated in Figure 2.42, the inserted column receives the previous column's label. All columns to the right of the inserted column are moved right, along with their contents. The moved columns have their labels changed accordingly. Thus, in Figure 2.42, a new column inserted in place of the original column D, is labelled D, and the original columns labelled D, E, and F are re-labelled as E, F, and G. Notice that the original contents in these moved columns have also been moved. Additionally, and equally important, is ***that any formula that used the original column labels is automatically changed to reflect the new column labels***.

In reviewing Figure 2.42, notice the Format Painter icon in column E. Clicking on this icon brings up the menu options shown in Figure 2.43. These options allow you to set the format in the newly inserted column to be the same as either the column to the left or the column to the right, or neither.

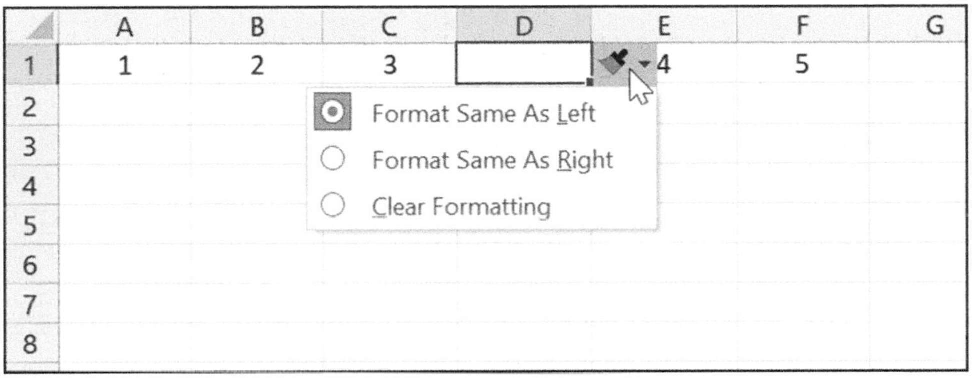

Figure 2.43 Formatting the column

Inserting or Deleting Multiple Columns

Multiple columns are inserted or deleted in the same manner as individual columns, with one modification. Once a single column is selected, as previously shown in Figure 2.40, and before right clicking the mouse to obtain the options menus shown in Figure 2.41, the left mouse button is held and the mouse moved either right or left to highlight and specify how many, and where, the new columns are to be inserted or deleted. Figure 2.44 shows how this appears when three new columns are to be inserted or deleted where existing columns D, E, and F currently exist.

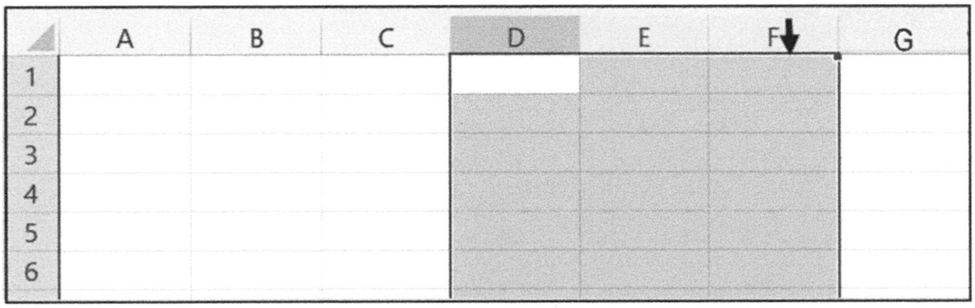

Figure 2.44 Inserting or deleting three new columns

Once the desired columns have been highlighted, releasing the left mouse button results in an arrow (see Figure 2.44) appearing over the last highlighted column. Right clicking the mouse then brings up the same menu options previously shown in Figure 2.41, from where the selected columns can either be inserted or deleted.

Inserting or Deleting a Single Row

A single row can be inserted or deleted using the same procedure as that used for individual columns. In this case, a new row will be inserted before the selected row; for deletion, the row is deleted.

The first step to insert or delete a row is to have the cursor pointed to the row that either will be deleted or will be moved down to make room for the inserted row. When positioned correctly, the cursor appears as shown in Figure 2.45a.

Once the desired row has been selected, right clicking the mouse brings up the options menu shown in Figure 2.45b. Selecting the Insert option results in a new row, as shown in Figure 2.45c, being inserted above Row 4; selecting the Delete option would remove Row 4 from the spreadsheet. As with column insertion and deletion and equally important, is *that any formula that used the original row labels are automatically changed to reflect the new row labels*. The Format Painter icon shown in Figure 2.45c allows an inserted row to be formatted as the same as the row above or below it, or neither (see Figure 2.46).

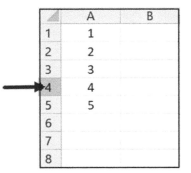

Figure 2.45a Selecting the desired row

Figure 2.45b Options menu

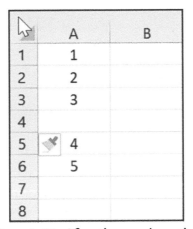

Figure 2.45c After the row insertion

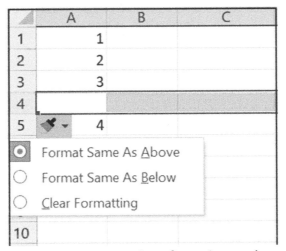

Figure 2.46 Format options for an inserted row

Inserting or Deleting Multiple Rows

Multiple rows are inserted or deleted exactly as individual rows, with one modification. Once a single row is selected and before right clicking the mouse to insert or delete a single row, the left mouse button is held; moving the mouse either up or down highlights and determines how many rows will be inserted or deleted. Figure 2.47 shows how this appears when the rows 2, 3, and 4 are highlighted. Releasing the left mouse button and pressing the right mouse button brings up the Options menu previously illustrated in Figure 2.45. Selecting the Insert option results in the spreadsheet shown in Figure 2.48, while selecting the Delete option results in that shown in Figure 2.49.

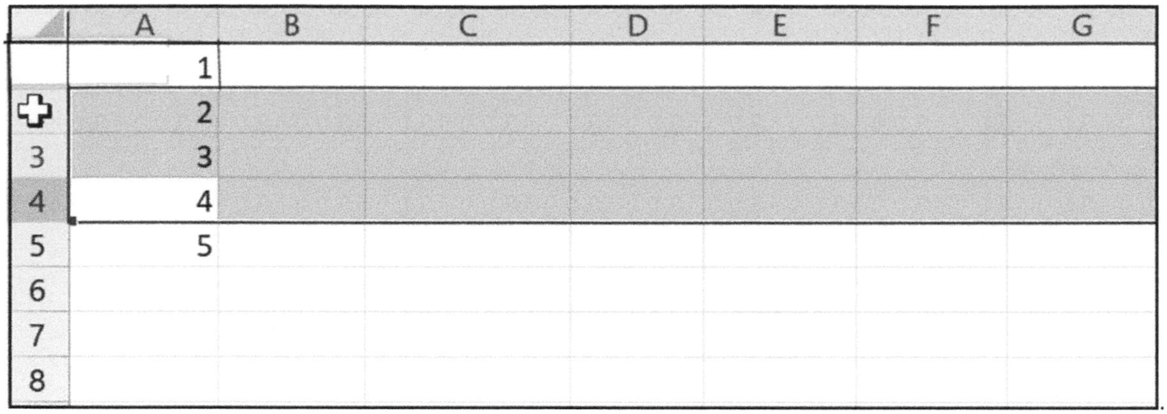

Figure 2.47 Highlighting 3 rows for insertion or deletion

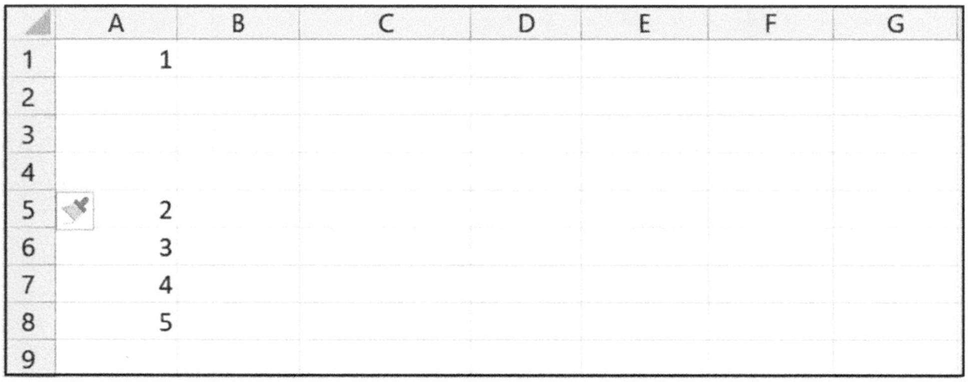

Figure 2.48 The selected 3 rows after insertion

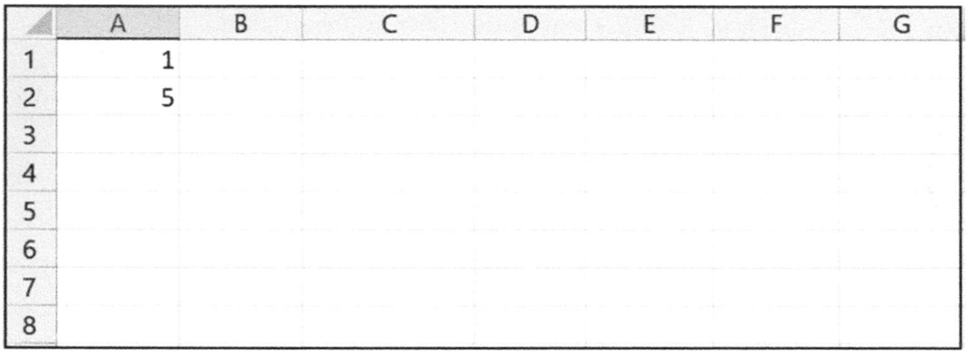

Figure 2.49 The spreadsheet after deleting the selected 3 rows

CHAPTER 3

FUNCTIONS AND CONDITIONAL FORMATTING

This Chapter Contains

Including the mathematical functions presented in Section 2.2, Excel provides over 200 functions for performing date, time, statistical, and financial calculations. These functions are grouped into thirteen sets organized around common types, such as, date and time, mathematical, statistical, and financial. Additionally, one set consists of all available functions listed in alphabetical order. These functions can be seen and accessed by clicking on the f_x icon shown in Figure 3.1 and then selecting the desired category set from the resulting dialog box.

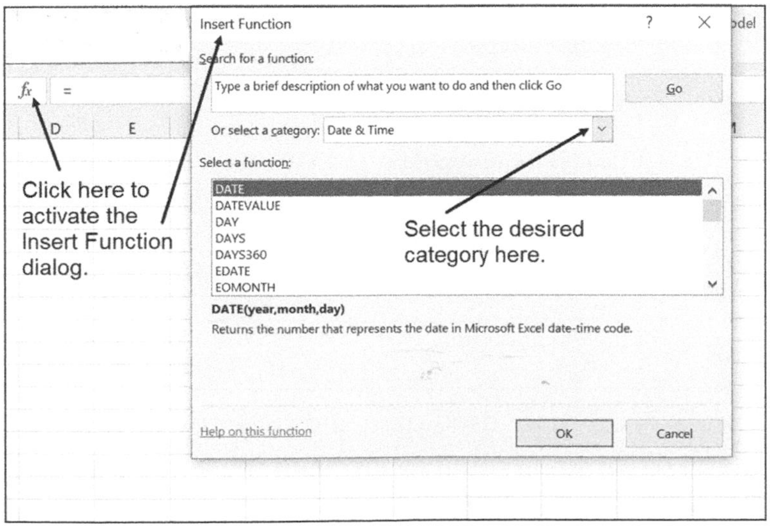

Figure 3.1 Activating the Excel function selection dialog

Excel also provides conditional formatting, which permits highlighting individual cells and rows using user-created criteria. This is helpful in isolating and pinpointing specifically relevant data in large data sets. Each of the topics in this chapter can be used independently or can be omitted on first reading with no loss of subject continuity.

3.1 DATE, TIME, AND TEXT FUNCTIONS

There are two main uses for Excel's Date and Time functions. The first is to place a date and/or time value directly on a spreadsheet. This provides a reference indicating when a spreadsheet was created or changed, and is referred to as a *date and/or time stamp.*

The second usage is for location and selection purposes. For example, sorting a list based on payment dates, or locating specific payments, such as those overdue by 30, 60, or 90 days. The selection of specific dates is typically made in conjunction with Excel's conditional formatting options. This option permits highlighting the selected dates and is presented in Section 3.4.

Table 3.1 Commonly used Date functions

Function	Description	Examples	Returns
DATE(year, month, day))	Returns a date in the cell's date or other number format	=DATE(2020,12,25)	12/25/2020
DATEVALUE(date as text)	Returns a number representing a text date in Microsoft's date-time code (serial number)	=DATEVALUE("2020/12/25")	44190
DAY(date)	Returns a number from 1 to 31 for Microsoft's date-time code (serial-number)	=DAY("2020/7/23") =DAY(TODAY( ))	23 Varies by day of month
DAYS(end-date, start-date)	Returns the number of days between two dates	DAYS("2020/8/15","2020/7/23")	23
MONTH(date)	Returns a number from 1 (Jan.) to 12 (Dec.)	= MONTH("2020/7/23") =MONTH(TODAY( ))	7 Today's Month
NOW( )	Returns the current date and time	=NOW( )	The current date and time
TODAY( )	Returns the current date	=TODAY( )	The current date
WEEKDAY(date)	Returns a number from 1 (Mon) to 7 (Sun)	=WEEKDAY("2018/7/23")	2
YEAR(date)	Returns a year from 1900 to 9999	=YEAR("2020/7/23") =YEAR(TODAY( ))	2020 Today's year

Table 3.1 lists Excel's commonly used date and time functions. Included in this table are examples of each of these function's usage and the value returned. When this value is a number, it is referred to as a Microsoft serial-number. These numbers are sequential numerical values that are used for the actual date storage (number of days elapsed

since January 1, 1900). This displayed value can be changed by formatting it using one of the available Date formats.

Figures 3.2 illustrates a spreadsheet segment using a number of these Date functions.

	A	B	C
1	**Description**	**Formula used**	**Return Value**
2	Today's Date is	=TODAY()	11/19/2019
3	Today's Date and Time is	=NOW()	11/19/2019 12:46
4	Today's Month is	=MONTH(TODAY())	11
5	Today's Day is	=DAY(TODAY())	19
6	Today's Year is	=YEAR(TODAY())	2019
7	The date 12/25/2025 is	=DATE(2025,12,25)	12/25/2025
8	The date value of 12/25/2025 is	=DATEVALUE("12/25/2025")	46016
9	The date value of 1/1/1900 is	=DATEVALUE("1/1/1900")	1

Figure 3.2 Examples using Date functions

Dates used as arguments to Excel's Date functions must adhere to the expected data types. For example, as seen in Table 3.1 and Figure 3.2, the DATEVALUE( ) function requires a text argument. Thus, for this function, a date, such as 12/25/20, must be entered as text, which requires the date be enclosed in double quotes, as "12/25/20." Other date functions may allow function arguments to be in either a text or numeric form.

Dates entered into a cell need not be entered as text. Thus, a date, such as 12/25/2020 or 1/18/25, can be entered as a combination of digits and forward slashes that accurately specify the date. If the provided argument to a Date or Time function is a cell reference, the value in the cell must be formatted as a Date and Time Value.

Dates Prior to 1/1/1900

Unfortunately, Excel stores dates as numbers representing the cumulative days from January 1st 1900, where dates before this must be stored as text. Practically, this means that the functions listed in Table 3.1 can only be used reliably for dates on or after 1/1/1900. Dates prior to this must be user-converted to a number format. One of the simplest conversion formulas is the following:

$$=Year * 10000 + Month * 100 + Day$$

where Year, Month, and Day are obtained using Excel's YEAR( ), MONTH( ), and Day( ) functions. Another alternative is to obtain a conversion routine from the Internet.

Application Note
Text Characters Are Stored as Numeric Values

In Excel, which is based on the C++ programming language, each character is stored as a unique numeric value. This permits the storage of special characters that have no printable equivalent, such as a line-feed or carriage return. These numeric codes can be represented in both binary and integer forms.

   An important consequence of using integer value codes for individual characters is that they can then be easily compared for alphabetical ordering. Because each subsequent letter in an alphabet is stored using a higher value than its preceding letter, the comparison of characters is reduced to the comparison of numeric values.

   Previously , the ASCII (American Standard Code for Information Interchange) code was used to store characters. This code was limited to representing 256 unique English language characters. To accommodate international applications using non-English character sets, Unicode was introduced in 1987. This code is now universally used and can represent 65,536 unique character codes. The first 256 Unicode characters have the same numerical values as the original 256 ASCII codes and are listed in Appendix A.

Text and Character Functions

As introduced in Chapter 1, text consists of a group of characters that can include one or more of the following:

- Letters
- Numbers
- Special Symbols (-, $, ., @, &)

Formally, a sequence of characters is referred to as a *string literal*. A string literal is also referred to as a *string constant* or *string value*, and more conventionally, as a *string* or *text string*, for short. By default, text is left aligned in a cell. Additionally, if the first character entered is an apostrophe ('), Excel considers the complete entry as text; it can also be designated as text by using formatting.

Text entered directly into a cell, such as a label, is recognized by Excel as text, just as numbers and formulas are recognized as their respective data types. However, when used as an argument to a function, text must be enclosed in double quotes. For example, "Pass," "Hello world!," and "xyz 123 *!#@&" are all examples of text strings that are acceptable as function arguments where a text string is appropriate.

Unlike a number, which is stored using a numerical code, text is stored in a character-by-character manner, with each individual character having its own unique numerical code. Table 3.2 lists the stored numeric code values and their corresponding characters for both uppercase and lowercase English letters (*see* Application Note above)[1].

---

[1] The first 256 ASCII and Unicodes can be found in Appendix A.

Table 3.2 Uppercase and lowercase numerical codes (ASCII and Unicode)

Letter	A	B	C	D	E	F	G	H	I
Code	65	66	67	68	69	70	71	72	73
Letter	J	K	L	M	N	O	P	Q	R
Code	74	75	76	77	78	79	80	81	82
Letter	S	T	U	V	W	X	Y	Z	
Code	83	84	85	86	87	88	89	90	
Letter	a	b	c	d	e	f	g	h	i
Code	97	98	99	100	101	102	103	104	105
Letter	j	k	l	m	n	o	p	q	r
Code	106	107	108	109	110	111	112	113	114
Letter	s	t	u	v	w	x	y	z	
Code	115	116	117	118	119	120	121	122	

The commonly used text functions available for processing characters are presented in Table 3.3. As previously noted for the Date and Time functions, when text is required as an explicit argument to any of these functions, it must be enclosed in double quotes ("string in here"). This permits a clear marking of where the string begins and ends. If the provided argument is a cell reference, the value in the cell must be formatted as text.

The CLEAN( ) Function

As is noted in the previous Application Note, not all characters are printable. There are times, however, when codes for these non-printable characters become embedded within text and are not seen when the text is displayed. For example, two names may appear to be the same but are not because one has a hidden, non-printable character within it. Such text can be an extremely troublesome problem when text is compared. Examples of these situations are described in Section 4.3, where a name is used in a look-up table or when an application must remove duplicate entries (see Section 8.5).

As a specific example, the two strings shown in cells A2 and A3 in Figure 3.3 look the same and have the same string length. However, they are not the same. The text in cell A2 contains two non-printable characters: one between the first and last name and one after the last name; each one is displayed as a single space, while the text in cell A3 uses a space character between the first and last name.

	A	B	C	D
1	**Text**	**Length**	**Cleansed Text**	**Length**
2	John Smith	11	JohnSmith	9
3	John Smith	11	John Smith	11

Figure 3.3 Same name, one with non-printable characters

Table 3.3 Commonly used text and character functions

Function	Description	Example	Result
CHAR(value)	Returns the character corresponding to the ASCII code number specified	=CHAR(122)	z
CLEAN(string)	Removes all non-printable characters from the string	=CLEAN("Hi"&CHAR(2)&"Ho")	HiHo
& operator CONCATENATE( ) CONCAT( ) is only available for Excel 2019 and Excel 365	Join arguments into a single string. Can be replaced by &	="Hi" & " " & "Ho" =CONCATENATE("Hi"," ","Ho") =CONCAT("Hi"," ","Ho")	Hi Ho
LEFT(string, num)	Returns the specified number of characters from the start of the string	=LEFT("Some Day",4)	Some
LEN(string)	Returns the number of characters in the string (includes spaces)	=LEN("This String")	11
LOWER(string)	Converts text string to all lowercase characters	=LOWER("Let's Go")	let's go
RIGHT(string, num)	Returns the specified number of characters from the end of the string	=RIGHT("Some Day",3)	Day
UPPER(string)	Converts text string to all uppercase characters	=UPPER("Excel")	EXCEL
TRIM(string)	Removes all spaces except single spaces between words in the string	=TRIM(" Hello ")	Hello
UNICHAR(value)	Returns the character corresponding to the Unicode value	UNICHAR(122)	z
UNICODE(char)	Returns the Unicode value corresponding to the character specified	=UNICODE("A")	65

Cells C2 and C3 contain cleansed versions of the strings in cells A2 and A3, respectively. The actual data and formulas used to produce Figure 3.3 are shown in Figure 3.4.

	A	B	C	D
1	Text	Length	Cleansed Text	Length
2	="John"&CHAR(2)&"Smith"&CHAR(2)	=LEN(A2)	=CLEAN(A2)	9
3	John Smith	=LEN(A3)	=CLEAN(A3)	11

Figure 3.4 Data and formulas used to produce Figure 3.3

In comparing text values, and in cases where text examples appear to produce unpredictable or "strange" results, using the CLEAN( ) function frequently clears up the matter.

EXERCISES 3.1

1. Enter the spreadsheet segment shown below and verify the display that is produced for the date and time you entered.

	A	B	C
1	**Description**	**Formula used**	**Return Value**
2	Today's Date is	=TODAY()	11/19/2019
3	Today's Date and Time is	=NOW()	11/19/2019 12:46
4	Today's Month is	=MONTH(TODAY())	11
5	Today's Day is	=DAY(TODAY())	19
6	Today's Year is	=YEAR(TODAY())	2019
7	The date 12/25/2025 is	=DATE(2025,12,25)	12/25/2025
8	The date value of 12/25/2025 is	=DATEVALUE("12/25/2025")	46016
9	The date value of 1/1/1900 is	=DATEVALUE("1/1/1900")	1

2. Write formulas for the following:

   a. cell B2 displays the text in cell A2 in uppercase letters

   b. cell C2 displays the text in cell A2 in lowercase letter

   c. cell D2 displays the text in cell A2 with all spaces in the text removed

   d. cell E2 displays the length of the text located in cell A2, after the CLEAN( ) function is applied to the text.

3. Write formulas to accomplish the following:

   a. cell C2 should display the first letter in cell A2 as an uppercase letter

   b. cell C2 should display the first letter in cell A2 as an uppercase letter followed by a period and a space.

   c. cell C2 should display the first letter in cell A2 as an uppercase letter, followed by a period, a space, and the first letter in cell B2 as an uppercase letter.

4. Write an Excel formula in cell D1 that inserts the text in cell B1 into the text in cell A1, where cell C1 contains the position where the insertion should begin.

5. The spreadsheet in Figure 3.5a contains first names in column A and last names in column B. These need to be processed so that they appear as shown in Figure 3.5b. For this, write a formula for cell C2 that can be copied down to produce the required display. (**Hint**: Review Exercise 3.)

	A	B	C
1	**First Name**	**Last Name**	**Name**
2	jean	KASTEN	
3	MOLLY	joNES	
4	bill	lanfrank	
5	lenny	Novik	

Figure 3.5a Spreadsheet for Exercise 5

	A	B	C
1	**First Name**	**Last Name**	**Name**
2	jean	KASTEN	J. Kasten
3	MOLLY	joNES	M. Jones
4	bill	lanfrank	B. Lanfrank
5	lenny	Novik	L. Novik

Figure 3.5b Spreadsheet results for Exercise 5

3.2   STATISTICAL FUNCTIONS

Excel provides two basic sets of statistical functions. The first set consists of descriptive statistical functions, while the second set provides more advanced inferential statistical functions.

Descriptive statistics describes and summarizes the relevant features of a data set. These include the data's mean (that is, its average), mode, and median, which are referred to as the data's *central tendency*, as well as the data's standard deviation, and maximum and minimum values, which are measures of the data's *dispersion* (spread). These measures, presented in this section, together with simple graphical charts form the basis of almost all data analysis.

Inferential statistics is the branch of statistics that draws conclusions about a population using random data samples taken from the population. Inferential functions are not directly included with the basic set, but can be easily added by using the Analysis Analysis Toolpak, and the procedure to install this Add-In is provided in Appendix B.

Table 3.4 lists the five most commonly used descriptive statistical functions: the complete set consists of 110 functions.

Table 3.4 Commonly used statistical functions

Function	Description	Example
AVERAGE( )	Returns the arithmetic average (mean) of its arguments	=AVERAGE(A2:A10)
COUNT( )	Returns the number of numbers in a range or set of arguments	=COUNT(A2:A10)
MAX( )	Returns the largest value in the range or set of arguments	=MAX(A2:A10)
MEDIAN( )	Returns the middle value of a range or set of arguments	=MEDIAN(A2:A10)
MIN( )	Returns the smallest value of a range or set of arguments	=MIN(A2:A10)
MODE.MULT( )	Returns a vertical array of the most frequently occurring values	=MODE.MULT(A2:A10)

Table 3.4 (*continued*)

Function	Description	Example
MODE.SNGL( )	Returns the single most frequently oc-curring value	=MODE.SNGL(A2:A10)
STDEV.P( ) (Earlier Excel versions named this function STDEVP( ).)	Calculates the standard deviation of its arguments. Considers the arguments the entire population and ignores text and logical values	=STDEV.P(A2:A10)
STDEV.S( ) (Earlier Excel versions named this function STDEV( ))	Calculates the standard deviation of its arguments. Considers the arguments a sample and ignores text and logical values	=STDEV.S(A2:A10)

Figure 3.6a illustrates the use of these functions as applied to the data in rows 4 through 7. The formulas used to produce the values shown are presented in Figure 3.6b.

	A	B	C	D	E
1		Examples of Statistical Functions			
2					
3	The Data:				
4	110	125	88	94	106
5	84	115	106	83	96
6	97	104	82	108	92
7	106	115	97	83	110
8					
9	Statistical Measures:				
10	Average:	100.05		Standard Dev:	12.04
11	Median:	100.50		Maximum Num:	125
12	Mode:	106		Minimum Num:	82
13	Count:	20		Range:	43

Figure 3.6a Examples of statistical functions

	A	B	C	D	E
1		Examples of Statistical Functions			
2					
3	The Data:				
4	110	125	88	94	106
5	84	115	106	83	96
6	97	104	82	108	92
7	106	115	97	83	110
8					
9		Statistical Measures:			
10	Average:	=AVERAGE(A4:E7)		Standard Dev:	=STDEV.P(A4:E7)
11	Median:	=MEDIAN(A4:E7)		Maximum Num:	=MAX(A4:E7)
12	Mode:	=MODE(A4:E7)		Minimum Num:	=MIN(A4:E7)
13	Count:	=COUNT(A4:E7)		Range:	=E11-E12

Figure 3.6b Formulas used to produce Figure 3.6a

Standard Deviations

Although the average of a set of data is a commonly used statistical result, it gives no indication of how the data is spread around the average. If the data is widely spaced, in fact, an average value can be extremely misleading. As an example, consider the two columns of house prices listed in Figure 3.7.

	A	B	C
1		House Prices	
2		Street 1	Street 2
3		$300,000	$100,000
4		315000	110000
5		320000	520000
6		325000	530000
7		315000	315000
8	Average Price =	$315,000	$315,000

Figure 3.7 Two datasets having the same average

Notice that the average prices for the prices listed in columns B and C are the same, but only the houses listed in column B are close to the average. Anyone expecting to buy a house near this average price in Street 2 may be disappointed by the houses available there.

In these situations, the standard deviation provides the missing information. In Figure 3.8, the standard deviation of each data set is listed. Notice that the standard deviation for the house prices in column B is $8,367, while that for the prices in column C is $187,883. This means that, on average, a house in Street 1 will be $8,367 above or below the average price of $315,000, while those in Street 2 will be $187,883 above or below the average price.

	A	B	C
1		House Prices	
2		Street 1	Street 2
3		$300,000	$100,000
4		315000	110000
5		320000	520000
6		325000	530000
7		315000	315000
8	Average Price =	$315,000	$315,000
9	Standard Dev. =	$8,367	$187,883

Figure 3.8 Comparing averages and standard deviations

Even more important than providing a measure of the average deviation of individual data points from the overall average, standard deviations provide a way of

1. Comparing averages obtained at different points in time (for example, comparing batting averages of professional baseball players across the decades)

2. A quick method, in certain situations, of determining the percentage of data contained within a bracket of ranges (for example, determining the percentage of students who scored within a given range of SAT scores)

How these two situations are accomplished is described next, after we understand how a standard deviation is obtained.

Calculating the Standard Deviation

At its most basic level, a standard deviation simply represents the typical difference between a data point and the overall data average, as was shown in Figure 3.8. To gain an understanding of this basic concept, consider the spreadsheet segment shown in Figure 3.9.

As seen in Figure 3.9, the sum and average of the four data values listed in column B are 48 and 12, respectively. The data in column C is simply the difference between each data point from the average. Thus, the − 8 in cell C2 is obtained as 4 − 12, and it indicates that the 4 in cell B2 is eight units below the average. Similarly, the value in cell C5 indicates that the data point in cell B5 is eight units above the average. Notice that the sum of all of the values in cells C2 through C5 is zero. This is always the case: the sum of the individual deviations of each data point from the average must be zero, because the average is calculated as the center point for all the data values. As such, the individual deviations tell us nothing about how far away a typical value is.

	A	B	C	D	E
1		Value	Deviation from Average	Absolute Value of Deviation	Squared Deviation
2		4	-8	8	64
3		8	-4	4	16
4		16	4	4	16
5		20	8	8	64
6	Sum =	48	0	24	160
7	Average =	12	0	6	40
8	Square Root =				6.32

Average Deviation

Standard Deviation

Figure 3.9 Measures of deviation from the average

Taking the absolute value of each deviation, however, does provide a meaningful measure of the average deviation. As shown in column D (again, in Figure 3.9), the sum of absolute value of each deviation is 24, and the average deviation, highlighted in cell D7, is 6. Thus, on average, each data point is 6 units away from the average of 12.

Now notice the highlighted value in cell E8, which is 6.32. Although it does not provide the exact average deviation of 6 in cell D7, it is very close. More importantly, however, it provides a measure of overall data spread that is much more useful than the exact average deviation. This number is the standard deviation of the data. As indicated, it is computed as the square root of the sum of each squared deviation. This value is computed using Excel's STDEV.P( ) function[2].

The Empirical Rule

When data is normally distributed, which means that it follows a bell-shaped curve, the following rule, known as the *Empirical Rule*, can be applied. This rule states that for normally distributed data,[3]

- 68% of the data will be between ± 1 standard deviations of the data's average value
- 95% of the data will be between ± 2 standard deviations of the data's average value
- 99.7% of the data will be between ± 3 standard deviations of the data's average value

Example 1

SAT scores are normally distributed, which means they follow a bell-shaped curve. The average SAT score in 2018 was 1060 with a standard deviation of 194. Using this data, determine

    a. the percentage of students who had scores between 866 and 1254

    b. the percentage of students who had scores between 672 and 1460

Solution: Because the data is normally distributed, the Empirical Rule can be used.

    c. A score of 1254 is one standard deviation (that is, $1254 - 1060 = 194$) above the average score of 1060, and a score of 866 is one standard deviation below the average score. Thus, 68% of all students had a score between these 866 and 1254.

---

[2] STDEV.P( ) divides the sum of the deviations by n, where n is the number of data points, while STDEV.S( ) divides by n-1. The P version is for populations and the S version for samples. The corresponding versions for Excel 2007 and earlier versions were named STDEVP() and STDEV(), respectively.

[3] For data that is not normally distributed, Chebyshev's Theorem, which is beyond the scope of this text, can be used.

d. A score of 1460 is two standard deviations above the average score of 1060, and a score of 672 is two standard deviations below the average score. Thus, 95% of all students had a score between 672 and 1460.

Example 2

A second use of the standard deviation provides a method of comparing two averages taken at different periods of time. For example, the lifetime batting average of Tris Speaker, who played in the 1920s, was .345, while Miguel Cabrera's current lifetime (at the end of the 2018 season) was .316. A direct comparison of these two averages to see who was the better hitter is not valid, because the equipment (bats, gloves, and baseballs) differed for these two players, and batting averages were more spread out in the 1920s. A better comparison is to see how these two players compared relative to their contemporary players. Doing this again requires using standard deviations to determine how far above the mean each of these players was relative to their contemporaries.

Solution: In the 1920s, the average batting average was .281, with a standard deviation of approximately .05, while in 2018, the average batting average of all players was .268 with a standard deviation of approximately .04. This means that the earlier players had, on average, higher batting averages with a wider spread between the players than the current players. Comparing each player to their contemporaries reveals that[4] Tris Speaker's batting average was $(.345 - .281)/.05 = 1.28$ above the average of his contemporaries, and Miguel Cabrera's batting average is $(.316 - .268)/.04 = 1.20$ above the average of his contemporaries. This indicates that both of these players are fairly equal as far as batting averages are considered.

---

[4] The resulting values are referred to as *z*-scores. A *z*-score represents how many standard deviations a given value is away from the average. It is most useful for bell-shaped data distributions, where 99.7% of all *z*-scores will lie between -3 and +3.

EXERCISES 3.2

1. Using Excel, reproduce the following spreadsheet so that the result appears as the second image (with column C). Use Excel text functions as needed.

	A	B	C
1	**First Name**	**Last Name**	**Name**
2	jean	KASTEN	
3	MOLLY	joNES	
4	bill	lanfrank	
5	lenny	Novik	

	A	B	C
1	**First Name**	**Last Name**	**Name**
2	jean	KASTEN	J. Kasten
3	MOLLY	joNES	M. Jones
4	bill	lanfrank	B. Lanfrank
5	lenny	Novik	L. Novik

2. Using Excel, reproduce the following spreadsheet.

	A	B	C
1		**House Prices**	
2		**Street 1**	**Street 2**
3		$300,000	$100,000
4		315000	110000
5		320000	520000
6		325000	530000
7		315000	315000
8	**Average Price =**	$315,000	$315,000
9	**Standard Dev. =**	$8,367	$187,883

3. Reproduce the following spreadsheet, using Excel statistical functions as needed.

	A	B	C	D	E
1		Value	Deviation from Average	Absolute Value of Deviation	Squared Deviation
2		4	-8	8	64
3		8	-4	4	16
4		16	4	4	16
5		20	8	8	64
6	Sum =	48	0	24	160
7	Average =	12	0	6	40
8	Square Root =				6.32

Average Deviation

Standard Deviation

4. Complete parts a and b.

  a. Using Excel's AVERAGE() and STDEV.P( ) functions, determine the average and standard deviations of the following salary data: $48,000, $53,000, $35,000, and $43,000.

  b. Use Excel functions to determine the median, mode, minimum, maximum, and number of salaries listed in Exercise 4a.

5. Complete parts a and b.

  a. Using Excel's AVERAGE() and STD.P( ) functions, determine the average and standard deviations of the following test grades: 85, 74, 88, 95, 65, 72, 79, 83, 90, 78, and 62.

  b. Use Excel functions to determine the median, mode, minimum, maximum, and number of grades listed in Exercise 5a.

3.3   FINANCIAL FUNCTIONS

Excel provides numerous financial functions. Table 3.6 provides a sampling of these functions, most of which require a knowledge of financial analyses, such as cash flows and bonds that are beyond the scope of this text. The PMT( ) function, however, is particularly useful in calculating loan payments, such as car loans and home mortgage payments. As these types of loans are in common usage for financing homes and cars, this particular function is discussed in detail.

The PMT( ) function

A loan used to buy a car or purchase a house, known as a *home mortgage*, or *mortgage*, for short, are common examples of commercial loans. Payments for these two types of loans are made on a monthly basis. Here, the amount of the loan, the length of the loan, and the interest rate are fixed when the loan is taken out. Based on these three variables, a fixed monthly required to pay off the loan can be calculated. In Excel this payment amount is determined using the PMT( ) function.

Table 3.6 A sampling of Excel's financial functions

Function	Description
COUPDAYS( )	Returns the number of days in the coupon period that contains the settlement date
CUMIPMT( )	Returns the cumulative interest paid on a loan between two specified periods
CUMPRINC( )	Returns the cumulative principal paid on a loan between two specified periods
DURATION( )	Returns the annual duration of a security with periodic payments
FV(rate, nper, pmt, [pv], [type])	Returns the future value of an investment assuming periodic, constant payments with a constant interest rate

Table 3.6 (*continued*)

Function	Description
IRR( )	Returns the internal rate of return for a series of cash flows that occur at regular intervals, but do not have to be the same amounts
NPV( )	Returns the Net Present Value of an investment, based on a supplied discount rate, and a series of payments and income
PMT(rate, nper, pv, [fv], [type])	Returns the payment for a loan having constant, periodic payments at a fixed interest rate
PPMT(rate, nper, pv, [fv], [type])	Returns the principal portion for a given period's payment for a payment based on a fixed interest rate and a payment schedule
PV(rate, nper, pmt, [fv], [type])	Returns the present value that a series of future payments is worth now

Figure 3.10 lists the monthly payments due for a $15,000 car loan made for four and seven years, respectively, and for a fifteen-year and thirty-year $200,000 home mortgage. The interest rates for all of these loans is 5%.

	A	B	C	D	E
1	Loan Type	Interest Rate	Loan Length (Years)	Loan Amount	Monthly Payment
2	Car	5%	4	$15,000	$345.44
3	Car	5%	7	$15,000	$212.01
4	Home Mortgage	5%	15	$200,000	$1,581.59
5	Home Mortgage	5%	30	$200,000	$1,073.64

Figure 3.10 Examples of car and home mortgage loans

Figure 3.11 shows the formulas in cells E2 through E5 needed for calculating the monthly payments. As indicated, the formula in Cell E2 can be copied down for cells E3 through E5. In each copy, the relative row designation in the function is changed appropriately.

	A	B	C	D	E
1	Loan Type	Interest Rate	Loan Length (Years)	Loan Amount	Monthly Payment
2	Car	5%	4	$15,000	=-PMT(B2/12,C2*12,D2)
3	Car	5%	7	$15,000	=-PMT(B3/12,C3*12,D3)
4	Home Mortgage	5%	15	$200,000	=-PMT(B4/12,C4*12,D4)
5	Home Mortgage	5%	30	$200,000	=-PMT(B5/12,C5*12,D5)

Figure 3.11 The data and formulas used to produce Figure 3.10

The PMT( ) function requires three parameters: the monthly interest rate, the length of the loan in months, and the amount of the loan. For the spreadsheet shown in Figure 3.11, the PMT( ) entry in cell E2 is

$$= -PMT(B2/12, C2*12, D2)$$

Because we are calculating monthly payments, the interest rate and the loan length used in the PMT( ) function must be in months. If the interest rate is in a yearly basis, it is necessary to divide the yearly interest rate by 12 to obtain a monthly rate. Similarly, if the loan length is in years, then there is a need to multiply the yearly loan length by 12.

The reason for the negative sign in front of the PMT( ) function has to do with the convention of money flows. Positive values, such as the amount of the loan, are considered funds that flow to the borrower. Negative values indicate funds that the borrower pays; as such, they are considered funds that flow away from the borrower. Thus, the PMT( ) function will report a negative amount as the monthly payment, because this is an amount that effectively flows away from the borrower. To counteract this, the negative sign in front of the PMT( ) function forces the calculated payment to appear as a positive value.

Note also that once a formula was entered in cell E2, it was then copied down for cells E3 through E5, as illustrated by the arrow in Figure 3.11.

Calculating Total Interest Paid

It is both instructive and easy to determine the total interest paid on a car loan or mortgage. The required formula is:

Total Interest Paid = (Monthly payment) *(Loan length in months)
$$- \text{ Original Loan Amount} \quad \text{(Eq. 3.1)}$$

For example, as seen in Figure 3.10, the monthly payment for a $200,000, 30-year, 5% mortgage is $1,073.64. Using Eq. 3.1, the total interest paid on this loan is

Total Interest Paid = ($1,073.64) *(360) – $200,000 = $186,511.57

Thus, after 30 years, when the $200,000 loan has been paid off, an almost equal amount of $186,511.57 has been paid in interest.

The highlighted columns in Figure 3.12 show the total amount and total interest paid on each of the loans listed in Figure 3.10. The values for the Total Amounts Paid that are listed in column F are calculated as follows:

(Monthly payment) *(Loan length in months)

Subtracting each loan's initial amount from this value, as presented in Eq. 3.1, yields the Total Interest Paid amounts highlighted in column G in Figure 3.12.

	A	B	C	D	E	F	G
1	Loan Type	Interest Rate	Loan Length (Years)	Loan Amount	Monthly Payment	Total Amount Paid	Total Interest Paid
2	Car	5%	4	$15,000	$345.44	$16,581.09	$1,581.09
3	Car	5%	7	$15,000	$212.01	$17,808.73	$2,808.73
4	Home Mol	5%	15	$200,000	$1,581.59	$284,686.20	$84,686.20
5	Home Mol	5%	30	$200,000	$1,073.64	$386,510.40	$186,510.40

Figure 3.12 The Total Interest Paid for the loans in Figure 3.10

Notice that as the length of a loan is extended, even though the monthly payment decreases, the total amount and total interest paid are greater for the longer loans than for the shorter ones. This is because more payments are required for the longer loans, which results in higher total amounts paid and higher total interest paid over the life of the loan.

Repayment Schedules: Amortization

The repayment of a loan over time is referred to as *amortization* (pronounced *am-or-ti-za-tion*), and loans paid over time are said to *amortized*. An *amortization schedule* is a table that shows how the loan is being paid down before and after each payment has been made.

Amortization schedules for car and home mortgage loans provide the monthly payments, interest paid, and remaining loan balance each month, until the loan is paid off. Although the monthly payment is the same each month, the dollar amount of the interest changes each month. The reason is that the interest is calculated on the remaining loan balance, which decreases each month as the loan is paid. This means that the dollar amount of the interest also decreases, with the remaining portion of the monthly payment, which increases, applied to paying off the loan.[5]

Figure 3.13 provides an amortization schedule for a one-year loan of $1,000 made at 5% annual interest. The required monthly payment for this loan is $85.61, which was determined using the PMT( ) function.

In reviewing Figure 3.13, first notice that the highlighted final outstanding balance at the end of the last column is zero, which means that the loan has been fully repaid. Next, notice that each payment in the second column is the same monthly payment of $85.61. This is always true, except possibly for the last payment. The reason for this is that the last payment is adjusted, if necessary, so that the balance of the loan is zero when the last payment is made. This can occur because of rounding to the nearest cent in the calculations of the monthly payment and interim balances.

---

[5] With adjustable-rate mortgages, known as ARMs, the interest rate is only fixed for an initial term, but then fluctuates with market interest rates. This provides an initially lower monthly payment than that of a traditional fixed-rate mortgage, but makes the monthly payments unpredictable after the initial term.

Notice that the outstanding balance at the end of each month, listed in column F, is reduced with each payment. This means the interest owed each month, which is calculated based on the outstanding balance, also declines from payment to payment. Thus, each month, a larger portion of the monthly payment, the amounts listed in column E, goes toward paying down the loan. The sum of these interest and principal amounts for each months equals the monthly payment. For larger mortgages having a longer life than the one in this example, the amount of the interest paid each payment, especially in the first few years of the mortgage, is significantly higher. In fact, for a typical 5-year car loan or 30-year mortgage, the total interest paid can amount to almost half of the original loan amount (see last section).

Amortization schedules are easy to create using Excel. The relevant formulas used to create the Figure 3.13's spreadsheet are shown in Figure 3.14. The formula used to create Figure 3.13 follows.

The PMT( ) function in cell B4 requires, as has been described previously, three parameters: the monthly interest rate, the length of the loan in months, and the amount of the loan. For the spreadsheet shown in Figure 3.11, the PMT( ) entry in cell E2 is

$$=-PMT(B2/12, C2*12, D2)$$

Again, as noted previously, the PMT( ) function reports a negative amount as the monthly payment, because this is an amount that effectively flows away from the borrower. To counteract this, the negative sign in front of the PMT( ) function forces the calculated payment to appear as a positive value.

	A	B	C	D	E	F
1	Amount of Loan:	$1,000				
2	Length of Loan (in years):	1				
3	Annual Interest Rate:	5%				
4	Monthly Payment:	$85.61				
5						
6			Payment Number	Payment Amount	Interest Paid	Principal Paid	Outstanding Balance
7			0				$1,000
8			1	$85.61	$4.17	$81.44	$918.56
9			2	$85.61	$3.83	$81.78	$836.78
10			3	$85.61	$3.49	$82.12	$754.66
11			4	$85.61	$3.14	$82.46	$672.20
12			5	$85.61	$2.80	$82.81	$589.39
13			6	$85.61	$2.46	$83.15	$506.24
14			7	$85.61	$2.11	$83.50	$422.74
15			8	$85.61	$1.76	$83.85	$338.89
16			9	$85.61	$1.41	$84.20	$254.70
17			10	$85.61	$1.06	$84.55	$170.15
18			11	$85.61	$0.71	$84.90	$85.25
19			12	$85.61	$0.36	$85.25	$0.00

Figure 3.13 Amortization schedule for a 12-month, $1,000 loan at 5% interest

The interest due each month is the monthly interest rate times the outstanding balance. Because this is a 5% annual loan, the monthly interest rate, i, is 0.05/12. Because the initial outstanding balance is $1,000, the first month's interest, I1, is calculated as

$$I1 = (0.05/12) * \$1{,}000 = \$4.17$$

This is the part of the $85.71 payment that is used to pay the first month's interest on the loan. Thus, we are left with $85.61 – $4.17 = $81.44 as the payment that is applied to the loan itself. This leaves an outstanding balance at the end of the first month, P1 of

$$P1 = \$1{,}000 - \$81.44 = \$918.56$$

For the second month the interest is again calculated as the monthly interest rate times the outstanding balance. Now, however, the outstanding balance is $918.56. Thus,

$$I2 = (0.05/12) * \$918.56 = \$3.83$$

and the amount of the payment that is left to paying the loan balance is $85.61 – $3.83 = $81.78. With this amount applied to the loan, the new outstanding balance at the end of the second month is

$$P2 = \$918.56 - \$81.78 = \$836.78$$

Continuing in this manner, the complete amortization schedule shown in Figure 3.13 in Table 3.5 is generated.

Note also that once the formulas have been placed in Row 8, they can be copied down to the end of the spread sheet, as shown by the arrowed lines in Figure 3.14. The dashed lines illustrate the data provided by the input section of the spreadsheet. Because the initial amount in cell B1 is only used once in the main body of the spreadsheet and is not copied, an absolute address is not required in cell F7 (see third dashed line).

	A	B	C	D	E	F
1	Amount of Loan:	1000				
2	Length of Loan (in years):	1				
3	Annual Interest Rate:	0.05				
4	Monthly Payment:	=-PMT(B3/12,B2*12,B1)				
5						
6		Payment Number	Payment Amount	Interest Paid	Principal Paid	Outstanding Balance
7		0				=B1
8		1	=$B$4	=$B$3/12*F7	=C8-D8	=F7-E8
9		2	=$B$4	=$B$3/12*F8	=C9-D9	=F8-E9
10		3	=$B$4	=$B$3/12*F9	=C10-D10	=F9-E10
11		4	=$B$4	=$B$3/12*F10	=C11-D11	=F10-E11
12		5	=$B$4	=$B$3/12*F11	=C12-D12	=F11-E12
13		6	=$B$4	=$B$3/12*F12	=C13-D13	=F12-E13
14		7	=$B$4	=$B$3/12*F13	=C14-D14	=F13-E14
15		8	=$B$4	=$B$3/12*F14	=C15-D15	=F14-E15
16		9	=$B$4	=$B$3/12*F15	=C16-D16	=F15-E16
17		10	=$B$4	=$B$3/12*F16	=C17-D17	=F16-E17
18		11	=$B$4	=$B$3/12*F17	=C18-D18	=F17-E18
19		12	=$B$4	=$B$3/12*F18	=C19-D19	=F18-E19

Figure 3.14 Amortization schedule

EXERCISES 3.3

1. Using Excel's PMT( ) function, determine the monthly payment for a 30-year, $36,000 mortgage, having a 4% annual interest rate.

2. Using Excel's PMT( ) function, determine the monthly payment for a 25-year, $30,000 mortgage, having an 8% annual interest rate.

3. Determine the total interest paid for the mortgage in Exercise 1.

4. Determine the total interest paid for the mortgage in Exercise 2.

5. Using Excel's PMT( ) function, determine the sum of the individual interest payments in column D of Figure 3.10 and then verify that this same sum is obtained using the following equation:

   Total Interest Paid = (Monthly payment) *(Loan length in months)
   – Original Loan Amount

   Total Interest Paid

6. Complete parts a-c.

   a. Using Excel, create the following spreadsheet.

	A	B	C	D	E	F
1	Amount of Loan:	$1,000				
2	Length of Loan (in years):	1				
3	Annual Interest rate:	5%				
4	Monthly Payment:	$85.61				
5						
6		Payment Number	Payment Amount	Interest Paid	Principal Paid	Outstanding Balance
7		0				$1,000
8		1	$85.61	$4.17	$81.44	$918.56
9		2	$85.61	$3.83	$81.78	$836.78
10		3	$85.61	$3.49	$82.12	$754.66
11		4	$85.61	$3.14	$82.46	$672.20
12		5	$85.61	$2.80	$82.81	$589.39
13		6	$85.61	$2.46	$83.15	$506.24
14		7	$85.61	$2.11	$83.50	$422.74
15		8	$85.61	$1.76	$83.85	$338.89
16		9	$85.61	$1.41	$84.20	$254.70
17		10	$85.61	$1.06	$84.55	$170.15
18		11	$85.61	$0.71	$84.90	$85.25
19		12	$85.61	$0.36	$85.25	$0.00

   b. Replace the absolute addresses with the relative references in cells C8 and D8, and then copy the formulas shown in Figure 3.14. Determine why the copied formulas produce incorrect results.

   c. Why is an absolute address for cell B1 not needed in cell F7?

7. Create an amortization table for a 5-year loan for $20,000 that is to be paid back monthly at a 5% annual interest rate. The schedule should include totals for the payments, interest paid, and outstanding balance. Use figures 3.13 and 3.14 as a model for your amortization table.

8. Create an amortization table for a 4-year loan for $45,000 that is to be paid back monthly at a 4% annual interest rate. The schedule should include totals for the payments, interest paid, and principal paid, and outstanding balance. Use figures 3.13 and 3.14 as a model for your amortization table.

9. Create an Excel spreadsheet that calculates the payment and produces the amortization schedule for the mortgage described in Exercise 1 in this section.

10. Create an Excel spreadsheet that calculates the payment and produces the amortization schedule for the mortgage described in Exercise 2 in this section.

3.4 INFORMATION (IS) FUNCTIONS[6]

Excel provides a set of functions that permit you to determine the data type of a cell's contents. All of these functions return either a Boolean value of TRUE or FALSE. These functions are needed wherever the goal is to test values before they are included in a formula or function. For instance, you may want to use the =ISBLANK( ) function in a situation where you want to perform an operation in a cell only if there was a value there. If not, it would ignore that cell. This would help avoid error messages and other problems that can develop when the wrong type of data is entered into a cell, in conjunction with doing some kind of calculation or text manipulation in that cell, for example. The most commonly used of Excel's Information (sometimes referred to as *IS*) functions are listed in Table 3.17.

Table 3.17 Commonly used Information (IS) functions

Function	Description	Example
ISBLANK(cell)	Returns TRUE if the cell is blank; otherwise, returns FALSE	=ISBLANK(A1)
ISEVEN(arg)	Returns TRUE if the argument is an even number; otherwise, returns FALSE. The argument must be numerical.	=ISEVEN(B1)
ISFORMULA(cell)	Returns TRUE if the cell contains a formula; otherwise, returns FALSE	=ISFORMULA(A1)
ISLOGICAL(arg)	Returns TRUE if the argument is a Boolean value; otherwise, returns FALSE	=ISLOGICAL(A1)
ISNONTEXT(arg)	Returns TRUE if the argument is not text (blanks are not text); otherwise returns FALSE	= ISNONTEXT(A1)
ISNUMBER(arg)	Returns TRUE if argument is a number; otherwise, returns FALSE	= ISNUMBER(A1)
ISODD(arg)	Returns TRUE if the argument is an odd number; otherwise, returns FALSE. The argument must be numerical.	=ISODD(B1)

---

[6] This topic can be omitted on first reading without loss of subject continuity.

3.5   CONDITIONAL FORMATTING

Highlighting selected cells based on meeting specific criteria is extremely useful, both for analysis and presentation purposes. For example, in a sales report, the highlighting of salespeople who have exceeded their sales goal might be required; in an inventory report, the highlighting of items that are below a certain quantity may be necessary; and in a class list the instructor may want to highlight grades that are above and/or below certain grade levels.

The highlighting of cells, using background cell color and/or font styles and color, is accomplished by formatting. The selection of which cells to highlight, based on meeting specified conditions, is accomplished using Excel's Conditional Formatting option. This option provides a complete sub-system of choices that permit you to select (or create your own) criteria, select (or create your own) highlighting formats, select where the conditional formats should be applied, and then permit you to add or change any of your individual choices. Additionally, Conditional Formatting provides other more advanced options, including in-cell bar graphs (data bars), color scales, and icon sets. In this section, we present the highlighting (Highlight Cells) option.

Conditional Formatting has as its main the goal the creation of specific rules that control the formatting of designated cells. This feature is activated by clicking on the Home tab's Conditional Formatting icon, as shown as item 1 on Figure 3.15. Although it is preferable to select the cells you want formatted before clicking on this icon, the cell selection can be made and changed later.

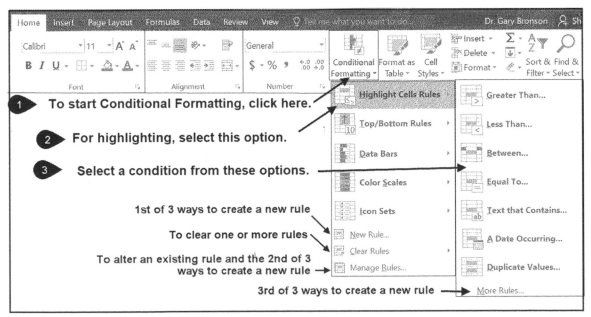

Figure 3.15 Activating Conditional Formatting

Application Note
Conditional Formatting Rules

A conditional formatting rule used for highlighting requires three elements:

1. Selecting where the formatting is to be applied
2. A specification of the conditional criteria
3. Applying the format to cells meeting the condition

Each separate area (group of cells being formatted) requires at least one rule. Multiple rules can be applied to the same area. If two separate areas are designated, at least two separate and distinct conditional rules must be constructed.

If more than one rule is specified, they are applied from the last rule entered down to the first rule entered, with each rule higher on the list having precedence over a rule lower on the list. Another way of saying this is that the last rule entered is placed on the top of the list of rules, and is applied first, and so on, until the first rule entered, which is at the bottom of the list, and is applied last. The rule order can be changed using the Manage Rules option.

When Conditional Formatting is selected, the drop-down menu shown in the figure appears. In this section, we will choose the first option **Highlight Cells Rules**, which is identified as item 2 in Figure 3.15. Selecting this option activates the second drop-down menu in the figure, from which a condition can be selected (item 3).

Note that the icons shown in this second drop-down menu permit the construction of simple criteria, such as cells with a value greater than (>) a certain amount, or equal to a certain amount. Multiple criteria, such as greater than or equal to (>=), can be created by using the **Highlight Cells Rules – More Rules – Format Only Cells that Contain** and selecting compound criteria (such as <= or >=). In particular, the **More Rules** option allows you to bypass the default choices in the list and create more complex conditions. When designating multiple conditions, the conditions are applied from the condition that was entered last on down to the condition that was entered first. This means that the last entered condition in the list is has a higher level of precedence (priority) compared with earlier rules.

The following three steps are those required to use the conditional formatting options shown in Figure 3.15:

1. Select the cells that are to be formatted.

2. Select one or more criteria (the conditions).

3. Select the highlighting format (how the highlighting should appear).

These three steps constitute a conditional formatting rule, and all three items (which cells, conditions, and how) must be specified for conditional formatting to take place.

To illustrate how a conditional format rule is created and used in practice, consider the following example.

Example 1

Creating a Simple Conditional Formatting Rule

The spreadsheet shown in Figure 3.16 provides a class list with each student's test grades and final average grade. Using conditional formatting, we want all final grades greater than 90 to be highlighted.

Solution:

Step 1: Select the cells. Highlight the cells that are to be conditionally formatted. For Figure 3.16, this requires highlighting cells F4 through F13.

Step 2: Select the conditions. From the Conditional Formatting Option, select *Highlight Cells Rules* and then *Greater Than*, as shown in both Figures 3.16 (see Figure 3.15 for more detail). This activates the Condition and Format dialog shown in Figure 3.17. In this dialog's Condition box on the left of this dialog, enter the value 90. This sets the condition that all the selected cells in Step 1 will be checked to see if their value is greater than 90. The cells that meet the criteria will be formatted as set in the next step.

	A	B	C	D	E	F
1						
2						
3	**Name**	**Test 1**	**Test 2**	**Test 3**	**Test 4**	**Final Grade (Average)**
4	Andrew	50	90	58	70	67
5	Anthony	90	70	65	72	74
6	Charles	95	85	90	95	91
7	Danielle	95	70	82	83	83
8	Denise	90	95	87	95	92
9	Jane	75	85	60	74	74
10	Jeffrey	50	55	70	58	58
11	Joseph	92	87	95	88	91
12	Mary	85	85	65	69	76
13	Matthew	80	85	85	82	83

Figure 3.16 Class list and grades

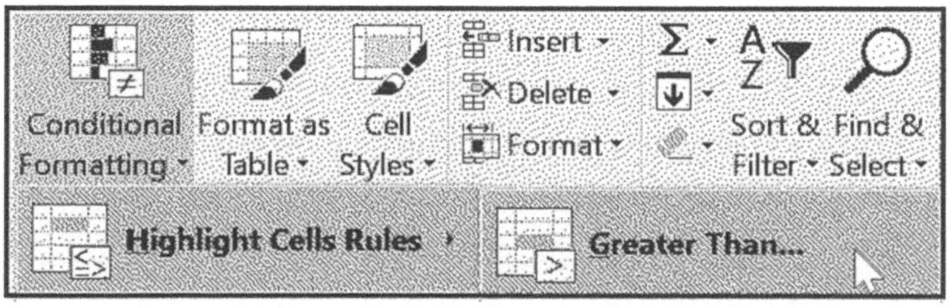

Figure 3.17 Selecting the Greater Than condition

Step 3: Select the Format. In the Format box on the right of the Condition and Dialog box shown in Figure 3.18, either select the default format shown, or click on the drop-down button to reveal the menu shown in the figure. From this drop-down menu, either select another default format or select the last option to create your own format. Clicking on this last option brings up a Format dialog box in which you can change the font style (bold, italic, or regular), font color, and cell fill color. In this example, the font style was set as white and bold, and the fill color as dark gray.

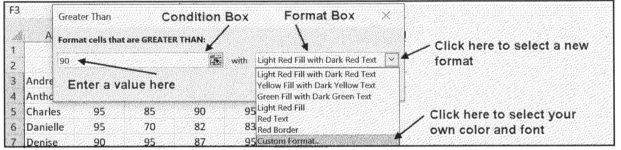

Figure 3.18 The Condition and Format dialog box

For the selections made in Steps 1 and 3, the class list will appear as shown in Figure 3.19. Notice that the cells in column F that are above 90 have been highlighted as bold white text on a dark gray background.

	A	B	C	D	E	F
1						
2						
3	**Name**	**Test 1**	**Test 2**	**Test 3**	**Test 4**	**Final Grade (Average)**
4	Andrew	50	90	58	70	67
5	Anthony	90	70	65	72	74
6	Charles	95	85	90	95	91
7	Danielle	95	70	82	83	83
8	Denise	90	95	87	95	92
9	Jane	75	85	60	74	74
10	Jeffrey	50	55	70	58	58
11	Joseph	92	87	95	88	91
12	Mary	85	85	65	69	76
13	Matthew	80	85	85	82	83

Figure 3.19 The selected and highlighted cells

Changing any or all of the three elements of a conditional formatting rule (cell selection, criteria, and format) is accomplished by clicking the Manage Rules option in the first drop-down box activated when the Conditional Formatting icon is selected (see Figure 3.15).

Selecting this option causes the dialog box shown in Figure 3.20 to appear. From this dialog box, you can verify and/or change any of the three elements constituting your conditional formatting rule. For example, to highlight all test grades above 90, all that is required is to either click on the Edit Rule... option or directly change the range currently in the *Applies to* box in Figure 3.20. To create a second rule, for example, including all grades equal to 90, either click on the New Rule... option or click on the Conditional Formatting icon and follow the sequence you used to create the greater than condition rule.

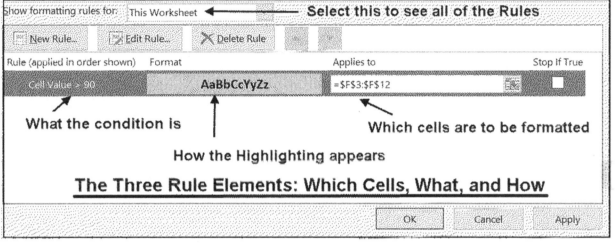

Figure 3.20 The Manage Rules dialog box

Example 2

Creating a User-Entered Conditional Value

In this example, we create a user-entered value for the greater than condition rule developed in Example 1. Note that cell B1 is used to enter the desired high grade.

	A	B	C	D	E	F
1	High Grade:		The value for the conditional			
2			rule will be user-entered in this cell.			
3	Name	Test 1	Test 2	Test 3	Test 4	Final Grade (Average)
4	Andrew	50	90	58	70	67
5	Anthony	90	70	65	72	74
6	Charles	95	85	90	95	91
7	Danielle	95	70	82	83	83
8	Denise	90	95	87	95	92
9	Jane	75	85	60	74	74
10	Jeffrey	50	55	70	58	58
11	Joseph	92	87	95	88	91
12	Mary	85	85	65	69	76
13	Matthew	80	85	85	82	83

Figure 3.21 Spreadsheet for Example 2

To alter the elements of the existing rule created in the previous example, click on the Manage Rules option from the drop-down menu after selecting Conditional Formatting (see Figure 3.15). This brings up the Conditional Formatting Rules Manager dialog box shown in Figure 3.22.

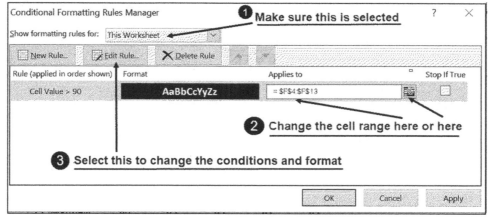

Figure 3.22 Changing the conditions, format, and cell range

Because we want to change the value in the conditional format formula from 90 to $B$1, the absolute address where the value is to be entered (an absolute address is necessary because the condition will be copied to each cell in the selected range), click on the Edit Rule button shown as item 3 in Figure 3.22. This brings up the dialog box shown in Figure 3.23.

NOTE *Changing the selected formatting range can be made directly to the dialog box shown on Figure 3.22 as item 2; this change cannot be made on the Figure 3.23's dialog box.*

Select a Rule Type:
- ▶ Format all cells based on their values
- ▶ Format only cells that contain
- ▶ Format only top or bottom ranked values
- ▶ Format only values that are above or below average
- ▶ Format only unique or duplicate values
- ▶ Use a formula to determine which cells to format

Edit the Rule Description:

Format only cells with:

| Cell Value | greater than | =$B$1 |

Enter the cell address here

Preview: AaBbCcYyZz   Format..

OK   Cancel

Figure 3.23 **Formatting** cells with a rule

Once the changes are made, clicking the OK button completes the desired changes.

Without the = sign, the address $B$1 is considered text, and will be stored surrounded by double quotes, as "$B$1." This will require you to activate the Manage Rules dialog and delete the quotes.)

When this is completed, the formatted worksheet will appear as shown in Figure 3.24, where the value 90 has been entered into cell B1.

	A	B	C	D	E	F
1	**High Grade:**	90				
2						
3	**Name**	**Test 1**	**Test 2**	**Test 3**	**Test 4**	**Final Grade (Average)**
4	Andrew	50	90	58	70	67
5	Anthony	90	70	65	72	74
6	Charles	95	85	90	95	**91**
7	Danielle	95	70	82	83	83
8	Denise	90	95	87	95	**92**
9	Jane	75	85	60	74	74
10	Jeffrey	50	55	70	58	58
11	Joseph	92	87	95	88	**91**
12	Mary	85	85	65	69	76
13	Matthew	80	85	85	82	83

Figure 3.24 The value 90 has been entered into cell B1

EXERCISES 3.5

1. Complete parts a and b.

   a. List the three items that define a conditional formatting rule.

   b. In what order should the three items that you listed be done?

2. Complete parts a and b.

   a. Enter the following spreadsheet and conditionally format column F as is done in Example 1.

	A	B	C	D	E	F
1						
2						
3	**Name**	**Test 1**	**Test 2**	**Test 3**	**Test 4**	**Final Grade (Average)**
4	Andrew	50	90	58	70	67
5	Anthony	90	70	65	72	74
6	Charles	95	85	90	95	91
7	Danielle	95	70	82	83	83
8	Denise	90	95	87	95	92
9	Jane	75	85	60	74	74
10	Jeffrey	50	55	70	58	58
11	Joseph	92	87	95	88	91
12	Mary	85	85	65	69	76
13	Matthew	80	85	85	82	83

   b. Put the label **Low Grade:** in cell A2. Then add a conditional formatting rule that highlights all values in column F that are below a user-entered value in cell B2.

3. Complete parts a-c.

   a. Enter the spreadsheet shown in Exercise 2a and conditionally format column B to highlight all Test 1 grades that are above 90.

   b. Add a second conditional rule that highlights all cells in column B that are equal to 90.

   c. Expand the selection range for both rules to include cells B4 through F13.

4. Complete parts a-c.

a. Enter the following spreadsheet and conditionally format column F, using a user-entered value in cell B1, as is done in Example 2.

	A	B	C	D	E	F
1	High Grade:		The value for the conditional rule will be user-entered in this cell.			
2						
3	Name	Test 1	Test 2	Test 3	Test 4	Final Grade (Average)
4	Andrew	50	90	58	70	67
5	Anthony	90	70	65	72	74
6	Charles	95	85	90	95	91
7	Danielle	95	70	82	83	83
8	Denise	90	95	87	95	92
9	Jane	75	85	60	74	74
10	Jeffrey	50	55	70	58	58
11	Joseph	92	87	95	88	91
12	Mary	85	85	65	69	76
13	Matthew	80	85	85	82	83

b. Put the label **Low Grade:** in cell A2. Then add a second conditional formatting rule that highlights all values in column F that are below a user-entered value in cell B2.

c. Expand the selection range for both rules to include cells B4 through F13.

3.6 COMMON EXCEL ERRORS

The typical errors associated with the functions presented in this section are as follows:

1. Forgetting to use the CLEAN( ) function whenever character and/or text processing functions produce unexpected results.

2. Not distinguishing between the standard deviation functions STD.P( ) and STD.S( ). The former is used when the standard deviation of a population is required, while the latter provides the standard deviation of a sample from a population. For most situations, unless you know a sample is being used, you should use the STD.P( ) function.

3. Not placing a minus sign in front of the PMT( ) function when a positive payment value is required.

4. When using the =PMT( ) function, forgetting to divide a yearly interest rate by 12 and/or multiply a yearly loan length by 12 when a monthly payment amount is calculated.

5. Forgetting to make the payments and interest rates absolute cell addresses when creating a loan repayment schedule.

3.7 CHAPTER APPENDIX: TRANSFERRING DATA BETWEEN SHEETS

In applications that use more than one sheet, it is frequently necessary to transfer one or more values from one sheet into a second sheet. This is known as *consolidation*, and is accomplished by using the general formula

$$=\text{SheetName-or-Num!cell-address}$$

Unlike the standard cell reference, a consolidation reference (following the =) has as its elements the worksheet name or number, followed by the "!" symbol, then the cell address or range of the desired cells. As a specific example, consider Figures 3.25a and b, which show the values and contents of a spreadsheet that resides in sheet 1.

	A	B	C
1	20	16	36
2	18	20	38
3	38	36	74

Figure 3.25a Cell values in Sheet 1's spreadsheet

	A	B	C
1	20	16	=A1+B1
2	18	20	=A2+B2
3	=A1+A2	=B1+B2	=C1+C2

Figure 3.25b Cell contents in Sheet 1's spreadsheet

Now, assume that the sum in cell C3 shown in Figure 3.25a is required in Sheet 2. For purposes of illustration, assume that the value needs to appear in cell M10 in Sheet 2's spreadsheet.

Placing the formula **=sheet1!C3** into cell M10 within Sheet 2's spreadsheet will cause the value in cell C3 on Sheet 1 to also be placed into cell M10 on Sheet 2. This placement is both dynamic and one-way.

That is, if the value in cell C3 on Sheet 1 changes, the new value will automatically appear in cell M10 on Sheet 2. It does not matter if the new value in C3 is caused by entering a new value directly or is derived from the formula currently in cell C3.

Clearly, this is a one-way transfer from Sheet 1 to Sheet 2. Any change in the contents of cell M10 will not be transferred back to Sheet 1. In fact, the specific transfer from Sheet 1 to Sheet 2 will be broken if any changes are made to the contents of cell M10, because a change in contents will replace the formula that causes the transfer to take place.

SELECTION

This Chapter Contains

Besides providing the ability to perform mathematical operations on data and determine simple statistical operations, what makes Excel so powerful is its ability to

- Select alternative operations based on individual data values
- Visually display data using charts and graphs
- Organize specific results using summary tables
- Organize and search data using database capabilities

This chapter presents the first item in this list, Excel's selection capabilities. This capability permits a formula in a cell to select the operation that will be performed and the resulting value displayed in the cell, based on the outcome of a comparison. The remaining three topics in the list are presented in the following three chapters. As selection requires choosing between alternatives, we begin this chapter with a description of Excel's selection criteria.

4.1   RELATIONAL EXPRESSIONS

Besides providing addition, subtraction, multiplication, and division capabilities, Excel provides the ability to compare quantities. Because many seemingly "intelligent" decision-making situations can be reduced to the level of choosing between two quantities, this comparison capability can be used to create a remarkable array of intelligent decisions. Some examples of this are providing a discount on a sales amount *only if* a person's age is 60 or above, or calculating an area *only if* all measurements are positive, or printing a letter grade *depending on* the grade's numerical value.

The expressions used to compare quantities are called *relational expressions*. A *simple relational expression* consists of a relational operator connecting two operands, as shown in Figure 4.1. Each operand can be a cell address, number, or any valid Excel expression. However, the relational operators must be one of those listed in Table 4.1.

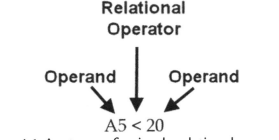

Figure 4.1 Anatomy of a simple relational expression

Table 4.1 Excel's relational operators

Relational Operator	Meaning	Example
<	less than	A1 < B1
>	greater than	B2 > 25
<=	less than or equal to	H5 <= $B$2
>=	greater than or equal to	H5 >= 75
=	equal to	T1 = 20000
<>	not equal to	C2 <> D2

The relational operators listed in Table 4.1 may be used with numbers, dates, and text, either as the contents of a cell or as an explicit value, but must be typed exactly as shown. Thus, the following examples are all valid:

A2 > 65   C2 = $B$2

3 < 5   95 > G1

L2 <= 50   F4 = 1

The following are not valid:

A5 =< B5   (operator out of order)

C10 << 20   (invalid operator)

T6 < = 98.6   (space not allowed between < and =)

Relational expressions are commonly referred to as *conditions*, and we will use both terms interchangeably. Like all Excel expressions, relational expressions are evaluated to yield a result. In the case of relational expressions, the value can only be evaluated as TRUE or FALSE. These are formally known as *Boolean values*, where a TRUE value corresponds to "Yes, the condition is met," and a FALSE value corresponds to "No, the condition is not met."[1]

In addition to numerical operands, character data can also be compared using relational operators. In Excel, which uses Unicode, the letter A is stored using a lower numerical value than the letter B, the numerical storage code for a B is lower in value than the code for a C and so on[2]. Additionally, all of the lowercase letters have a higher numerical code than the uppercase letters. This means that, in alphabetical order, lowercase letters appear after the uppercase letters., Examples of relational expressions using characters and their resulting Boolean values are[3]

Expression	Boolean Value
"A" < "B"	TRUE
"C" <= "D"	TRUE
"B" <> "C"	TRUE
"E" = "F"	FALSE
"G" >= "M"	FALSE
"Z" < "a"	TRUE

When longer text data is compared, individual characters are evaluated a pair at a time (both first characters, then both second characters, and so on). If no differences are found, the texts are equal; if a difference is found, the text with the first lower character is considered the smaller text. Thus, "Hello" is greater than "Good Bye" because the first H in "Hello" is greater than the first G in "Good Bye." "Hello" is less than "hello" because the first H in "Hello" is less than the first h in "hello." "SMITH" is greater than "JONES" because the first S in "SMITH" is greater than the first J in "JONES."

Relational operators have a hierarchy of execution and associativity similar to that of the arithmetic operators. Table 4.2 lists the operators in order of precedence in relation to the other operators we have used. The operator with the highest precedence is at the top of the table, and the operator with the lowest precedence is at the bottom.

Table 4.2 Excel operators listed from highest precedence to lowest precedence

Operator	Associativity
^	Left to Right
* /	Left to Right
+ −	Left to Right
< <= > >=	Left to Right
=	Left to Right

---

[1] Internally, a TRUE value is stored as the integer 1 and a FALSE value as the number 0.

[2] The numeric codes used to store characters can be found in Appendix A.

[3] To yield a result, the expression must be entered in a cell as a formula, such as, ="A" > "C". Otherwise, it will appear as text, just like any other label.

The examples listed in Table 4.3 illustrate the use of precedence and associativity to evaluate more involved relational expressions, and the results of each comparison assuming cell A1 contains a 5, cell B1 contains a 7, and cell C1 contains a 12.

Table 4.3 Examples of Relational Expressions

Relational Expression	Equivalent Expression	Value
A1 + 2 = C1 − 1	(A1 + 2)= (C1 − 1)	FALSE
3 * A1 − B1 < 22	((3 * A1) − B1) < 22	TRUE
A1 + 2 * B1 > C1	(A1 +(2 * B1)) > C1	TRUE
C1 + 3 <= -B1 + 3 + A1	(C1 + 3) <= ((-B1) + (3 + A1))	FALSE

As with all expressions, parentheses can be used to alter the assigned operator priority and improve the readability of relational expressions. Expressions within parentheses are evaluated starting with the innermost set of parentheses and working toward the outer parentheses.

Logical Functions[4]

In addition to using relational expressions as conditions, more complex conditions can be created using the logical functions AND( ), OR( ), XOR( ), and NOT( ). Note that these are functions that require arguments, and not operators that appear between two operands.

When the AND( ) function is used with two simple expressions, the function returns a value of TRUE only if both single expressions are true by themselves.[5] Thus, the formula

$$=AND(A1 > 40, T2 < 10)$$

returns TRUE only if the contents of cell A1 is greater than 40 and the contents of cell T2 is less than 10.

The logical OR( ) function also requires two or more expressions as arguments.[6] The function returns a value of TRUE when either one or more of its arguments are true by themselves. Thus, the formula

$$=OR(B1 > 40, B2 < 10)$$

returns TRUE if either the value in cell B1 is greater than 40, the value in cell B2 is less than 10, or both conditions are TRUE.

---

[4] This topic can be omitted without loss of subject continuity.

[5] The AND( ) function can take up to 255 arguments; to return TRUE, each individual argument must be TRUE; otherwise, the function returns FALSE.

[6] The OR( ) function can take up to 255 arguments; to return TRUE, only one of the individual arguments must be TRUE; otherwise, the function returns FALSE.

The XOR( ) function only returns TRUE if an odd number of its conditions are TRUE; otherwise, it returns FALSE.

The last logical function, NOT( ), is used to change a single condition to its opposite state; that is, if its argument is FALSE to begin with the function returns TRUE; if its argument is TRUE to begin with, the function returns FALSE.

EXERCISES 4.1

1. Write relational expressions to express the following conditions:

a. a person's age, which is located in cell A2, is equal to 20.

b. a person's height, which is located in cell B2, is less than 6 feet.

c. a person's temperature, which is located in cell C2, is greater than 98.6.

d. a letter, located in cell D2, is "m".

2. Determine whether the following relational expressions are TRUE or FALSE, for the cell contents shown in Figure 4.2:

a. A1 = 4

b. A1 <= 6

c. D1 <= 4

d. A1 = D1

e. B1 <= C1

f. B1 = C1

3. Determine whether the following relational expressions are TRUE or FALSE, for the cell contents shown in Figure 4.2:

a. B1 * D1 < A1 * C1

b. C1/B1 > D1/A1

c. D1-C1 > C1/B1

d. A1*B1*2 = C1 *D1

e. A1*B1*C1*D1 > 200

	A	B	C	D
1	5	2	4	5

Figure 4.2 Spreadsheet for Exercise 2 and Exercise 3

4. Write AND( ) functions to express the following conditions:

   a. a person's age, located in cell A2, is equal to 25 and the person's height, located in cell B2, is taller than 6 feet.

   b. a person's age, located in cell A2, is greater than 20 and they have been employed at the company, located in cell B2, for more than 5 years.

   c. a person's identification number, located in cell F3, is less than 500 and the person's age, located in cell G3, is less than 25.

   d. a rectangle's length, located in cell H5, and its width, located in cell I5, are both positive.

5. Determine whether the following relational expressions are TRUE or FALSE, for the cell contents shown in Figure 4.3:

   a. AND(B1 = 4, C1 = 2)

   b. AND(A1 = 3, D1 <= 8)

   c. AND(B1 = 4, C1 < 2)

   d. AND(B1*C1 > 5, D1 < 6)

   e. AND(B1*C1 > 5, B1*D1 < 7)

	A	B	C	D
1	3	4	2	6

Figure 4.3 Spreadsheet for Exercise 5

6. Determine whether the following relational expressions are TRUE or FALSE, for the cell contents shown in Figure 4.3:

   a. OR(B1 = 3, C1 = 2)

   b. OR(A1 = 3, D1 <= 8)

   c. OR(B1 = 4, C1 < 2)

   d. OR(B1*C1 > 5, D1 < 6)

   e. OR(B1*C1 < 5, B1 *D1 < 7)

7. Write OR( ) functions to express the following conditions:

   a. a person's age, located in cell A2, is less than 25 or the person's height, located in cell B2, is taller than 6 feet.

   b. a person's age, located in cell A2, is greater than 20 or they have been employed at the company, located in cell B2, for more than 5 years.

c. a person's identification number, located in cell F3, is less than 500 or the person's age, located in cell G3, is less than 25.

d. the length of a fence, located in cell M3, is greater than 2 and less than 10 feet.

4.2   THE IF( ) FUNCTION

The IF( ) function directs Excel to select a value based on the result of a comparison. For example, in a particular Pass/Fail course, a passing grade is assigned to any numerical grade greater than or equal to 65; otherwise, a failing grade is assigned. The IF( ) function can be used in this situation to determine the final grade based on whether the numerical grade is greater than or equal to 65. The general form of the IF( ) function, used within a formula is

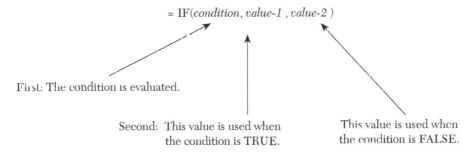

The condition (sometimes known as a *conditional test*) is evaluated first. If the condition is TRUE, *value-1* is displayed in the cell using the IF( ) function. If the condition is FALSE, *value-2* is displayed in the cell. Both *value-1* and *value-2* can be a number, text, an expression, or a function. If an expression or function is used for these values, they will be evaluated to yield a single value.

Note that when an IF( ) function is used by itself, it must be preceded by an equal sign. (This may not be true when an IF( ) function is used as an argument within another function or as a part of a larger expression.)

Example 1

Selecting a Text Value

Consider Figure 4.4a, which contains a list of final grade averages of the first five students from a much larger list. A "Pass" grade is to be assigned for each final average equal to or above 65; otherwise the grade is "Fail."

	A	B
1	**Final Average**	**Grade**
2	95	
3	64	
4	65	
5	58	

Figure 4.4a Spreadsheet for Example 1

Solution: The IF( ) function, used within the formula shown in cell B2 (see Figure 4.4b) determines the correct grade ("Pass" or "Fail"). The grade is displayed in cell B2, based on the numerical grade listed in cell A2. Here we have used the relational operator >= to represent the condition "greater than or equal to." If the grade in cell A2 is greater than or equal to 65, the text string "Pass" is displayed in cell B2; otherwise, the text string "Fail" is displayed. Note that text values used as arguments to the IF( ) function ***must be*** included within double quotes.[7]

	A	B
1	**Final Average**	**Grade**
2	95	=IF(A2>= 65, "Pass", "Fail")
3	64	
4	65	
5	58	

Figure 4.4b Pass and Fail appear in quotes

When the formula in cell B2 is copied down through cell B5, the following spreadsheet is displayed:

	A	B
1	**Final Average**	**Grade**
2	95	Pass
3	64	Fail
4	65	Pass
5	58	Fail

Figure 4.4c Spreadsheet showing Pass/Fail grades

The advantage of using an IF( ) function here is that a Pass/Fail determination is automatically made once a grade is entered into column A. If a numerical grade changes, the Pass/Fail determination is automatically updated. Additionally, only one formula was entered and copied down for as many grades needed.

---

[7] As noted previously, text that is used within an expression or as a function argument must be enclosed in double quotes. Text entered into a cell as a label or data should not be enclosed in double quotes.

Example 2

Selecting a Numeric Value

Consider Figure 4.5a, which is a partial list of people's ages. Here, anyone 62 or older is to be assigned a 10% discount, while anyone younger is assigned a 5% discount.

	A	B
1	**Age**	**Discount**
2	61	
3	62	
4	18	
5	32	

Figure 4.5a Spreadsheet for Example 2

Solution: The IF( ) function, used within the formula shown in cell B2 (see Figure 4.5b) determines the correct discount (10% or 5%) for the age listed in cell A2. Here, we have again used the relational operator >= to represent the condition "greater than or equal to." If this age is greater than or equal to 62, the 10% value is displayed in cell B2; otherwise, the 5% value is displayed.

Again, the advantage of using an IF( ) function is that should an age change, the correct discount is automatically assigned. More importantly, however, is that only one formula need be entered and then copied for as many additional cells as needed.

	A	B
1	**Age**	**Discount**
2	61	=IF(A2 >=62, 10%, 5%)
3	62	
4	18	
5	32	

Figure 4.5b Copying the discount =IF function down

Copying cell B2's formula down through cell B5 produces the spreadsheet display shown in Figure 4.5c.

	A	B
1	**Age**	**Discount**
2	61	5.00%
3	62	10.00%
4	18	5.00%
5	32	5.00%

Figure 4.5c Results after applying the discount formula

Unlike text, cell addresses and numbers used within the IF( ) function **must not** be surrounded by quotes *or* contain commas; commas are used to separate the three arguments within the IF( ) function.

In addition to using text or numeric values as IF( ) function arguments, as in the last two examples, any expression or function that yields a value can also be used, as seen in the next example.

Example 3

Selecting a Calculation

The personal state income tax levied in New Jersey depends on a person's income as follows:

If a person's income is less than or equal to $20,000, then the State Tax is 2% of income; Otherwise, the State Tax is $400 + 2.5% of income over $20,000.

Because one of two possible calculations must be made depending on a person's income, this is ideal for an IF( ) function. To illustrate the selection process in action, consider Figure 4.6a, which shows a section of a spreadsheet containing NJ incomes for three individuals.

	A	B
1	**NJ Income**	**NJ State Tax**
2	$24,000	
3	$18,000	
4	$34,000	

Figure 4.6a A section of a spreadsheet

An appropriate formula for determining the taxes on the income in cell A2 is

$$=IF(A2 <= 20000 , 0.02*A2, 400 + .025 * (A2{-}20000))$$

Here we have used the relational operator <= to represent the condition "less than or equal to." The first argument in this IF( ) function tests the condition A2 <= 20000. If the value in A2 is less than or equal to 20000, the condition is TRUE. In this case the computation 0.02*A2, which is the second function argument, is calculated and the resulting value displayed in cell B2. However, if the condition is FALSE, the expression 400 + .025 *(A2–20000) is evaluated and its result displayed in cell B2. The quantity (A2–20000) in this calculation is the amount of income that is over the $20,000.

Placing this formula into cell B2 (note that IF can be typed in either uppercase form, as IF, or lowercase form, as if), and copying the formula into cells B3 and B4 produces the cell formulas shown in Figure 4.6b.

	A	B
1	**NJ Income**	**NJ State Tax**
2	24000	=IF(A2<=20000,0.02*A2,400+0.025*(A2-20000))
3	18000	=IF(A3<=20000,0.02*A3,400+0.025*(A3-20000))
4	34000	=IF(A4<=20000,0.02*A4,400+0.025*(A4-20000))

Figure 4.6b The required formulas

The values calculated and displayed by the formulas in Figure 4.6b produces the spreadsheet display shown in Figure 4.6c.

	A	B
1	**NJ Income**	**NJ State Tax**
2	$24,000	$500
3	$18,000	$360
4	$34,000	$750

Figure 4.6c The values produced by the IF( ) statements

Because the income values in cells A2 and A4 are above $20,000, the tested condition for these incomes is FALSE (they are not less than $20,000) and the last IF( ) function's argument is computed and the value displayed. In cell B3, the value used in the condition is less than $20,000, which makes the condition TRUE; thus the state tax is computed using the expression 0.02 * A3.

Nested IF( ) Functions[8]

Either or both of the arguments in an IF( ) can also be an IF( ) function. Including one or more IF( ) functions as arguments to an IF( ) function is referred to as a *nested IF*.

The most useful nested IFs occurs when the nested IF( ) is used as the last IF( ) argument, which takes the form

IF(condition-1, argument-1, IF(condition-2, argument -2, argument-3)

Nested IFs rapidly become cumbersome, with three IFs in one formula usually being a practical limit however more complex ones are possible and have been used. For example, the following formula

=IF(C7 >= 90, "A", IF(C7 >=80,"B", IF(C7 >=70,"C","D")))

assigns a letter grade of A, B, C, or D depending on the numerical value in cell C7. Notice that the formula looks rather complicated.

The reason that nested =IF( ) functions are necessary in certain cases, is because of the fact that the standard function only supports the testing of one condition, and 2

---

[8] This topic can be omitted on first reading without loss of subject continuity.

alternate choices based on whether the result is TRUE or FALSE. If more conditions need to be tested, then one solution is to use nested =IF( ) functions.

In Excel 2019, it is possible to created nested =IFs using the =IFS ( ) function. This is a function which allows one to create more complex multi-level IF structures without the need for complex nesting.

While the setup and arrangements are quite different from the =IF ( ), yet another way to examine multiple conditions is to use the vertical and horizontal lookup functions.

It also should be mentioned that there is another class of functions which may be confused with the =IF( ) and =IFS( ) functions, which are the Conditional =IF functions. These are especially useful with lists and tables, and will be discussed briefly in the section on advanced filters, later in this book.

Logical Conditions[9]

The conditions used in the majority of IF( ) functions are typically relational, using the relational operators (<, <=, =, >=, and >) to compare operands. However, more complex conditions can be created using the logical functions AND( ), OR( ), XOR( ), and NOT( ) presented in the prior section.

For example, in the spreadsheet shown in Figure 4.7, the text "Teenager" is displayed in cell B2 if the value in cell A2 is between 13 and 19, inclusive, and the text "Not a Teenager" is displayed for any other value in A2. This formula can then be copied down into cells B3 through B5.

	A	B
1	**Age**	**Category**
2	13	=IF(AND(A2>=13,A2<=19), "Teenager", "Not a Teenager")
3	20	
4	12	
5	19	

Figure 4.7 "Teenager" and "Not a Teenager" text

EXERCISES 4.2

   1. Complete parts a-c.

      a. How many arguments are required by an IF( ) function?

      b. What must the first argument provided to the IF( ) function be?

      c. What do the remaining arguments provide?

---

[9] This topic can be omitted on first reading without loss of subject continuity.

2. Complete parts a-b.

    a. Enter the data shown in the following spreadsheet (on the left) and add the appropriate IF( ) functions to produce the spreadsheet results shown in the figure on the right. A "Pass" grade is to be assigned for each final average equal to or above 65; otherwise, the grade is "Fail".

	A	B
1	**Final Average**	**Grade**
2	95	
3	64	
4	65	
5	58	

	A	B
1	**Final Average**	**Grade**
2	95	Pass
3	64	Fail
4	65	Pass
5	58	Fail

    b. Change the IF( ) formula used in Exercise 2a to =IF(A2 < 65, "Fail", "Pass"). Does this produce the same results?

3. Complete parts a-b.

    a. Enter the data shown in the spreadsheet on the left and add the appropriate IF( ) functions to produce the spreadsheet results shown on the right. Anyone 62 or older is to be assigned a 10% discount, and anyone younger is assigned a 5% discount.

	A	B
1	**Age**	**Discount**
2	61	
3	62	
4	18	
5	32	

	A	B
1	**Age**	**Discount**
2	61	5.00%
3	62	10.00%
4	18	5.00%
5	32	5.00%

    b. Change the IF( ) formula in this problem to =IF(A2 < 62, 5%, 10%). Does this produce the same results as in Exercise 3a?

4. Enter the data shown in the spreadsheet on the left and add the appropriate IF( ) functions to produce the spreadsheet shown in the right. If a person's income is less than or equal to $20,000, then the State Tax is 2% of the income, otherwise, the State Tax is $400 + 2.5% of the income over $20,000.

	A	B
1	**NJ Income**	**NJ State Tax**
2	$24,000	
3	$18,000	
4	$34,000	

	A	B
1	**NJ Income**	**NJ State Tax**
2	$24,000	$500
3	$18,000	$360
4	$34,000	$750

5. On a blank worksheet, write IF( ) functions for the following:

   a. if the value in cell C1 is 1, display "OKAY," otherwise, display "NOT OK"

   b. if the sum of the values in cells C1 through C4 is equal to 1, display "OKAY," otherwise, display "NOT OK"

   c. if the value in cell A2 is less than 60, display "PASS," otherwise, display "Fail"

   d. if the value in cell C3 is greater than 5, display the value .045; otherwise, display the value .035

6. On a blank worksheet, write IF( ) functions for the following:

   a. If the character in cell A2 is either an "f" or an "F," calculate the value of (5/9)(values in cells B2 –32); otherwise, calculate the value (9/5)(value in cell B2) + 32. (**Hint:** the condition should check the value UPPER(A2) rather than just the value in A2.)

   b. If the value in cell B2 is either an "s" or an "S," display the value 800; otherwise, display the value 450. (**Hint:** the condition should check the value UPPER(B2) rather than just the value in B2.)

7. Write an IF( ) function to calculate the overtime pay for an employee as follows: If the hours worked, which is located in Cell D5 is greater than 40, the overtime pay is calculated as 1.5 (the value in Cell C5) times (the hours greater than 40); otherwise, the overtime pay is 0. (**Hint:** the hours greater than 40 is found using the expression (D5 – 40)).

8. Complete the spreadsheet shown below so that all of the ages between 13 and 19, inclusive, are categorized as "Teenager"; otherwise they should be categorized as "Not a Teenager."

	A	B
1	**Age**	**Category**
2	13	=IF(AND(A2>=13,A2<=19), "Teenager", "Not a Teenager")
3	20	
4	12	
5	19	

4.3   THE VLOOKUP( ) FUNCTION

Whenever a decision is based on one of two possible alternatives, an IF( ) function should be used. However, when multiple conditions must be evaluated, using multiple IF( ) statements involving multiple levels of nesting within another can be complex and prone to errors.

For example, although the following IF( ) function can be used to determine a letter grade for the numerical grade contained in cell F4, it should not be used, because it is overly complicated and not easy to understand[10].

=IF(F4 < 60, "F", IF(F4 < 70, "D", IF(F4 < 80, "C", IF(F4 < 90, "B", "A"))))

or the equivalent using the =IFS( ) function.

The =IFS( ) function (Excel 2019) allows for greater flexibility in terms of doing multi-level nested conditional tests.

The general form is as follows:

= IFS(logical_test1, Value1 [logical_test2, Value2] …, [logical_test127, Value127])

So

IFS(F4<60,"F",F4<70,"D",F4<80,"C",F4<90, "B",TRUE, "A")

would be the equivalent of the earlier nested function presented. Basically, the conditions to be tested, up to 127, are listed as pairs, first as the conditional test, followed by the result if TRUE. If the test evaluates to TRUE, the result is displayed. Otherwise, it proceeds on to the next condition(s) to be tested. If it does not match any of the other conditions, then the default choice, here listed as TRUE, gives the student the grade of "A." The use of this function simplifies the testing for multiple conditions. However, it is not available in Excel 2016 and earlier versions.

For situations requiring multiple conditions that necessitate more than one IF( ) function as an argument to another IF( ) function, another viable option would be to use the VLOOKUP( ) and HLOOKUP ( ) functions. The difference is that a VLOOKUP( ) function requires a range of cells consisting of at least two columns, referred to as a *vertical lookup table*. This kind of lookup table lists items vertically, as the one shown in Figure 4.8. The HLOOKUP( ) function requires a lookup table that is oriented horizontally, as shown in Figure 4.9.[11]

---

[10] Excel 2019 permits the nesting of up to 64 IF( ) functions.

[11] Although it is formally referred to as a lookup table, this kind of table is just a range of regular spreadsheet cells. The table heading and labels form no part in the actual lookup. They are there for informational purposes only.

In the majority of applications, vertical lookup tables predominate. Thus, the VLOOKUP( ) function, which uses this type of table, tends to be used more than its HLOOKUP( ) equivalent. The VLOOKUP( ) function is described in this section and the HLOOKUP( ) function in Section 4.4.

ID	Hourly Rate
2755	$15.62
2904	$21.84
3752	$18.80
3891	$16.20
4205	$14.40
4628	$17.25

Figure 4.8 A vertical lookup table

Grade Range	0	60	70	80	90
Letter Grade	F	D	C	B	A

Figure 4.9 A horizontal lookup table

The vertical lookup table needed for a VLOOKUP( ) function conceptually resembles the index in a book.

In a book index, a topic is located in the first column and the corresponding page number is located next to it, in the second column. As with an index, in a vertical lookup table, it is only the table's first column that is searched for a match. This column must list values that will be "looked up." This first column can contain names, ID numbers, or grade values, for example, as listed in Figure 4.8. When labels are included in a lookup table, as they are in Figure 4.8, the labels *are not* included in the search for a match.

Two major differences, however, are that in a book index, the index table is at the back of the book, and there are only two columns. A vertical lookup table can contain more than two columns, and its placement can be on any part of a spreadsheet, or even on a different spreadsheet from the main application. When there are more than two columns in the lookup table, the data in each row must be related to the item in the row's first column, and the table expands downward in the same manner as new lookup items are inserted or added into the table.

The VLOOKUP( ) function accepts a numeric or text value, such as a numeric code or name, and uses that value to locate its exact or closest match in the first column of the lookup table. The value that is being searched for is referred to as the *lookup value*. Because the lookup table's location can be anywhere, its location must also be provided to the VLOOKUP( ) function. Finally, because the lookup table can contain more than two columns, the column containing the desired returned value must also be specified.

Application Note
VLOOKUP( ) Alerts

When using VLOOKUP( ), be aware of the following:

1. VLOOKUP( ) ***is not*** case sensitive. Thus, if the looked-up value is the word "computer," a match occurs for "Computer," "COMPUTER," or any combination of upper- and lowercase letters in the lookup table's first column that spell "computer."

2. VLOOKUP( ) stops looking for a match once a match is found. This can be either because an exact match was located or an approximate match occurred, and depends on the value of the 4th argument.

3. If the 4th argument is FALSE, an exact match (again, not case-sensitive) stops the lookup table search, regardless if there is another match later in the table. If the 4th argument is TRUE or omitted, an approximate match stops the search (see the next Application Note for what an approximate match entails.)

As an example, consider the vertical lookup table shown in Figure 4.10. What defines it as a vertical table is that, like an index, the item being looked for is always and only looked for in the first column of the table.

	D	E	F	G
4	**Item**	**Desc.**	**Qty. in Stock**	**Price**
5	C-2400	Chair	4	$230.00
6	C-2476	Chair	2	$415.00
7	T-8624	Table	12	$195.00
8	T-8701	Table	8	$341.00

Figure 4.10 An example of a vertical lookup table

The first argument provided to the VLOOKUP( ) function is the value that the lookup table is searched for to determine if there is a match. In the table shown in Figure 4.10, it is an item code number that the table will be searched for a match. The remaining arguments required by the VLOOKUP( ) function tell it where the lookup table is located, what matching value is to be returned, and whether an exact or closest match to the lookup value is required.

For example, the table shown in Figure 4.10 is located in the range D5 through G8. Note that the column labels are not included in the location, because they are not included in the search. Because a lookup table can be located anywhere within a spreadsheet, even on a different sheet than the main application, its location must be provided to the VLOOKUP( ) function, and it is the function's second argument.

The third argument required by the VLOOKUP( ) function is the column number of the value to be returned when a match to the looked up value is found.[12] For

---

[12] If no match is found, the return value is #N/A, which denotes Not Available.

example, if the code T-8624 is searched for in Figure 4.10's lookup table, a match is found in cell D7. Now, the corresponding Description, Quantity in Stock, or Price can be returned, as specified by the third argument. Finally, the last argument specifies whether an exact or closest match is required. The general syntax of the VLOOKUP( ) function is as follows.

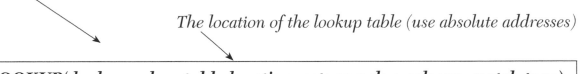

A lookup value or a cell address where the value is located

The location of the lookup table (use absolute addresses)

VLOOKUP(*lookup value, table location, return value column, match type*)

A number indicating the column of the returned value

Either TRUE (or omitted) for the closest match, or FALSE for an exact match
*The **return value column** can also be referred to as the **column index number**.*

To better understand the arguments required by the VLOOKUP( ) function, consider the function

=VLOOKUP(A2, $D$5:$G$8, 3, FALSE)

in cell B2 shown in Figure 4.11. Here, the lookup value is located in cell A2, which is VLOOKUP( )'s first argument. For any data entered into cell A2, the items in the first column of the lookup table will be automatically searched. VLOOKUP( ) knows where the table is, because its address, in this case $D$5:$G$8, was provided as the function's second argument. Notice that absolute addresses were used to specify the table's location. Absolute addresses should always be used in specifying the table's location because it ensures that if or when the VLOOKUP( ) formula is copied, the table's address will not change.

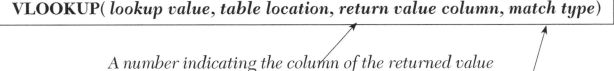

Figure 4.11 VLOOKUP table example

The search for a match always and only occurs by comparing the lookup value, provided by the function's first argument, to each value in the in the lookup table's first column, one item at a time. When a match is found (the type of match is determined by the function's 4th argument) the search stops, and the corresponding value in the column specified by the 3rd argument (which in this example is 3) is returned.

To see how a match is determined, a clear understanding of the function's 4th argument is required. The simplest match criterion is provided when this 4th argument is specified as FALSE. This indicates that an exact match is required, and it is most useful when ID numbers or name matches are needed. Example 1 illustrates this criterion.

When a search involves a range of values, such as a commission based on a range of monthly sales, or postage due on a range of weights, an approximate match, also referred to as a closest match, should be used. This type of match is selected by either explicitly specifying the function's 4th argument as TRUE, or omitting it altogether. Thus, the default search, when the 4th argument is omitted, is an approximate match. It is important to realize that this type of match *requires* that the data in the lookup table's first column be in sorted ascending order, from lowest to highest. This is necessary because the search stops once a value greater than the lookup value is encountered. Example 2 illustrates this criterion.

Example 1

Exact Match

For the function, located in cell B2, determine the following:

	A	B
1	Name	Grade
2	Roberts	=VLOOKUP(A2, $F$1:$H$10, 3, FALSE)

   a. the location of the lookup value

   b. the lookup value

   c. the location of the lookup table

   d. the number of columns in the lookup table

   e. the lookup table's column containing the return value, if an exact or "closest-to" match is specified

   f. the cell that displays the return value

Solution:

   a. The lookup value is located in cell A2.

   b. The lookup value is Roberts.

   c. The lookup table is located in cells F1 through H10.

d. The lookup table contains three columns (F, G, and H).

e. If a match is found, the return value is in the 3rd column of the table; otherwise, #N/A is returned.

f. An exact match is specified because the last argument is FALSE.

g. The return value is displayed in cell B2.

Give It a Try

For the function, located in cell D3, determine the following:

	C	D
3	96.8	=VLOOKUP(C3, $E$10:$H$10, 3, FALSE)

a. the location of the lookup value

b. the lookup value

c. the location of the lookup table

d. the number of columns in the lookup table

e. the lookup table's column containing the return value, if an exact or "closest-to" match is specified

f. the cell that displays the return value

Example 2

Approximate (Closest) Match

Consider the student list shown in Figure 4.12a. The lookup table, located in cells I2 through J6, provides the correspondence between the numerical and letter grades. It is used as follows: a numerical grade starting at 0 and less than 60 corresponds to a grade of F, grades from 60 to less than 70 correspond to a grade of D, and so on. Here, the lookup table consists of two columns, which is the minimum number of columns for a lookup table. Exact matches are not required. This ensures that a grade such as 75, which lies above 70 but below 80, will be assigned a C grade.

	A	B	C	D	E	F	G	H	I	J
1	Name	Test 1	Test 2	Test 3	Final	Average Grade	Letter Grade		Cut-Off Grade	Letter Grade
2	Bronson, Gary	70	90	85	85	82.5			0	F
3	Best, Harriet	90	70	83	92	83.75			60	D
4	Flavano, Louis	70	85	72	70	74.25			70	C
5	Glover, Jane	85	92	89	95	90.25			80	B
6	Restin, Ann	60	70	80	80	72.5			90	A
7	Williams, Bill	79	72	63	60	68.5				

Figure 4.12a The vertical lookup table is located in the range I2 through J6

Application Note
A Requirement for Approximate Matches

When VLOOKUP( )'s fourth argument is omitted or explicitly entered as TRUE , a closest, or approximate, match criterion is used. As in an exact match, the lookup value in an approximate match is compared to each value in the lookup table's first column, starting at the first value.

Unlike an exact match, however, an approximate match means that the search continues down the first column until either an exact match *or* a value higher in value than the lookup value is encountered. In this latter case, when a value higher than the lookup value is located, the first column's prior value is taken to be the matching value. This means that for an approximate search, the following is required:

For an approximate search, which is specified whenever VLOOKUP( )'s fourth argument is TRUE *or omitted*, the lookup table's first column values must be in sorted order, from the lowest to highest values.

Solution: The lookup table in Figure 4.12a consists of the shaded cells contained in the range I2 through J6. This is a vertical lookup table because items of the same type are listed vertically; all the cut-off grades (beginning of each letter grade's range) are in column I and their corresponding letter grades are in column J.

The letter grade for the numerical grade in cell G2, which is the first cell requiring a function, is found using

=VLOOKUP(F2, $I$2:$J$6, 2, TRUE)

In this function, the first argument, in this case F2, tells the VLOOKUP( ) function that it is the value in cell F2 that will be searched for in the lookup table. As with all vertical lookups, the search for a match is always made with the data in the lookup table's first column. It is the second parameter in the VLOOKUP( ) function, which in this case is $I$2:$J$6, that specifies where the lookup table is located (for convenience, this range of data has been shaded in Figure 4.12a). Absolute addresses are used to ensure that if or when the function is copied, the designation of the lookup table's location will not be changed. Additionally, notice that the table range does not include the labels above the data.

This function uses cell F2's value to search through the lookup table's first column for the closest match. It is the last parameter in the VLOOKUP( ) function, which in this case is TRUE, that tells the function that if an exact match is not found in column one, the closest value in column one that is less than the value that is being looked for should be selected.[13]

The value 2, which is VLOOKUP( )'s third parameter in the VLOOKUP( ), tells the function to return the value in the 2nd column of the table when a match is found. In this case, the lookup table only has two columns, but in many applications, lookup

---

[13] If this parameter is omitted, a default value of TRUE is used. Because a value of TRUE permits an approximate match that is less than the searched value, this option always requires that the values in the first column are arranged in ascending (lowest to highest order).

tables with more than two columns are needed and you may have to return a value from a column other than the second one.

If an exact match is required, the last argument would be specified as FALSE. In this case, the values in the first column can be placed in any order, as only an exact match is permitted. If there are more than one value in the first column that match the lookup value, the first found match value is used. In both cases, TRUE or FALSE, if an exact match is not found, an error value of #N/A is returned.

When the function in cell G2 is entered and copied down through cell G7, the spreadsheet will appear as shown in Figure 4.12b. Because the lookup table's cell addresses were written using absolute addresses, each copy of the VLOOKUP( ) function contains the correct table location.

	A	B	C	D	E	F	G	H	I	J
						Average	Letter		Cut-Off	Letter
1	Name	Test 1	Test 2	Test 3	Final	Grade	Grade		Grade	Grade
2	Bronson, Gary	70	90	85	85	82.5	B		0	F
3	Best, Harriet	90	70	83	92	83.75	B		60	D
4	Flavano, Louis	70	85	72	70	74.25	C		70	C
5	Glover, Jane	85	92	89	95	90.25	A		80	B
6	Restin, Ann	60	70	80	80	72.5	C		90	A
7	Williams, Bill	79	72	63	60	68.5	D			

Figure 4.12b VLOOKUP( ) results for Letter Grade

EXERCISES 4.3

1. Complete parts a-d.

    a. What information does the first argument of the VLOOKUP( ) function provide?

    b. What information does the second argument of the VLOOKUP( ) function provide?

    c. What information does the third argument of the VLOOKUP( ) function provide?

    d. What information does the fourth argument of the VLOOKUP( ) function provide?

2. For the following function, which is located in cell D2,

    =VLOOKUP(A2, $H$1:$J$14, 2, TRUE),

    do the following:

    a. determine the location of the lookup value.

b. determine the location of the lookup table.

c. determine the column in the lookup table of the located item.

d. What cell will display the looked-up item?

3. For the following function, which is located in cell C2,

=VLOOKUP(A2, $H$1:$J$14, 3, TRUE), do the following:

a. determine the location of the lookup value.

b. determine the location of the lookup table.

c. determine the column in the lookup table of the located item.

d. What cell will display the looked-up item?

4. On a blank worksheet, write the VLOOKUP( ) function to perform the following:

a. the lookup value is in cell A2, the lookup table is located in cells C5 through D20, the return value column is in the second column of the table, and an approximate match is required. The function is to be copied from cell B2 through B10.

b. the lookup value is in cell D3, the lookup table is located in cells G1 through H15, the return value column is in the third column of the table, and an approximate match is required. The function is to be copied from cell E2 through E10.

c. the lookup value is in cell B2, the lookup table is located in cells G1 through H18, the return value column is in the second column of the table, and an exact match is required. The function is to be copied from cell C2 through C15.

d. the lookup value is in cell B2, the lookup table is located in cells G1 through H18, the return value column is in the third column of the table, and an exact match is required. The function is to be copied from cell C2 through C15.

e. the lookup value is in cell C2, the lookup table is located in cells E5 through F25, the return value column is in the second column of the table, and an approximate match is required. The function is to be copied from cell D2 through D15.

5. Complete parts a-b.

a. Write a VLOOKUP( ) function that returns the value from column 2 of a vertical lookup table residing in cells C10 through F25. The lookup value is located in cell A2, and an approximate data match is required.

b. Modify the function written for Exercise 5a so that the returned value is located in column 3 of the lookup data table.

6. Create the following spreadsheet and complete the spreadsheet by entering a function in cell G2 to locate and display the correct grade from the lookup table for the data in cell A2. Copy your function down through G7 and verify that the correct grades are displayed for all of the students.

	A	B	C	D	E	F	G	H	I	J
1	Name	Test 1	Test 2	Test 3	Final	Average Grade	Letter Grade		Cut-Off Grade	Letter Grade
2	Bronson, Gary	70	90	85	85	82.5			0	F
3	Best, Harriet	90	70	83	92	83.75			60	D
4	Flavano, Louis	70	85	72	70	74.25			70	C
5	Glover, Jane	85	92	89	95	90.25			80	B
6	Restin, Ann	60	70	80	80	72.5			90	A
7	Williams, Bill	79	72	63	60	68.5				

7. Replace the lookup table data in Exercise 6 with that shown below. Then, modify the VLOOKUP( ) function used to calculate the grades for the students in the Exercise 7 spreadsheet using this new lookup table.

	F	G
12	Cut-Off Grade	Letter Grade
13	0	F
14	60	D
15	70	C-
16	73	C
17	77	C+
18	80	B-
19	83	B
20	87	B+
21	90	A-
22	93	A

Figure 4.13 Data for Exercise 7

8. Using the spreadsheet section shown in Figure 4.14, complete parts a-d.

   a. What data type can be used for a lookup value and what column is searched for this value?

   b. What is the range that should be used for the lookup table?

c. What column number (1,2,3,4, or 5) would you use if you wanted the Last Name to be returned for the looked-up value?

d. What column number (1,2,3,4, or 5) would you use if you wanted the Grade to be returned for the looked-up value?

	G	H	I	J	K
9	**ID No.**	**Last Name**	**First Name**	**Final Average**	**Grade**
10	DS101	Barron	Harriet	84.6	B
11	DS104	Benson	James	91.5	A-
12	DS232	DeSanto	Louise	62.4	D
13	DS325	Harrison	Samantha	95.8	A-
14	DS408	Jones	Robert	76.2	C
15	DS110	Smit	Michael	78.7	C+

Figure 4.14 Exercise 8 spreadsheet

9. Modify the Exercise 8 data to have the data placed in Columns A through E, with the labels placed in cells A1 through E1 (note the row and column addresses). This arrangement is shown in Figure 4.15. For any ID number entered in cell A2, the spreadsheet should use the lookup data in cell G9 through K15 to display the correct information in columns B1 though E1.

	A	B	C	D	E
1	**ID No.**	**Last Name**	**First Name**	**Final Average**	**Grade**
2					

Figure 4.15 Exercise 9 spreadsheet

10. Enter the spreadsheet shown in Figure 4.16. Then complete the spreadsheet by supplying the appropriate VLOOKUP( ) functions to correctly fill-in the discount percentages in cells B2 through B8. Your lookup function should use the vertical lookup table located in cell C13 through D18.

	A	B	C	D
1	Amount	Discount Percentage		
2	$800			
3	$5,425			
4	$9,250			
5	$2,760			
6	$8,300			
7	$1,645			
8	$12,450			
9				
10				
11				
12			Dollar Amount	Discount Percentage
13			0	0%
14			1000	2%
15			2500	4%
16			4000	6%
17			8000	8%
18			10000	10%

Figure 4.16 Spreadsheet for Exercise 10

11. Complete parts a-b.

a. The interest rate used on funds deposited in a bank is determined by the amount of time the money is left on deposit. For a particular bank, the following schedule is used.

Time on Deposit	Interest Rate
Less than 1 year, but greater than 0	2%
Less than 2 years, but greater than or equal to 1 year	2.5%
Less than 3 years, but greater than or equal to 2 years	3%
Less than 4 years, but greater than or equal to 3 years	3.5%
Less than 5 years, but greater than or equal to 4 years	4%
Greater than 5 years	4.5%

Using this schedule, which is included in the spreadsheet shown in Figure 4.17, determine the function that should be placed in cell C2 to check the value in cell B2 and display the corresponding interest rate in cell C2.

	A	B	C	D	E	F
1	Amount	Years on Deposit	Interest Rate			
2	$1,000	2.50			Time (Yrs)	Int. Rate
3	$2,400	1.80			0	2.0%
4	$1,500	3.20			1	2.5%
5	$6,000	0.75			2	3.0%
6	$3,200	6.20			3	3.5%
7	$5,300	4.30			4	4.0%
8					5	4.5%

Figure 4.17 Spreadsheet for Exercise 11

b. Enter the spreadsheet shown in Figure 4.17 and complete it, using the VLOOKUP( ) function determined in Exercise 11a, to fill in the corresponding interest rates in cells C2 through C7.

12. Complete parts a-b.

a. The monthly income of a salesperson is calculated using the following commission schedule.

Monthly Sales	Income
Less than $10,000 but greater than $0	$1,200 plus 3% of sales
Less that $20,000 but greater than or equal to $10,000	$2,000 plus 6% of sales
Less that $30,000 but greater than or equal to $20,000	$2,500 plus 9% of sales
Less that $40,000 but greater than or equal to $30,000	$3,500 plus 12% of sales
Less that $50,000 but greater than or equal to $40,000	$4,500 plus 14% of sales
Greater than $50,000	$5,000 plus 16% of sales

Using this schedule, which is included in Figure 4.18 as a lookup table in cells G7 through I12, determine

 i. the function that should be placed in cell C2 to check the value in cell B2 and display the corresponding Base Pay.

 ii. the function that should be placed in cell D2 to check the value in cell B2 and display the corresponding Percent of Sales.

 iii. the function that should be placed in cell E2 that calculates the Net Pay, where

Net Pay = Base Pay + (Percent of Sales) * (Monthly Sales)

b. Enter the spreadsheet shown in Figure 4.18 and complete it, using the functions and formulas determined in Exercise 12a.

	A	B	C	D	E	F	G	H	I
1	Name	Monthly Sales	Base Pay	Percent of Sales	Net Pay				
2	Yolanda	$35,000							
3	Billy	$25,250							
4	Janet	$9,200							
5	Bobby	$10,000							
6	Joe	$40,000					Sales	Base	Percent of Sales
7	Linda	$48,000					$0	$1,200	3%
8	Bonnie	$19,400					$10,000	$2,000	5%
9	Neal	$30,000					$20,000	$2,500	9%
10	Harriet	$50,000					$30,000	$3,500	12%
11	John	$52,700					$40,000	$4,500	14%
12	Sydney	$20,000					$50,000	$5,000	16%

Figure 4.18 Spreadsheet for Exercise 12

4.4   THE HLOOKUP( ) FUNCTION

The IF( ) function should always be used when a decision based on one of two possible alternatives is required. Although IF( ) functions can be nested, as described at the end of Section 4.2, this becomes cumbersome quickly, and should be avoided if more than one IF( ) function is used as an argument within an outer IF( ) function.

For situations requiring multiple conditions that would require more than one IF( ) function as an argument to another IF( ) function, either a VLOOKUP() or HLOOKUP( ) function can be used. As their names imply, a VLOOKUP( ) function, as described in the previous section, requires a vertical lookup table, while the HLOOKUP() function requires a horizontal lookup table, as shown in Figure 4.19.

Code	1020	1030	1040	1050	1060
Flavor	Mango	Bergamot	Raspberry	Orange	Cherry
Price	$2.50	$2.75	$2.05	$1.95	$1.95

Figure 4.19 A horizontal lookup table

What defines it as a horizontal table is that data *in each row* are the same data category. Thus, the items listed in Figure 4.19's first row are code numbers, the items listed in the second row are descriptions, and items listed in the third row are prices. In a horizontal lookup table, the item being looked for is always, and only, looked for in the table's first row. The table itself can be placed anywhere on a spreadsheet, and can contain two or more rows. However, the first row must contain values that will be searched using the HLOOKUP( ) function.

The general syntax for the HLOOKUP( ) function is as follows:

A lookup value or a cell address where the value is located.

The location of the lookup table (use absolute addresses)

HLOOKUP(*lookup value, table location, return value row, match type*)

A number indicating the row of the returned value

Either TRUE (or omitted) for the closest match, or FALSE for an exact match
*The **return value row** can also be referred to as the row index number.*

The value to be looked up, which is referred to as the *lookup value*, is the first argument provided to the HLOOKUP( ) function. The remaining three items, provide the location of the lookup table, the row number of the return value, and whether an exact or approximate (closest) match to the lookup value is required.

The HLOOKUP( ) function searches the specified table's first row looking for a match to the lookup value (if no match if found, an error message is displayed). Once a match is located, either exact or approximate, as specified by the fourth argument, the third argument provides the *row* of the return value.

Figure 4.20 illustrates the relationship between the arguments provided to the HLOOKUP( ) function and other cells in the spreadsheet.

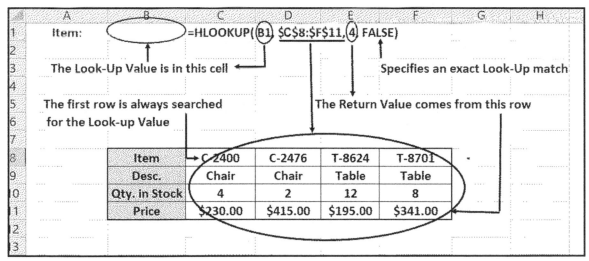

Figure 4.20 The relationship between the arguments provided to the HLOOKUP( )
function and other cells in the spreadsheet

Consider the HLOOKUP( ) function in cell C1, repeated below for convenience

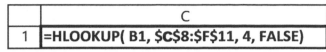

	C
1	=HLOOKUP(B1, $C$8:$F$11, 4, FALSE)

The function's first argument specifies that the lookup value is contained in cell B1. The next argument, $C$8:$F$11, specifies that the lookup table is located in the cell range from C8 through F11. This is the area circled in the spreadsheet. Notice that the lookup table does not include the highlighted row labels in cells B8 through B11. Also notice that the cell addresses specifying the lookup table's location use absolute addresses. This ensures that if or when the function in cell C1 is copied, the lookup table's addresses will not be changed.

The search for a match always, and only, occurs by comparing the lookup value, provided as the function's first argument, to each value in the lookup table's first row, one item at a time. When a match is found (the type of match is determined by the function's fourth argument) the search stops, and the corresponding value in the row specified by the third argument (which in this example is 4) is returned.

To understand how a match is determined, a clear understanding of the function's fourth argument is required. The simplest match criterion is provided when this fourth argument is specified as FALSE. This indicates that an exact match is required, and it is most useful when code numbers or name matches are needed.

When a search involves a range of values, such as the amount of commission based on recent orders, or spending towards various loyalty program rewards categories, an approximate match, also referred to as a closest match, should be used. This type of match is indicated by either explicitly specifying the function's fourth argument as TRUE, or omitting it altogether. Thus, the default search, when the fourth argument is omitted, is an approximate match. It is important to realize that this type of match *requires* that the data in the lookup table's first row be in sorted ascending order, from lowest to highest. This is necessary because the search stops once a value greater than the lookup value is encountered.

Example

For the function, located in cell D3, determine the following:

	C	D
3	1020	=HLOOKUP(C3, $D$6:$H$8, 2, FALSE)

a. the location of the lookup value

b. the lookup value

c. the location of the lookup table

d. the number of rows in the lookup table

e. the lookup table's row containing the return value, if an exact or "closest-to" match is specified

f. the cell that displays the return value

Solution:

a. The lookup value is located in cell C3.

b. The lookup value is 1020.

c. The lookup table is located in cells D6 through H8.

d. The lookup table contains three rows (6, 7, an 8).

e. If a match is found, the return value is in the second third row of the table; otherwise #N/A is displayed.

f. An exact match is specified because the last argument is FALSE.

Give It a Try

For the function, located in cell D3, determine the following:

	C	D
3	96.8	=HLOOKUP(C3, $E$6:$H$7, 2, TRUE)

a. the location of the lookup value

b. the lookup value

c. the location of the lookup table

d. the number of rows in the lookup table

e. the lookup table's row containing the return value, if an exact or "closest-to" match is specified

f. the cell that displays the return value

EXERCISES 4.4

1. Complete parts a-d.

   a. What information does the first argument of the HLOOKUP( ) function provide?

   b. What information does the second argument of the HLOOKUP( ) function provide?

   c. What information does the third argument of the HLOOKUP( ) function provide?

   d. What information does the fourth argument of the HLOOKUP( ) function provide?

2. For the following function, which is located in cell D2,

$$=HLOOKUP(A2, \$H\$1:\$P\$3, 2, TRUE)$$

   a. determine the location of the lookup value.

   b. determine the location of the lookup table.

   c. determine the row in the lookup table of the located item.

   d. What cell will display the return value from the HLOOKUP( ) function?

3. For the following function, which is located in cell C2,

$$=HLOOKUP(A2, \$H\$1:\$P\$4, 3, TRUE)$$

   a. determine the location of the lookup value.

   b. determine the location of the lookup table.

   c. determine the row in the lookup table of the located item.

   d. What cell will display the return value from the HLOOKUP( ) function?

4. Use a blank worksheet to write HLOOKUP( ) functions to perform the following:

   a. The lookup value is in cell A2, the lookup table is located in cells C5 through H3, the return value row is in the second row of the table, and an approximate match is required. The function is to be copied from cell B2 through B10.

   b. The lookup value is in cell D3, the lookup table is located in cells G1 through M3, the return value row is in the third row of the table, and an approximate match is required. The function is to be copied from cell E2 through E10.

   c. The lookup value is in cell B2, the lookup table is located in cells G1 through M4, the return value row is in the second row of the table, and an exact match is required. The function is to be copied from cell C2 through C15.

d. The lookup value is in cell B2, the lookup table is located in cells G1 through N4 the return value row is in the third row of the table, and an exact match is required. The function is to be copied from cell C2 through C15.

e. The lookup value is in cell C2, the lookup table is located in cells E5 through M5, the return value row is in the second row of the table, and an approximate match is required. The function is to be copied from cell D2 through D15.

5. Enter the spreadsheet shown in Figure 4.21. Then complete the spreadsheet by supplying an appropriate HLOOKUP( ) function to correctly fill-in the description in cell D2 and the unit price in cell D2. The Total Price in cell E2 is the quantity times the unit price. Then copy the functions down to complete the spreadsheet. Make sure to check the Descriptions and Unit Prices to see that the lookup is working correctly.

	A	B	C	D	E	F	G	H	I	J	K	L
1	Code	Quantity	Description	Unit Price	Total Price		Code	1020	1030	1040	1050	1060
2	1030	5					Flavor	Mango	Bergamot	Raspberry	Orange	Cherry
3	1010	8					Price	$2.50	$2.75	$2.05	$1.95	$1.95
4	1040	2										
5	1060	7										
6	1050	6										
7	1020	4										
8	1060	9										
9	1040	3										

Figure 4.21 Exercise 5 spreadsheet

6. Create the spreadsheet shown in Figure 4.22. Then complete the spreadsheet by supplying an appropriate HLOOKUP( ) function to correctly fill in the letter grades in cells C2 through C7. Your lookup function should use the horizontal lookup table located in cell C9 through G10.

	A	B	C	D	E	F	G
1	Name	Final Aveage	Grade				
2	Barron, Harriet	84.6					
3	Benson, James	91.5					
4	Harrison, Louise	62.4					
5	DeSanto, Robert	95.8					
6	Smith, Clare	76.2					
7	Jones, Michael	78.7					
8							
9		Average	0	60	70	80	90
10		Grade	F	D	C	B	A

Figure 4.22 Exercise 6 spreadsheet

4.5   COMMON EXCEL ERRORS

In using the material presented in this chapter, be aware of the following possible errors:

1. Forgetting to enclose a string literal within double quotes when used as an operand in a condition or as an argument within an IF( ) function. The only time double quotes **should not** be used is when text is user-entered into a cell. Here, Excel automatically recognizes the entry as text.

2. Assuming the IF( ) function is selecting an incorrect choice. Typically, the designer mistakenly concentrates on the tested condition as the source of the problem. As a general rule, whenever an IF( ) function does not act as you think it should, make sure to test your assumptions about the values assigned to the cells within the tested condition. If an unanticipated value is displayed by the IF( ) function, you have at least isolated the source of the problem to the cell values being tested, rather than the structure of the IF( ) function. From there, you need to determine where and how the incorrect value or values were obtained.

3. Not listing the data in the first column of a vertical lookup table in ascending (that is, increasing) order when an approximate match is specified. This error can cause the search for an approximate match to stop prematurely before a closer match is located. Where an approximate match is specified in a horizontal lookup table, the data in the first row must be in ascending order.

4. Forgetting to use absolute addresses for the range of cells that define a lookup table in the VLOOKUP( ) and HLOOKUP( ) functions. This results in an error, usually #VALUE, when the function containing the lookup function is copied. The reason is that the relative addresses are changed when copied, while absolute addresses remain fixed.

4.6   CHAPTER APPENDIX: TESTING AND DEBUGGING

The ideal in creating a spreadsheet is to produce error-free applications that work correctly and can be modified or changed with a minimum of testing. You can work toward this ideal by keeping in mind the two main types of errors that can occur, when they are typically detected, and how to correct them. An error is typically detected in two situations:

1. While entering and copying formulas as the spreadsheet is being developed

2. After a spreadsheet's results are being examined, either when it is being used or at some later date

And clearly, in some cases, an error may not be detected at all.

By now, you have probably encountered numerous errors while developing your spreadsheets. Although beginning developers tend to be frustrated by these errors, experienced developers understand that detecting errors and correcting them is part of the process of becoming an experienced Excel developer and user. Additionally, any errors that are detected in the development stage, and not when a user is attempting to perform an important task with it, ensures that no one but the developer ever knows they occurred; you fix them and they go away. Having someone else report an error while they are using one of your spreadsheets not only requires you to find and fix the error, as you would do during the development stage, but hurts your credibility as a knowledgeable Excel designer.

Although there are no hard-and-fast rules for locating and correcting errors, some useful techniques can be applied.

First, the primary ingredient needed for successful isolation and correction of errors is the attitude and spirit you bring to the task. After you enter a formula, and copy it, it is natural to assume it is correct. It is difficult to back away and honestly find the cause of an error in your own spreadsheet after an error message, such as "#N/A," "#VALUE," or "#NAME," appears. As a developer, you must constantly remind yourself that just because you think a formula is correct does not make it so. Just because a formula produces a correct result in one cell does not ensure that it will be correct when copied. Having an error appear in your own spreadsheet is a sobering experience, but one that will help you to become a better developer. It can also be exciting and fun if approached as a detection problem with you as the master detective.

A second technique is purely preventative. Frequently, many errors are introduced in a rush to create your spreadsheet without fully understanding what is required and how the result is to be achieved. Take the time to understand what each formula is supposed to do, and, if necessary, do a few hand calculations to ensure you know what cell values are needed for your formula.

A third technique is to check the result, using a calculator, of the initial entry of each formula used in your spreadsheet. Then, immediately after the formula is copied, check the first copy produced. This typically reveals whether an absolute address should have been used or was used incorrectly.

Finally, when using cells that contain IF( ), VLOOKUP( ), or HLOOKUP( ) functions, change the values in the cells being tested, so that as many as possible of the results can be verified.

Part 2

PRESENTATIONS

Presenting results clearly, in an easily understood manner, is as important as producing correct results. In fact, your work will almost always be judged on its presentation. Here, providing simple and clear visual aids, that is, graphs, charts, and summary tables that highlight and quickly show appropriate relationships, are indispensable. These permit users to focus on significant results and rapidly see and understand relevant associations.

In this unit, Chapter 5 presents basic Excel charting and graphing presentations. Chapter 6 presents PivotTables, which are used to easily create concise summary tables. Together, these represent Excel's basic visual presentation tools.

GRAPHICAL PRESENTATIONS

This Chapter Contains

5.1 INTRODUCTION

While the main goal of a spreadsheet is to present numerical data and the results of calculations and analyses in a clear and logical way, often the need for presenting numerical information in a graphical way can be highly useful and valuable. This is especially the case if the results of the quantitative results can be presented in an easy-to-understand manner. For instance, sales trends can be presented in the form of appropriate charts and graphs, or the results of a firm's performance over a past year can be summarized in the form of a graphical dashboard display. Sometimes referred to broadly as *visualizations*, the availability of charts and graphs allow for colorful and easy-to-interpret representations of spreadsheet data.

While there are a number of chart types available in Excel, three of the most basic and frequently used are column/bar charts, pie charts, and line graphs. Each of these graphical presentations provide visual aids for highlighting specific relationships between data values.

A *column chart* presents data with rectangular bars whose lengths are proportional to the represented values. In a column chart, the bars are plotted vertically, as shown in Figure 5.1a. A *bar chart* is the same as a column chart, except that the bars are drawn horizontally, as shown in Figure 5.1b.

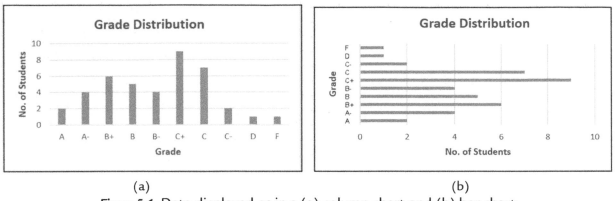

(a) (b)

Figure 5.1 Data displayed as in a (a) column chart and (b) bar chart

A *pie chart* is a circular pie-shaped graphic that is divided into slices. Each slice in a pie chart, like each bar in a bar chart, is proportional to the quantity it represents. Two pie chart examples are illustrated in Figure 5.2.

Pie charts are typically used to highlight relationships among two to ten quantities; additional slices make the chart difficult to read.

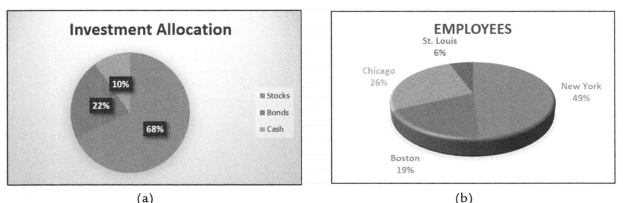

(a) (b)

Figure 5.2 Pie chart examples (a) 2-D pie chart (b) 3D pie chart

In a *line graph*, data points are plotted and then physically connected by straight line segments between each successive data point. Examples of this type of graphic are shown in Figure 5.3.

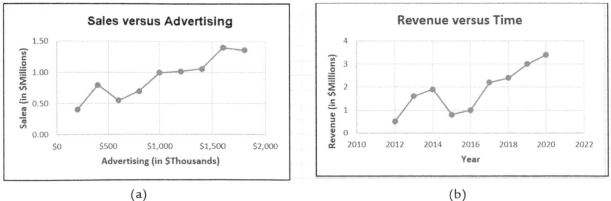

(a) (b)

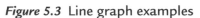

Figure 5.3 Line graph examples

Line graphs are typically used to highlight multiple pairs of data points, as shown in Figure 5.3. A line graph without lines connecting data points is referred to as a *scatter diagram*. This type of graph is typically used when trend lines are added (*see* Section 5.5).

Each of the basic chart types is presented in the following sections, and each may be read independently. It is suggested that you initially select only one of these sections to clearly understand the basics of creating the specific visual graphic most appropriate to your work, and then explore the other types as needed.

EXERCISES 5.1

1. Complete parts a-b.

    a. What type of graph is typically more appropriate for displaying the relationship between two variables?

    b. What type of graphic is typically more appropriate for displaying the relationship between two to ten variables?

2. Complete parts a-b.

    a. Obtain at least three examples of any combination of line, pie, or bar/column charts from the Internet, a newspaper, or magazine.

    b. Did one type of chart appear more often in your response to Exercise 2a? If so, which type of chart appeared most frequently?

3. Determine the type of chart, line, pie, or bar/column that is most appropriate for the following:

    a. the populations of the ten largest cities in the United States

    b. the dollar amounts and percentages of stocks, bonds, and cash held in an individual's investment account

    c. a supermarket's yearly sales of raspberries, blackberries, blueberries, and strawberries

    d. the median home price in the eight largest cities in the United States

    e. an outlet's yearly sales of shoes, dresses, and accessories

5.2   CREATING COLUMN AND BAR CHARTS[1]

Since column and bar charts are relatively easy to create, and are widely used, they are typically the first to be examined when learning how to create and work with Excel charts and graphs. At this point, we are creating column and bar charts with only a *single data series*, that is with one set of labels (text) and one set of numerical data (numbers).

This is the simplest form of chart, which results in a single set of columns and bars as a result. More complex charts may typically involve two data series, where there are two sets of data and two sets of labels (often referred to as a *multiple data series* chart). In general, the labels (text) are referred to as *category labels*, while the data can be differentiated between the *data series* (a group of numbers being charted) and each individual number within the series, known individually as a *data point*.

An important note: You don't necessarily need to memorize these terms, since you can easily create charts and graphs with only a basic working understanding of what the process is based on what is detailed in this chapter. However, if you ever consult any resources on charts and graphs and these terms are mentioned, you can understand the explanations and tutorials better.

Column and bar charts are essentially the same chart with their respective displays rotated ninety degrees. Thus, as seen in Figure 5.4, a column chart displays its data vertically, in column form, while a bar chart displays its data horizontally, as bars across the chart.

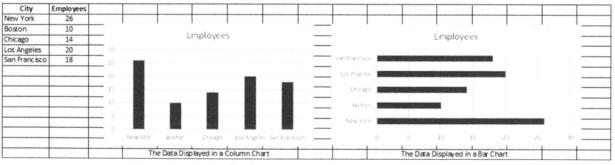

Figure 5.4 Data displayed as a column chart and bar chart

Both column and bar charts are created using the following four-step procedure, illustrated in Figure 5.5:

1.   Highlight the data to be charted. The data can be listed in either column form (item 1 in Figure 5.5) or in row form. In the case of the single data series chart, the set of relevant category labels (to identify the columns or bars) must be selected, together with a single row or column of numerical data.

---

[1] This section may be read independently of any other sections in this chapter.

2. Select the Insert tab, (Charts Group) on the Excel ribbon (item 2 in Figure 5.5).

3. Select the Column Chart Icon (item 3 in Figure 5.5).

4. Choose either the 2-D or 3-D Column or Bar Chart display type, (item 4 in Figure 5.5).

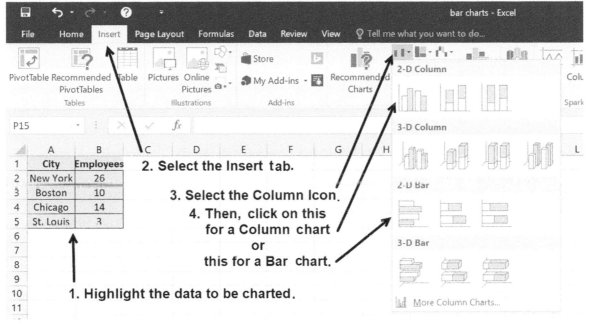

Figure 5.5 Creating a column or bar chart

In reviewing Figure 5.5, notice that selecting either the 2-D or 3-D Column icon produces a column chart, while choosing either the 2-D or 3-D Bar chart icon produces a bar chart. Although the data charted in Figure 5.5 is listed in column form, this is not a required data format. The data for both the column and bar charts can also be listed in rows.

Changing a Column Chart's and Bar Chart's Elements and Appearance

Once you have created a chart, normally, by default, it is created as a chart object on your spreadsheet. A *chart object* is a part of a worksheet, but it is also a dynamic object that can be resized and moved, and operates as though it is "floating above" the surface of the worksheet. It is an OLE (Object Linking and Embedding) object that can then be shared, pasted, and exported to other Windows applications. An alternate means of display is as a *chart sheet*, which is a special kind of worksheet that only holds a chart.

Once your chart is created, and the chart is selected (highlighted), a new tab appears on the ribbon. This is known as the Chart Tools tab, below which are two submenus, Design and Format. Since we are starting charts at a very basic level, we will only reference those commands on the menu which are relevant to the tasks currently described, rather than reviewing the entire set of menus in detail.

Depending on your needs, you can make your chart as either a chart object or a chart sheet. The way to change a chart object to a chart sheet is to use the Excel ribbon Chart Tools tab and Design submenu, and click on the Move Chart command. Select the New Sheet command and click OK to convert the chart object to a chart sheet. You will note that the chart figures given in this chapter are *chart objects*. A chart sheet has a somewhat larger sized chart, laid out as a separate sheet, with an assigned default sheet name starting with *Chart1*.

The various elements which can be included in a column, bar (and for other chart types), such as titles, legends, and the like are known as Chart Elements. The way to add and modify chart elements to your chart is through the ribbon tab sequence **Chart Tools – Design- Chart Elements-Add Chart Elements**. There, you are given a list of the various chart elements available.

In practical terms, once a column or bar chart has been created, its title, axes labels, data labels, and grid lines can be added, changed, or deleted using the Chart Elements submenu. As shown in Figure 5.6, this submenu is activated by either right or left clicking within a chart, and then selecting the displayed cross-hairs icon.

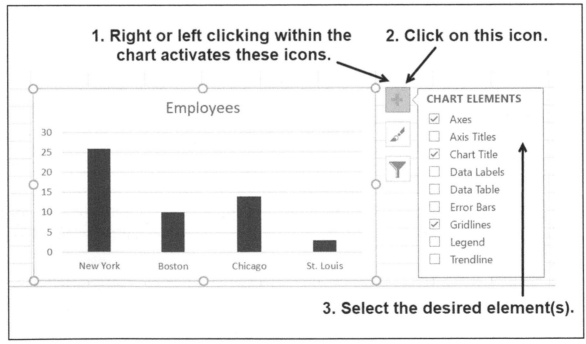

Figure 5.6 Changing the chart elements

For example, checking the Axis Titles and Legend checkboxes shown in Figure 5.6 produces the chart shown in Figure 5.7a. Simply clicking within each element allows you to change the titles to those of your own choosing, including the font type and size. This was done to produce the titles shown in Figure 5.7b.

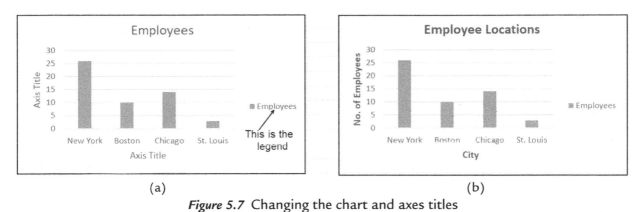

(a)   (b)

Figure 5.7 Changing the chart and axes titles

In addition to changing a chart's title and labels, a number of differing chart appearances (chart styles) can be selected, such as those shown in Figure 5.8.

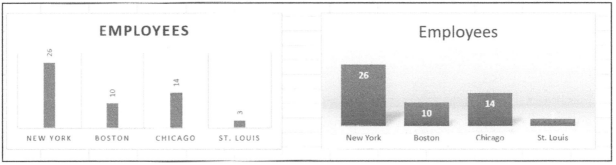

Figure 5.8 Two column chart variations

Changing a chart's appearance is accomplished by first double-clicking anywhere within the chart. Doing this brings up the ribbon's Chart Tools tab, and its submenu, Design, as shown in Figure 5.9.[2] Clicking on any of the pre-constructed Chart Styles changes the chart to the selected appearance.

Figure 5.9 Pre-constructed chart styles

---

[2] The Design submenu shown in Figure 5.5 can also be activated by single clicking (selecting) the chart and then selecting the Chart Tools' Design option at the top of Figure 5.5.

Notice that the chart elements previously shown in Figure 5.5 can also be accessed by clicking on the left-most icon in the Excel ribbon Chart Tools – Design menu (see the figure's dotted arrow).

Changing Chart Types

Once a chart is created, it can easily be changed to a different chart type, which simply changes how the data is displayed. For example, Figure 5.10 shows how Figure 5.4's data appears in a number of chart types.

Figure 5.10 Different chart types

An existing chart's type is changed by

1. Right-clicking within the chart (or selecting the chart)

2. Clicking on the **Change Chart Type** option on the pop-up submenu (or the same option on the ribbon **Chart Tools – Design**).

3. Selecting the desired chart type from the resulting pop-up sub-menu (or from the **Chart Tools – Design – Type – Change Chart Type**).

The first two steps are illustrated in Figure 5.11.

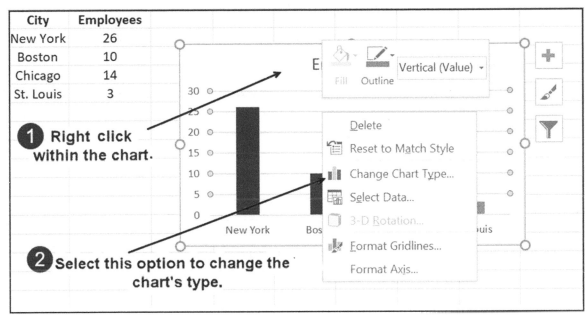

Figure 5.11 The first two steps in changing a chart's type

EXERCISES 5.2

1. Create both the column and bar charts shown in the figure.

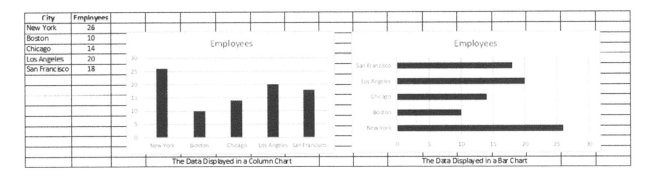

2. Create the same column and bar charts shown below the data.

	A	B	C	D	E
1	**City**	New York	Boston	Chicago	St. Louis
2	**Employees**	26	10	14	3

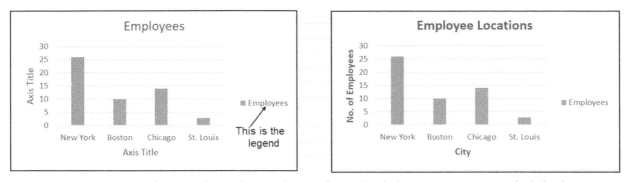

3. Construct a column chart (as a chart object) of the percentage of global Internet users for the data listed in the table below. An Internet user is defined as someone having access to the Internet in their home, using a computer or mobile device. (*Source: worldometers.info/licensing-how.php*)

Year	Internet Users (Billions)
1998	0.208
2000	0.415
2002	0.665
2004	0.913
2006	1.163
2008	1.575
2010	2.023
2012	2.494
2014	2.956
2016	3.424

4. Construct a column chart as a chart sheet, for the following population data:

City	2019 Population (in Millions)
New York	8.550
Los Angeles	3.972
Chicago	2.721
Houston	2.296
Philadelphia	1.567
Phoenix	1.563
San Antonio	1.470
San Diego	1.395
Dallas	1.300
San Jose	1.027

5. Construct a column chart as a chart object, for the following Median House Price data.

City	2019 Median House Price
New York	$849,000
Los Angeles	$775,000
Chicago	$245,000
Houston	$282,000
Philadelphia	$165,000

5.3 CREATING PIE CHARTS[3]

Figure 5.12 illustrates Excel's two basic pie chart types (with an related alternate option as a doughnut chart). The chart on the left is a 2-D type (short for two-dimensional), while the one on the right is a 3-D type (short for three-dimensional).

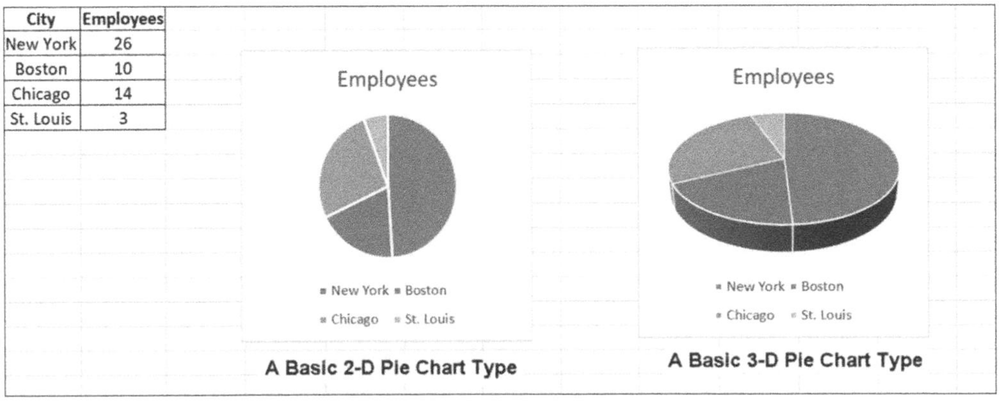
City Employees
New York 26
Boston 10
Chicago 14
St. Louis 3
Employees
New York Boston
Chicago St. Louis
A Basic 2-D Pie Chart Type
Employees
New York Boston
Chicago St. Louis
A Basic 3-D Pie Chart Type

Figure 5.12 Data displayed as a pie chart

[3] This section may be read independently of any other sections in this chapter.

Both 2-D and 3-D pie charts are created as follows:

1. Highlight the data to be displayed (Item 1 in Figure 5.13). You need to highlight one set of text (category labels) and one set of numerical data values (data series).

2. Select Insert from the Excel ribbon Insert tab (Item 2 in Figure 5.13).

3. Select the Charts group, and click on the Pie Chart icon (Item 3 in Figure 5.13).

4. Choose either the 2-D or 3-D chart type (Item 4 in Figure 5.13).

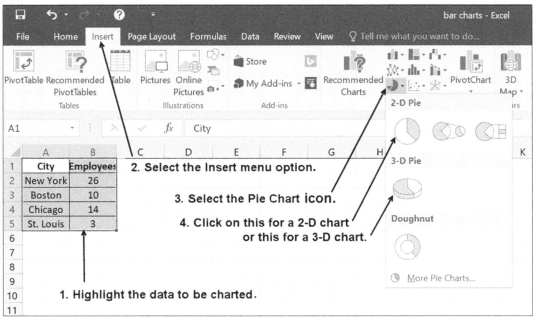

Figure 5.13 Creating a pie chart

In terms of the chart data needed (much like the data for the column and bar charts, although the data is presented in column form), having the data in rows is also acceptable.

Changing a Pie Chart's Elements and Appearance

A pie chart's title, data labels, legend, and other chart elements can be activated, changed, or deactivated by either clicking or clearing the respective item within the Chart Elements submenu, as shown in Figure 5.14. This submenu (item 3 in Figure 5.14) is activated by either right or left clicking within the pie chart, and then selecting the displayed cross-hairs icon.

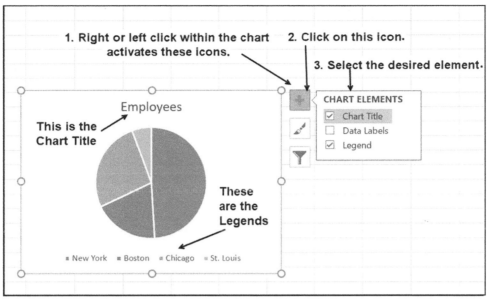

Figure 5.14 Pie Chart: Change chart elements

For example, checking the Data Labels checkbox shown in Figure 5.14 activates the labels within each pie slice, as shown in Figure 5.15a. Here, the labels provide the percentage of employees within each city. Note that a Chart Title and Legend are activated by default, when the chart is created.

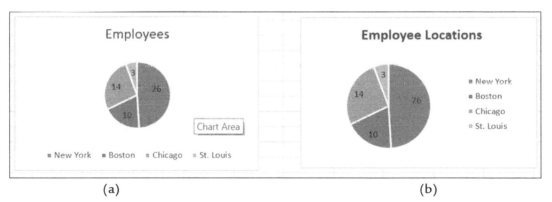

Figure 5.15 Adding data labels to a pie chart

Once activated, a chart title's text, font, and type size are changed by directly clicking on the title. A legend's position is changed by clicking on the Legend checkbox, and then selecting one of the positions offered in the activated Legend submenu. These procedures were done to produce the chart shown in Figure 5.15b.

In addition to changing a chart's title and labels, a number of different chart variations, such as those illustrated in Figure 5.16, are easily produced.

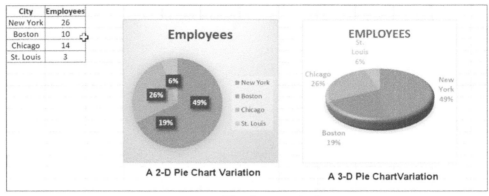

Figure 5.16 Pie chart variations

Variations in a chart's appearance are accomplished by first double-clicking anywhere within the chart. Doing this brings up the Chart Tools - Design menu shown in Figure 5.17. Clicking on any of the preconstructed chart styles changes the chart to the selected appearance.[4]

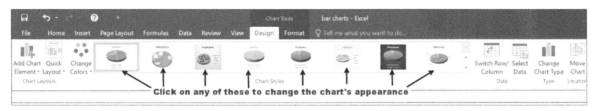

Figure 5.17 Pre-constructed pie chart styles

Changing Chart Types

Once a pie chart is created, it can easily be changed to different chart types, which changes how the data is displayed. For example, Figure 5.18 shows how Figure 5.12's 2-D chart appears using different chart types.

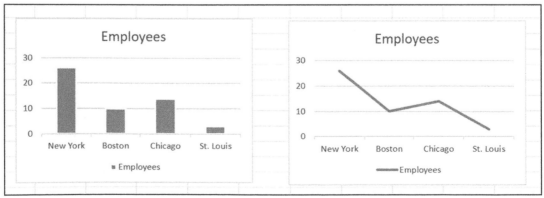

Figure 5.18 Different chart types

---

[4] The Design submenu shown in Figure 5.17 can also be activated by single clicking within a chart and then selecting the Chart Tools' Design option at the top of Figure 5.17.

A pie chart's type is changed by

1. right-clicking within the chart (or selecting the chart)

2. clicking on the Change Chart Type option

3. selecting the desired chart type from the resulting pop-up sub-menu

The first two steps are illustrated in Figure 5.19.

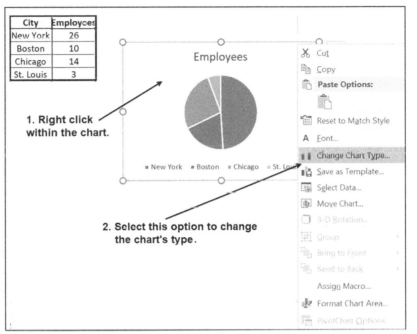

Figure 5.19 The first two steps in changing a chart's type

The change made above can also be done through the Excel ribbon Chart Tools-Design menu.

EXERCISES 5.3

1. Create the 2-D and 3-D pie charts shown in the figure.

2. Create the same column and bar charts shown in Exercise 1 using the following data.

	A	B	C	D	E
1	**City**	New York	Boston	Chicago	St. Louis
2	**Employees**	26	10	14	3

3. Complete parts a-b.

   a. Construct a 2-D pie chart of the percentage of Internet users in the world for the data listed in the following table as a chart sheet. (*Source: worldometers. info/licensing-how.php*)

Area	Percentage
Africa	9.8%
Americas	21.8%
Asia	48.4%
Europe	19.0%
Oceania	1.0%

   b. Convert the 2-D pie chart created for Exercise 3a into a 3-D pie chart.

4. Complete parts a-b.

   a. Construct a 2-D pie chart for the following data, as a chart object.

City	2019 Median House Price
New York	$849,000
Los Angeles	$775,000
Chicago	$245,000
Houston	$282,000
Philadelphia	$165,000

   b. Convert the 2-D pie chart created for Exercise 4a into a 3-D pie-chart.

5. Construct a 3-D pie chart for the following data in its own chart sheet:

Investment	Amount
Stocks	$72,000
Bonds	$26,000
Cash	$15,000

5.4   CREATING LINE GRAPHS[5]

Figure 5.20 illustrates an example of a line graph. The majority of line graphs show the relationship between two variables, such as Sales versus Advertising or between quantities, such as revenue or profit, as they change over time. Either straight or curved lines can be used to connect individual points on the graph.[6]

Rain(In.)	1	1.7	2.3	3.2	3.8	4.3	4.8
Yield (Bu.)	9	18	25	30	34	40	45

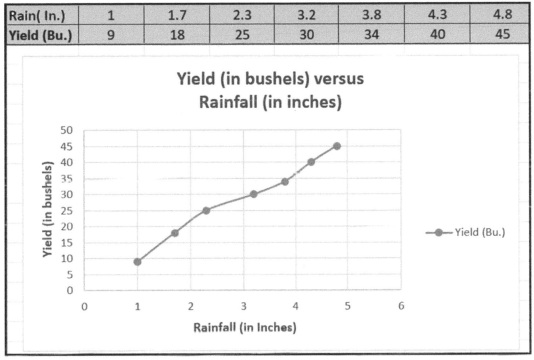

Figure 5.20 A line graph example

Creating a line graph requires that the data first be entered into either consecutive rows, as shown in the upper-left corner of Figure 5.20, or consecutive columns. Once entered, the data is highlighted, as shown as Step 1 in Figure 5.21, and the remaining steps shown in the figure can then be completed.

Although any two consecutive rows or columns can be used for the data, when rows are used, the data entered in the upper-most row become the x-axis values, and the data in the lower row become the y-axis values. Similarly, for data listed in columns, the data in the left-most column is plotted on the x-axis and the data in the right-most column on the y-axis.

---

[5] This section may be read independently of any other sections in this chapter.

[6] A line graph without connecting lines between data points is a *scatter diagram*. Scatter diagrams are typically used with trend lines, as presented in the next section.

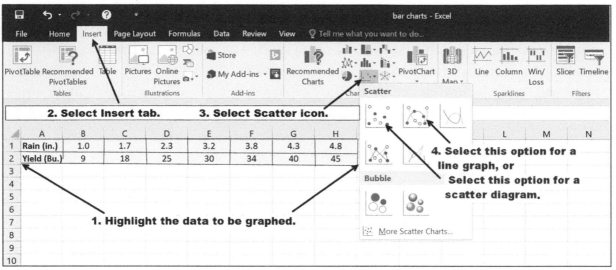

Figure 5.21 The steps needed to create a line graph

After selecting the line graph option shown as Step 4 in Figure 5.21, the line graph shown in Figure 5.22 is automatically created. Notice that the figure has no axes titles and that the chart's title is a copy of the data label in cell A2, which is the y-axis data label.

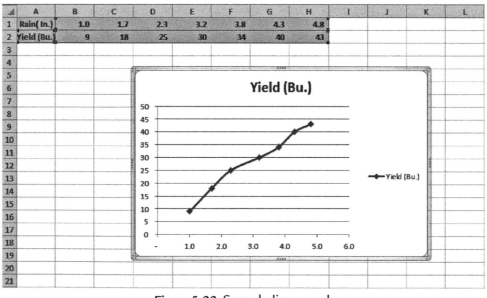

Figure 5.22 Sample line graph

Changing a Line Graph's Chart Elements and Appearance

Figure 5.23 shows the initial position and description of the four descriptive chart elements associated with line-graphs. These consist of a chart title, axis labels, legend, and grid lines. When any of these textual elements are present, the text, font type and size of each can be changed by clicking on the desired element and then entering new text and font attributes.

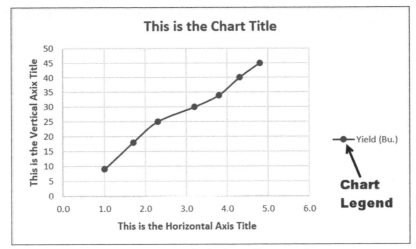

Figure 5.23 Labels for a line graph

Deleting or adding a chart element is accomplished using the Chart Elements sub-menu shown in Figure 5.24. As shown in the figure, this submenu is activated by either right or left clicking within the chart, and then clicking on the cross-hairs icon and selecting the desired element.

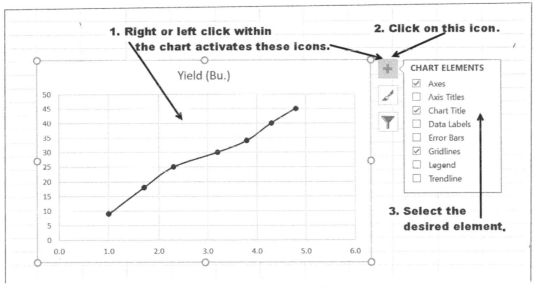

Figure 5.24 Working with a line graph

Additionally, a line graph's legends and line colors can be changed using the Change Colors option in the Chart Tools Design menu, shown in Figure 5.25. The Design menu is obtained by either double clicking within the chart or single clicking and then selecting the Chart tool's Design tab (seen at the top of Figure 5.25).

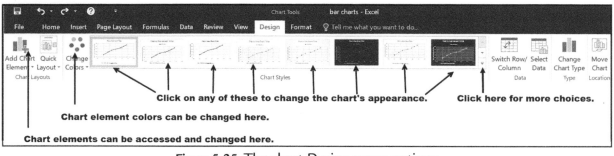

Figure 5.25 The chart Design menu options

Finally, a line graph's appearance is changed by selecting one of the chart styles shown within the Chart Tools - Design menu (again, see Figure 5.25). Clicking on any of the pre-constructed styles changes the chart to the selected choice.[7]

Changing Chart Types

As with all Excel charts, a chart can easily be changed to a different chart type. Figure 5.26 illustrates two variations for the line graph previously illustrated in Figure 5.24.

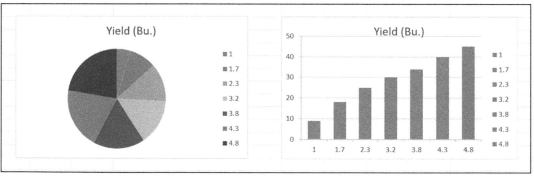

Figure 5.26 Different chart types

As with all of Excel's charts, a line graph can be changed to another type by

1. Right-clicking within the chart

2. Clicking on the Change Chart Type option

3. Selecting the desired chart type from the resulting pop-up sub-menu (or by using the Chart Tools – Design menu.)

---

[7] Notice that the chart elements previously shown in Figure 5.24 can also be accessed and changed by clicking on the leftmost icon in the Chart Tools – Design menu.

The first two steps are illustrated in Figure 5.27.

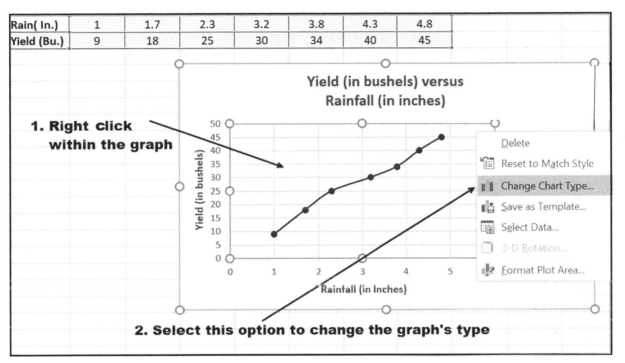

Rain(In.)	1	1.7	2.3	3.2	3.8	4.3	4.8
Yield (Bu.)	9	18	25	30	34	40	45

Figure 5.27 The first two steps in changing a chart's type

In addition to creating a graph with a single line, Excel permits multiple lines to be plotted on the same graph. The multiple line graph shown in Figure 5.28 was created using the same technique as presented above, with the exception that all of the data in rows 1, 2, and 3 were highlighted before selecting the line graph option.

Year	2014	2015	2016	2017	2018	2019	2020
Advertising ($1,000)	35	40	46	38	30	42	44
Sales ($1,000)	150	160	175	180	160	170	170

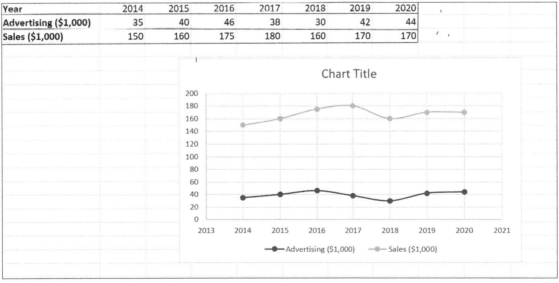

Figure 5.28 An example of a multiple line graph

EXERCISES 5.4

1. Construct a line graph for the following data as a chart object.

Day	Closing Price
1	$ 172.50
3	$ 174.25
4	$ 177.10
5	$ 182.35
6	$ 173.40
7	$ 168.60

2. Construct a line graph for the following data as a chart sheet.

Year	Sales (in $Millions)
2012	0.5
2013	1.7
2014	1.9
2015	1.4
2016	1.6
2017	2.0
2018	2.2
2019	2.4
2020	2.9
2021	3.3

3. Complete parts a-b.

   a. Construct a line graph for the following data as a chart object.

Rain (inches)	2	2.2	2.3	3.2	3.8	4.9	5.6
Yield (bushels)	23	25	25	34	40	50	58

   b. Add the appropriate chart and axes titles to the line graph created for Exercise 3a.

4. Complete parts a-b.

   a. Construct a line graph for the following data in its own chart sheet.

Advertising ($1,000)	Sales ($Millions)
$20	0.40
$40	0.80
$60	0.55
$80	0.70
$100	1.00
$120	1.02
$140	1.06
$160	1.40
$180	1.36

   b. Add appropriate chart and axes titles to the line graph created for Exercise 4a.

5. Complete parts a-b.

   a. The number of air conditioners sold each year by one department in an outlet store is given below. Construct a line graph for this data as a chart object.

Year	1	2	3	4	5	6
Units	197	164	210	191	236	205

   b. Add the appropriate chart and axes titles to the line graph created for Exercise 5a.

6. Complete parts a-b.

   a. Construct a line graph, in its own chart sheet, for the sales data given below.

Year	1	2	3	4	5	6	7	8
Sales	$15,000	$18,000	$16,000	$20,000	$18,000	$22,000	$19,000	$24,000

   b. Add the appropriate chart and axes titles to the line graph created for Exercise 6a.

7. Complete parts a-b.

   a. The share of people in the world with water available from a protected source is given in the following table (*Source: World Health Organization*). Construct a line graph, as a chart object, for this data. (**Hint:** Code Year 1980 as 1, 1990 as 10, and so on.)

Year	1980	1990	2000	2010	2015
Percentage	58%	68%	76%	84%	88%

   b. Add the appropriate chart and axes titles to the line graph created for Exercise 7a.

8. Complete parts a-b.

    a. Construct a line graph for the following data in its own chart sheet (*Hint:* Code Year 2012 as 1, 2013 as 2, and so on).

Year	Revenue ($Millions)
2012	0.5
2013	1.6
2014	1.9
2015	0.8
2016	1.0
2017	2.2
2018	2.4
2019	3.0
2020	3.4

    b. Add the appropriate chart and axes titles to the line graph created for Exercise 8a.

5.5   TREND LINES AND SCATTER DIAGRAMS

In business, economics, and science, a line used to fit empirically obtained data is referred to as a *trend line*. A trend line can be linear, quadratic, exponential, or any other line that best fits the data. Mathematically, a best fit is accomplished by minimizing the total squared error between the trend line and the actual data.[8] The dotted line shown in Figure 5.29 is an example of a straight line trend line.

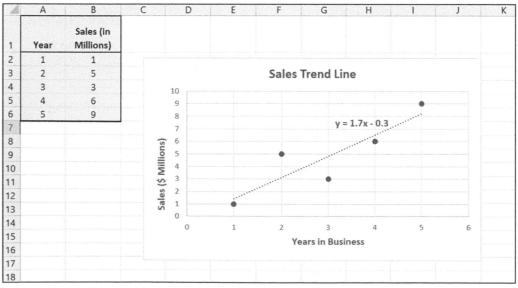

Figure 5.29 An example of a straight line trend line

---

[8] This procedure is known as the least-squares minimization method. Refer to *Mathematics for Business*, by Bronson, Bronson, and Kieff for a presentation of this method.

In constructing a trend line, the first step is to create a scatter diagram. A scatter diagram is a graph containing multiple data points, with no connecting lines between the points.[9] Figure 5.30 illustrates two examples of scatter diagrams. Trend lines are graphed on the resulting scatter diagram.

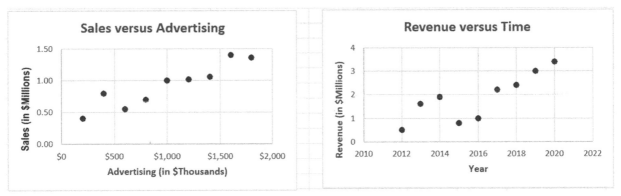

Figure 5.30 Examples of scatter diagrams

Creating a Scatter Diagram

Creating a scatter diagram requires that the data is first entered into either consecutive columns, as shown in the upper-left corner of Figure 5.31, or consecutive rows. The data is then highlighted, as shown as Step 1 in the figure, and the remaining steps listed in the figure are then completed.

Although any two consecutive columns or rows can be used for the data, when columns are used, the data entered in the left-most column become the x-axis values, and the data in the right-most column become the y-axis values. For data listed in the rows, the upper-most row data is plotted on the x axis and the lowest-row data on the y axis.

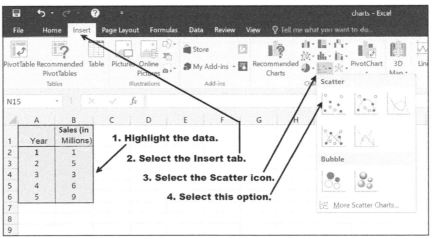

Figure 5.31 The steps required to produce a scatter diagram

---

[9] When the data points are connected with lines between them, the scatter diagram is referred to as a *line graph*. Connecting lines are not used so that they do not clutter the graph and obscure the trend line.

After selecting the scatter option listed as Step 4 in Figure 5.31, the scatter diagram shown in Figure 5.32 will appear. Notice that the figure has no axes titles and that the chart's title is a copy of the data label in cell B2, which identifies the y-axis values.

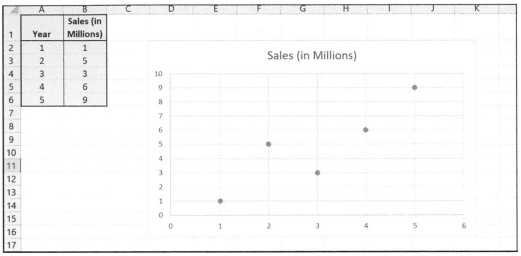

Figure 5.32 The scatter diagram created with the given data

Changing a Scatter Diagram's Elements and Appearance

Figure 5.33 shows the initial position and description of the descriptive Chart Elements associated with line graphs. These consist of a chart title, axes labels, legend, and grid lines. When any of the four textual elements are present (title, axes labels, and legend) the text, font type, and size of each of these elements can be changed by clicking on the desired element and directly entering new text and font attributes.

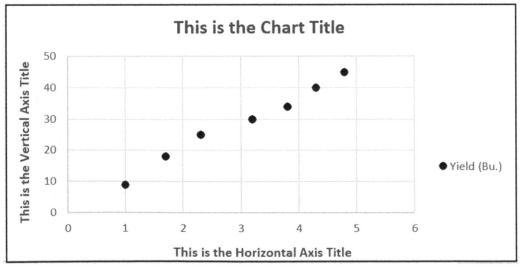

Figure 5.33 Scatter Diagram with labels

Adding or deleting a scatter diagram's title, axes labels, legend, and grid lines is done using the Chart Elements submenu shown in Figure 5.34. This submenu is activated by either clicking on the Chart Tools – Design menu, or right or left clicking within the chart itself (item 1 in the figure), and then selecting the cross-hairs icon (item 2 in the figure). Clicking on a chart element within the submenu adds the element to the chart, while clearing a checkbox removes the element.

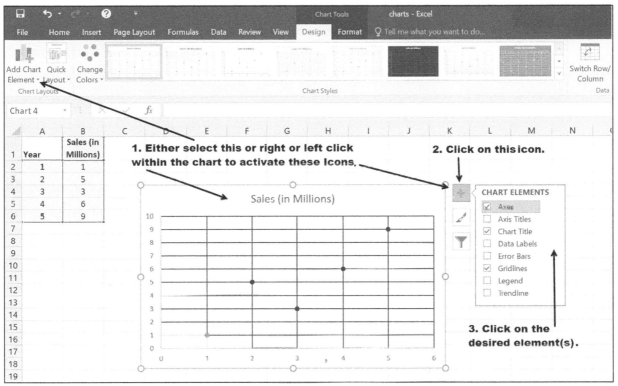

Figure 5.34 Adding or deleting chart elements

A scatter diagram's colors can be changed using the Change Colors option in the Excel ribbon Chart Tools Tab, Design submenu, as shown at the upper left in Figure 5.35. The Design submenu is activated either by double clicking within the chart or single clicking and then selecting the Design tab under the Chart Tools option (at the top of Figure 5.35).

For example, checking the Axis Titles and Legend checkboxes shown in Figure 5.34 produces the chart shown in Figure 5.35a. Simply double clicking within each element allows you to change the titles to those of your own choosing, including the font type and size. This was done to produce the titles shown in Figure 5.35b.

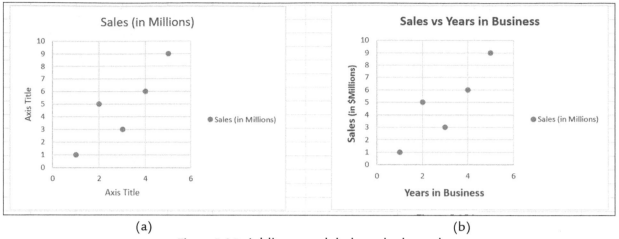

(a)   (b)

Figure 5.35 Adding axes labels and a legend

A scatter diagram's appearance is changed by selecting one of the chart styles shown within the Chart Tools - Design menu (see Figure 5.36). Clicking on any of the pre-constructed styles changes the chart to the selected choice. Note that the chart elements previously shown in Figure 5.34 can also be accessed and changed by clicking on the leftmost icon in the Chart Tools - Design menu.

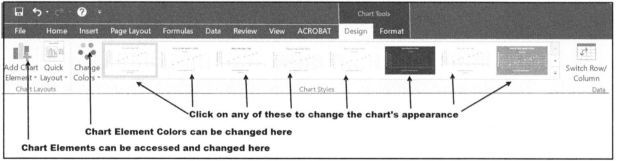

Figure 5.36 The Chart Tools Design ribbon

Adding a Trend Line

To add a trend line for the data shown on a scatter diagram, either click on the Add Chart Elements in the Chart Tools - Design Tools menu, as shown in Figure 5.37 (if this menu is not shown, double clicking anywhere within the scatter diagram causes it to be displayed), or click on the Chart Elements icon (if this icon is not displayed, either right or left clicking within the scatter diagram activates it). Either of these actions produces the submenus shown in Figure 5.37.

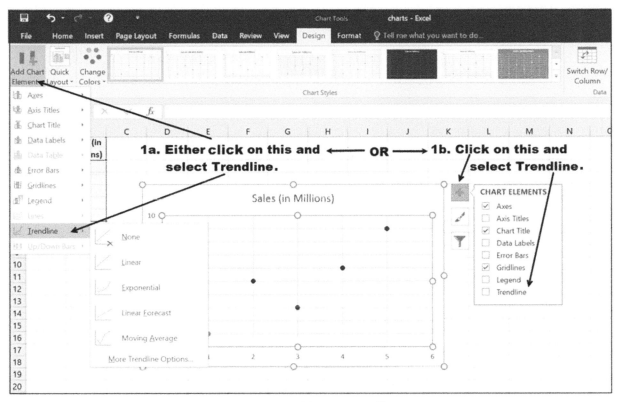

Figure 5.37 Adding a trendline

Clicking on the arrow to the right of the Trendline option from either of the submenus displayed in Figure 5.37 (hover over the Trendline option to activate the arrow) triggers the menu shown in Figure 5.38

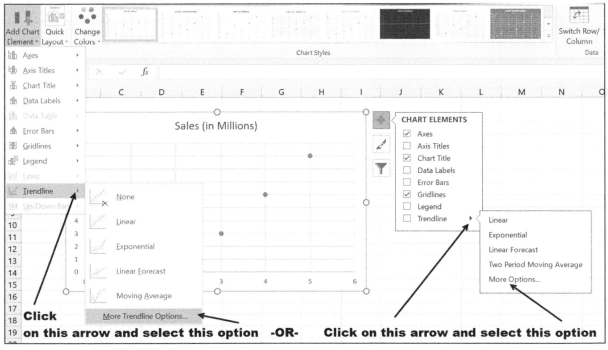

Figure 5.38 Selecting Trendline Chart Elements

When the Trendline drop-down menu shown in Figure 5.38 is displayed, you are ready to add the Trendline and its equation onto the scatter diagram. To do so, click on the last option, which is labeled More Trendline Options. Selecting this option will bring up the last menu needed, which is that shown on Figure 5.39.[10]

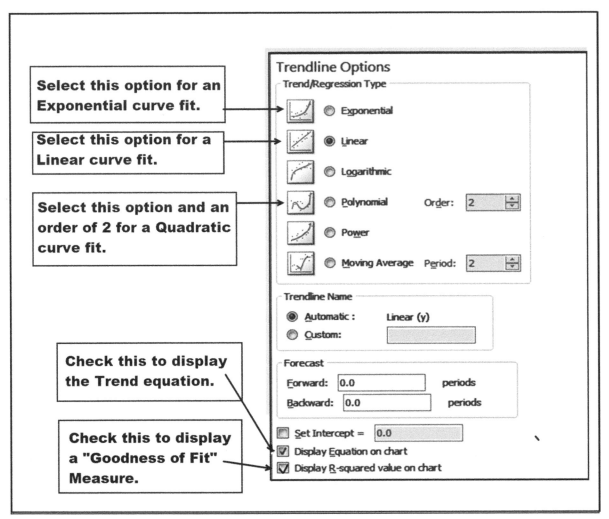

Figure 5.39 Trendline options

When the menu shown in Figure 5.39 is displayed, click on the desired trend line type as shown in the figure. Then check the *Display Equation on chart* and Display *R-squared value on chart* checkboxes at the bottom of the menu and click on the Close button. This will produce a display of the chosen trend line with its associated equation and R-squared value directly on the scatter diagram. Selecting a Linear Trend line for the Year and Sales data used throughout this example produces Figure 5.40.

---

[10] **Note:** Checking the Trendline box on the Chart Elements submenu immediately produces a linear trend with no equation.

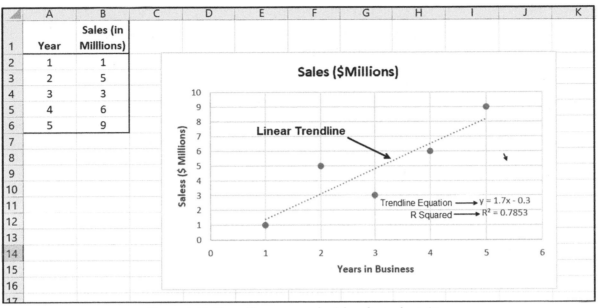

	A	B
1	Year	Sales (in Milllions)
2	1	1
3	2	5
4	3	3
5	4	6
6	5	9

Figure 5.40 Trendline created with selected options

R² and Selecting an Appropriate Trend Line

The example in this section illustrated modeling of the data using a linear trend line. In practice, the choice of which trend line to use is always based on the data itself. Thus, in practice, after a scatter diagram has been produced, the next step is to determine which, if any, of the curve types considered in this section best fits the data. The starting point is always the same. Use a scatter diagram to plot the data and then carefully examine the resulting plot.

Typically, a pattern develops. Based on the emergent pattern and knowledge of various curves, a curve type that appears to fit the data reasonably well is then selected. As shown in Figure 5.41, Excel provides a number of Trendline options.

Trendline Options

Trend/Regression Type

- Exponential
- ● Linear
- Logarithmic
- Polynomial   Order: 2
- Power
- Moving Average   Period: 2

Figure 5.41 Excel's Trendline options

Once a selection has been made, the Trendline is superimposed on the scatter diagram. The final step is then to determine whether the resulting line does, in fact, adequately model the data. It is here that the R^2 value, which is formally known as the *Coefficient of Determination*, is used.

Mathematically, an R^2 of 0 indicates that the variable plotted on the y-axis cannot be predicted from the value plotted on the x-axis. Similarly, an R^2 of 1 indicates that the variable on the y axis can be predicted, without error, from the corresponding value on the x axis, assuming all other variables remain the same. An R^2 between 0 and 1 indicates the degree to which the y-axis variable is predictable. Thus, an R^2 of 0.25 indicates that 25% of the y-axis value is predictable from x-axis value, and an R^2 of 0.80 means that 80% is predictable. In all cases, this requires that all other variables remain constant. Interestingly, the coefficient of determination, R^2, is the square of the Correlation Coefficient between the y-axis values and x-axis values.[11] An R^2 value of 1 indicates a perfect correlation, while a value of 0 indicates no correlation. ***It is important to understand that even if two quantities are perfectly correlated, correlation does not imply causation.*** All that correlation implies is that when one quantity occurs, the other quantity tends to occur to the degree indicated by the correlation coefficient. It never means that one quantity causes the other quantity to occur.

This chapter addressed a number of the commonly used chart types in Excel, and how to use the chart features within Excel to create charts, change charts, and enhance the charts that have been created. Besides the most commonly used kinds that were covered in detail in the chapter, there are other types available, some of which are variations of the basic types, and others which are more advanced or for specialized purposes. These types include area charts, radar charts, stock charts, waterfall charts, sunburst charts, and combo charts. You can consult various resources for more information on these other chart types.

---

[11] Although the correlation coefficient squared yields the coefficient of determination, the square root of the coefficient only provides the *value* of the correlation coefficient, not whether it is positive of negative. In addition to its value, correlation coefficients have a sign, either + or –, indicating either a positive or negative correlation, respectively.

EXERCISES 5.5

1. Construct a scatter diagram chart for the following data (chart object).

Year	Sales ($Millions)
1	0.5
2	1.7
3	1.9
4	1.4
5	1.6
6	2.0
7	2.2
8	2.4
9	2.9
10	3.3

2. Complete parts a-b.

a. Construct a scatter diagram for the following sales data (chart sheet).

Year	1	2	3	4	5	6	7	8
Sales	$15,000	$18,000	$16,000	$20,000	$18,000	$22,000	$19,000	$24,000

b. Add the appropriate chart and axes titles to the scatter diagram created for Exercise 2a.

3. Complete parts a-b.

a. The share of people in the world with water available from a protected source is given in the following table *(Source: World Health Organization)*. Construct a scatter diagram chart (chart object) for this data. (**Hint:** Code Year 1980 as 1, 1990 as 10, and so on.)

Year	1980	1990	2000	2010	2015
Percentage	58%	68%	76%	84%	88%

b. Add the appropriate chart and axes titles to the scatter diagram created for Exercise 3a.

4. Complete parts a-b.

a. Construct an Excel scatter diagram and a linear trend line for the following data (chart sheet).

x	0	1	2	3	4	5	6
y	1	5	8	7	12	14	13

b. Add the appropriate chart and axes titles to the scatter diagram created for Exercise 4a and make sure that the trend line's equation and R^2 value are shown on the chart.

5. Complete parts a-b.

a. Construct an Excel scatter diagram and a linear trend line for the following data (chart object).

x	0	1	2	3	4	5	6	7
y	36	49	55	56	67	69	76	85

b. Add the appropriate chart and axes titles to the scatter diagram created for Exercise 5a and make sure that the trend line's equation and R^2 value are shown on the chart.

6. Complete parts a-b.

a. Construct an Excel scatter diagram and a linear trend line for the following data (chart sheet).

Year	2014	2015	2016	2017	2018	2019	2020
Sales ($Thousands)	15	18	16	20	18	22	19

b. Add the appropriate chart and axes titles to the scatter diagram created for Exercise 6a and make sure that the trend line's equation and R^2 value are shown on the chart. (***Hint:*** Code Year 2014 as 1, 2015 as 2, and so on.)

7. Complete parts a-b.

a. Construct an Excel scatter diagram and a 2nd order polynomial (quadratic) trend line for the following data as a chart object.

x	-2	-1	0	1	2
y	10	11	15	16	23

b. Add the appropriate chart and axes titles to the scatter diagram created for Exercise 7a and make sure that the trend line's equation and R^2 value are shown on the chart.

8. Complete parts a-b.

   a. Construct an Excel scatter diagram and a 2nd order polynomial (quadratic) trend line for the following data as a chart sheet.

x	-3	-2	-1	0	1	2	3
y	8.1	2.9	0	-1	0	3.1	7.8

   b. Add the appropriate chart and axes titles to the scatter diagram created for Exercise 8a and make sure that the trend line's equation and R^2 value are shown on the chart.

9. Complete parts a-b.

   a. Construct an Excel scatter diagram and an exponential trend line for the following data (as a chart object).

x	0	1	2	3	4
y	2	16	90	500	2,500

   b. Add the appropriate chart and axes titles to the scatter diagram created for Exercise 9a, and make sure that the trend line's equation and R^2 value are shown on the chart.

10. Complete parts a-b.

   a. Construct an Excel scatter diagram and an exponential trend line for the following data (chart sheet).

x	0	1	2	3	4	5
y	16	20	38	60	90	130

   b. Add the appropriate chart and axes titles to the scatter diagram created for Exercise 10a, and make sure that the trend line's equation and R^2 value are shown on the chart.

11. Complete parts a-c.

   a. Construct an Excel scatter diagram and an exponential trend line for the following data (chart object).

Year	0	1	2	3	4
Sales ($1,000)	0.9	2.9	9.5	28.8	100

   b. Add the appropriate chart and axes titles to the scatter diagram created for Exercise 11a, and make sure that the trend line's equation and R^2 value are shown on the chart.

   c. Use the trend equation found in Exercise 11a to project sales for the 6th year.

12. Complete parts a-c.

    a. Construct an Excel scatter diagram and an exponential trend line for the following data as a chart sheet (***Hint:*** Code Year 2014 as 1, 2015 as 2, and so on).

Year	2016	2017	2018	2019	2020
Population	4,953	7,398	11,023	16,445	24,532

    b. Add the appropriate chart and axes titles to the scatter diagram created for Exercise 12a, and make sure that the trend line's equation and R^2 value are shown on the chart.

    c. Use the trend equation found in Exercise 12a to project the population in 2022.

13. Complete parts a-b.

    a. Using R^2 values, determine whether a linear, quadratic, or exponential trend line best fits the following data.

Years in Business	1	2	3	4	5
Sales ($Millions)	10	14	26	38	55

    b. Use the trend line found to be best in Exercise 13a to project sales for the company's 6th and 7th year in business.

5.6 COMMON EXCEL ERRORS

Errors common to the material presented in this section are:

1. Not realizing how much visual elements such as charts and graphs add to a presentation and, thus, not making the maximum use of them.

2. Not adding the R^2 value to trend lines superimposed on scatter diagrams. The R^2 value provides important information as to the validity of the trend line.

3. Mistaking correlation with causation. It is extremely important to understand that even if two variables are 100% correlated, *it does not mean* that one variable causes the other.

5.7 CHAPTER APPENDIX: CREATING HISTOGRAMS

A *histogram* is a specialized bar graph used to display the frequency (that is, how often something happens) in successive groups of equal size, such as 10-19 or 20-29. The individual groups are generally known as *bins*, and are also termed "intervals" or "buckets." As an example, consider Figure 5.42, which shows the distribution of student ages from 17 to 21. The first column in the figure lists the ages that will be analyzed and charted, while the second column lists the upper value of the bin. A bin's values are determined to be the values below the upper value, but higher than the next upper value bin number.

In Figure 5.42, only the data and bin values are entered. The Bin/Frequency table and histogram chart were produced using Excel's Histogram option.

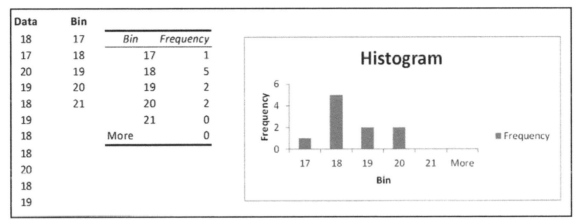

Figure 5.42 Histogram with the bin and frequency

As noted above, the only data entered in the spreadsheet used to produce Figure 5.42 are the data and bin values listed in the first two columns, one for the data and one for the bins, and consist of the following:

- **Data Column:** This is your data. It will be analyzed and displayed in the histogram.
- **Bin Column:** A bin value represents the upper bound for the bin. Bin values must be in increasing order. The difference between two successive values represents the bin's range.

Each bin value sets the upper bound for the bin. When you create a histogram, a data value is included in a bin if it is less than or equal to the bin's value (thus, it is the bin's upper bound) and greater than the prior bin's value (thus, this is the lower bound for the current bin).[12] Thus, in Figure 5.42, the first bin will contain the number of students up to 17 years of age, the second bin will contain the number of students between 17 and 18 years of age, and so on.

There are two procedures for creating a histogram; the first works with all Excel versions, the second was introduced in Excel 2016. All that is required for the first procedure are the data and bin columns, as shown in Figure 5.42. From this data, the procedure calculates and displays both a bin and frequency table and a histogram, examples of which are shown in Figure 5.42. The second method requires you to first

---

[12] If a bin range is omitted, Excel will create a set of evenly distributed bins between the minimum and maximum values of the data.

create a bin and frequency table and uses the data in this table to create the histogram. As the separate creation of a bin and frequency table is typically accomplished using Excel's advanced array processing formulas, this method is not presented.

Procedure to Produce a Histogram in All Excel Versions

Before you can create a histogram in Excel, you need to load the Analysis ToolPak add-in into Excel. This can be accomplished by going to the File tab on the ribbon, selecting Options, then Add Ins on the Excel Options submenu; selecting the Analysis ToolPak option, then click OK. When you enable this Add In, then you will be presented with a new option on the Data Tab, Analysis group, named "Data Analysis." Once loaded, then you will be able to start creating histograms.

The first step in creating a histogram is to click on the main menu's Data tab and then click the Data Ribbon's Data Analysis option, as shown on Figure 5.43. This activates the Data Analysis sub-menu. From this menu select the Histogram option, noted as callout 3 in the figure.

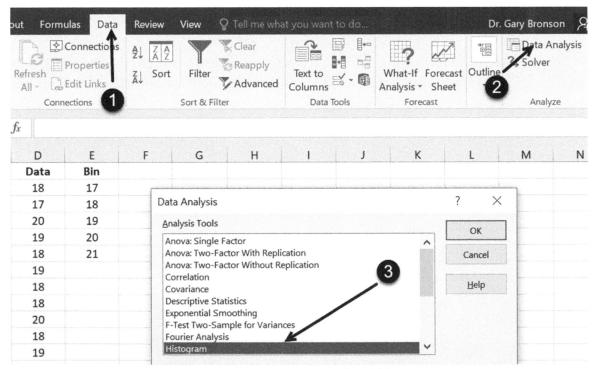

Figure 5.43 Steps to start creating a histogram

Selecting the Histogram option causes the Histogram dialog box, shown in Figure 5.44, to be displayed. It is within this dialog that the location of the input data and bin specifications are entered. Both of these data must be located in columns. If these columns have headers, the Labels box must be checked.

To view the histogram on the same spreadsheet as the data, both the Chart Output box and Chart Output range must also be checked, as indicated in callout 3.

Omitting these, only the bins and the number of data points in each bin are displayed and not the histogram chart itself. To locate the histogram, only the upper left cell of the output needs to be entered.

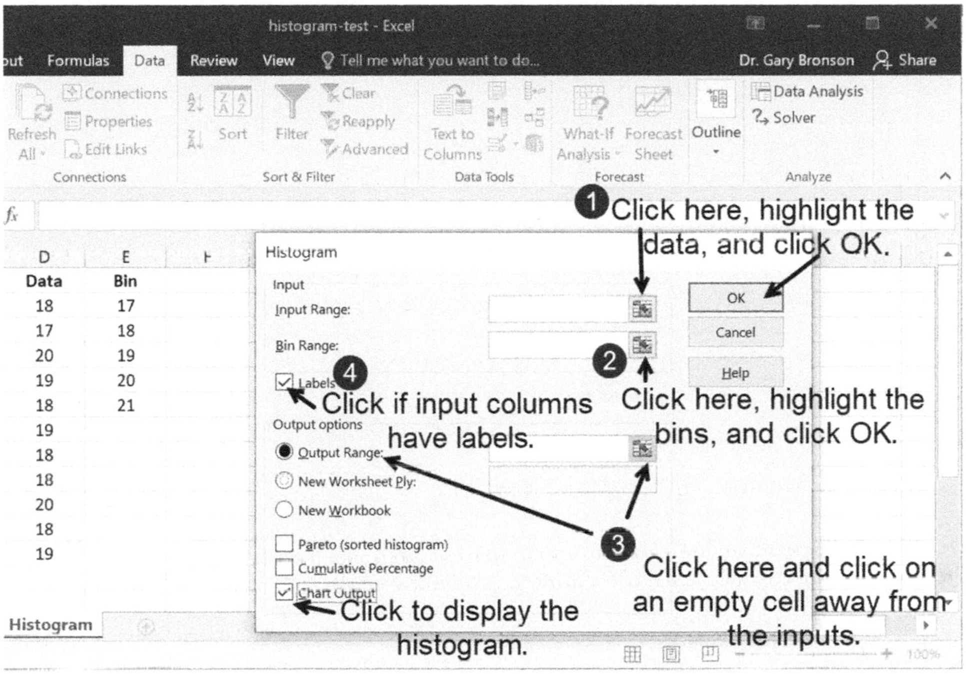

Figure 5.44 Options for the histogram

Figure 5.45 illustrates the information filled in for the Histogram dialog box that produced the display previously shown in Figure 5.42.

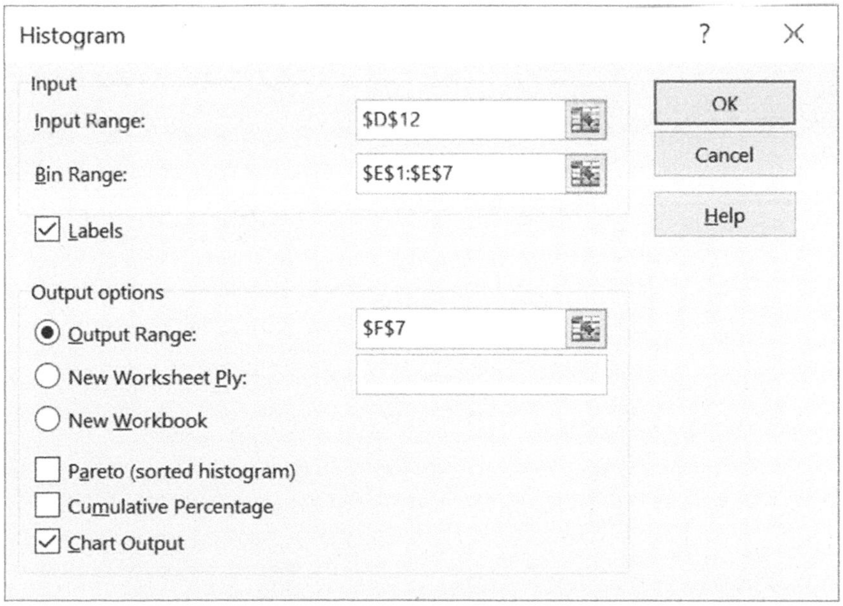

Figure 5.45 The information that produced the display in Figure 5.42

PIVOTTABLES

In addition to visually highlighting significant relationships using graphs and charts, the vast majority of business and scientific reports also include summary tables. In Excel, summary tables are known as **PivotTables** (one word). A PivotTable can automatically sort, count, sum, and average the data in one spreadsheet, and display these summary results in a second spreadsheet. The summary tables provided by Excel's PivotTable option are easy to produce: two clicks start the process, and one or more additional clicks produces a complete summary table. This chapter presents the basics of creating and modifying PivotTables.

6.1   INTRODUCTION

One of the more powerful Excel features is its ability to quickly and easily create summary tables. Summary tables play an important part in almost all business and research reports for highlighting significant relationships and important details. Summary tables are essential when an underlying spreadsheet may contain hundreds of rows and multiple columns containing several types of data, which is typical of many business and research databases.

The ability to rapidly create comprehensive summary tables is provided by Excel's **PivotTable** option. The name itself refers to the ability to switch, or *pivot*, from row summaries to column summaries. Unfortunately, the term PivotTable masks other important aspects of this feature, including the ability to quickly create convenient and easily understood summary tables.

As an example, consider the spreadsheet shown in Figure 6.1. The data is simply a detailed listing of individual sales in date order; it does not provide any specific or easily-understood summaries.

Order No	Date	Sales Person	Mall Location	Product	Quantity	Unit Price	Sale
261-10010	1/7	A. Smith	Oak Ridge	Lounge Chair	3	$425	$1,275
322-10010	1/10	H. Smith	Oak Ridge	Sofa	4	$895	$3,580
265-10010	1/20	D. Shea	Oak Ridge	Straight Chair	8	$370	$2,960
282-10010	1/22	T. Wang	Oak Ridge	Tables	5	$580	$2,900
282-10011	2/4	T. Wang	Oak Ridge	Ottoman	2	$125	$250
322-10011	2/6	H. Smith	Oak Ridge	Recliner	1	$675	$675
261-10011	2/10	A. Smith	Freeman Ave.	Lounge Chair	6	$425	$2,550
265-10011	2/16	D. Shea	Freeman Ave.	Rocking Chair	5	$230	$1,150
322-10012	2/18	H. Smith	Freeman Ave.	Table	2	$580	$1,160
322-10013	2/22	H. Smith	Freeman Ave.	Recliner	3	$675	$2,025
265-10012	2/25	D. Shea	Oak Ridge	Rocking Chair	1	$230	$230
282-10012	2/25	T. Wang	Freeman Ave.	Ottoman	1	$125	$125
282-10012	2/25	T. Wang	Freeman Ave.	Straight Chair	4	$370	$1,480

Figure 6.1 The initial sales spreadsheet

To see how various summary tables can display meaningful information from the raw data in Figure 6.1, consider the summary tables shown in Figures 6.2 through 6.5.

Figure 6.2 provides a summary of total sales for each product. This summary table was produced using only four mouse clicks (an additional two mouse clicks produced the formatting of the second column).

Row Labels	Sum of Sale
A. Smith	$3,825
D. Shea	$4,340
H. Smith	$7,440
T. Wang	$4,755
Grand Total	$20,360

Figure 6.2 Summary of total sales by salesperson

Figure 6.3 provides a quick summary of total sales for each salesperson. Again, this summary table was produced using only four mouse clicks, with an additional two clicks needed for the second column's currency formatting. The only difference in producing Figures 6.2 and 6.3 was that in Figure 6.2, the Sales Person field was used for the row field, while for Figure 6.3 the Product field was selected for the row field. The Sale sums in each figure were automatically calculated to correspond to its respective row field.

Row Labels	Sum of Sale
Lounge Chair	$3,825
Ottoman	$375
Recliner	$2,700
Rocking Chair	$1,380
Sofa	$3,580
Straight Chair	$4,440
Table	$4,060
Grand Total	$20,360

Figure 6.3 Summary of total sales by product

Although Figures 6.2 and 6.3 consist of only two columns, more complicated, but equally easily-produced summary tables can be created. For example, with one more mouse click, Figure 6.3 is expanded to Figure 6.4. This table not only provides total sales for each salesperson, but additionally lists the individual products sold by the salesperson. It should be noted that "Sum of Sale" refers to the calculation of total sales for each combination of Sales Person and Product. The Sales Person is found in rows, and the Product in columns.

Sum of Sale Row Label	Column Label Lounge Chair	Ottoman	Recliner	Rocking Chair	Sofa	Straight Chair	Table	Grand Total
A. Smith	$3,825							$3,825
D. Shea				$1,380		$2,960		$4,340
H. Smith			$2,700		$3,580		$1,160	$7,440
T. Wang		$375				$1,480	$2,900	$4,755
Grand Total	$3,825	$375	$2,700	$1,380	$3,580	$4,440	$4,060	$20,360

Figure 6.4 Summary of sales by salesperson and product

Again, using one more mouse click, Figure 6.4 is expanded into Figure 6.5, which further breaks out total sales for each salesperson by mall location and product.

Sum of Sale Row Labels	Column Labels Lounge Chair	Ottoman	Recliner	Rocking Chair	Sofa	Straight Chair	Table	Grand Total
A. Smith	$3,825							$3,825
Freeman Ave.	$2,550							$2,550
Oak Ridge	$1,275							$1,275
D. Shea				$1,380		$2,960		$4,340
Freeman Ave.				$1,150				$1,150
Oak Ridge				$230		$2,960		$3,190
H. Smith			$2,700		$3,580		$1,160	$7,440
Freeman Ave.			$2,025				$1,160	$3,185
Oak Ridge			$675		$3,580			$4,255
T. Wang		$375				$1,480	$2,900	$4,755
Freeman Ave.		$125				$1,480		$1,605
Oak Ridge		$250					$2,900	$3,150
Grand Total	$3,825	$375	$2,700	$1,380	$3,580	$4,440	$4,060	$20,360

Figure 6.5 Summary of sales by salesperson, location, and product

The degrees and types of summary reports that can be produced using PivotTable features are almost endless. Interestingly, the procedures for creating PivotTables, such as those shown in Figures 6.2 through 6.5, are not difficult or involved. In creating basic summary tables, however, you need to understand the elements that make up a PivotTable's rows and columns.

Basic PivotTable Elements

There are four main elements provided for constructing PivotTables. These are

- Row fields
- Column fields
- Value fields
- Report Filter fields

The first three of these field types and how they are used to create PivotTables are described in detail in this chapter.

Many useful, yet simple, PivotTables, such as those shown in Figures 6.2 and 6.3 can be constructed using only a single Row field and a single Value field (the third field type, Column, is used in Figures 6.4 and 6.5 and explained in Section 6.3). From an applications viewpoint, the two required column types for a basic PivotTable consist of

- A *Row Labels* column (created as a Row Field with at least one required)
- A *Summary* column (created as a Value Field with at least one required)

The headings for each of these columns come from the column headings in the original spreadsheet. These headings are formally referred to as *fields*. Using Excel's PivotTable terminology, a Row Label is a specific row field, and a Summary column is a specific value field.

For example, if a summary table (that is, a PivotTable) is required for the spreadsheet shown in Figure 6.6, the available fields for the PivotTable are the six column headings shown at the top of the figure.

These are the fields

Date	Sales Person	Mall Location	Sale	Quantity	Product
1/7	A. Smith	Oak Ridge	$1,275	3	Lounge Chair
1/10	H. Smith	Oak Ridge	$3,580	4	Sofa
1/20	D. Shea	Oak Ridge	$2,960	8	Straight Chair
1/22	T. Wang	Oak Ridge	$2,900	5	Tables
2/4	T. Wang	Oak Ridge	$250	2	Ottoman
2/6	H. Smith	Oak Ridge	$675	1	Recliner
2/10	A. Smith	Freeman Ave.	$2,550	6	Lounge Chair
2/16	D. Shea	Freeman Ave.	$1,150	5	Rocking Chair
2/18	H. Smith	Freeman Ave.	$1,160	2	Table
2/22	H. Smith	Freeman Ave.	$2,025	3	Recliner
2/25	D. Shea	Oak Ridge	$230	1	Rocking Chair
2/25	T. Wang	Freeman Ave.	$125	1	Ottoman
2/25	T. Wang	Freeman Ave.	$1,480	4	Straight Chair

Figure 6.6 The column headings become a PivotTable's fields

Figure 6.7 shows how two of the fields shown in Figure 6.6 become the elements of a two column PivotTable.

Row Labels Column
(from SalesPerson field)

Summary Column
(from Sale field)

Row Labels	Sum of Sale
A. Smith	$3,825
D. Shea	$4,340
H. Smith	$7,440
T. Wang	$4,755
Grand Total	$20,360

Figure 6.7 PivotTable with a Row Label and Summary column

The labels in the *Row Labels* column (also known as a *row fields* column), which is typically the first column in a basic PivotTable, consists of the data in one of the original spreadsheet columns. A *Summary* column, technically referred to as a *values* column, is created from the values contained in a second selected field.

Although the basic two column PivotTable shown in Figure 6.7 is useful for a wide variety of summary tables, additional row fields, Column fields, a Report Filter field, and Value/Summary fields can easily be included. For example, Figure 6.8 shows a PivotTable with two Row Label fields (Sales Person and Mall Location) and two Summary columns (Sale and Quantity). Each Set of Row Label fields and each set of Summary fields requires a single mouse click selection (they may also be "dragged and dropped," as explained in the next section.)

Row Labels	Sum of Sale	Sum of Quantity
A. Smith	$3,825	9
Freeman Ave.	$2,550	6
Oak Ridge	$1,275	3
D. Shea	$4,340	14
Freeman Ave.	$1,150	5
Oak Ridge	$3,190	9
H. Smith	$7,440	10
Freeman Ave.	$3,185	5
Oak Ridge	$4,255	5
T. Wang	$4,755	12
Freeman Ave.	$1,605	5
Oak Ridge	$3,150	7
Grand Total	$20,360	45

Figure 6.8 A two element PivotTable, each with multiple categories

The initial field in the Row Labels column is referred to as the *Primary Row Field*. This distinction becomes important when more than one set of row fields is selected. For example, notice that in Figure 6.8 there is a second set of row fields. These row fields do not form a new column, but are indented under the Primary Row fields. When a second set of Row Labels is included, it is referred to as a *Subsidiary Row Field (level)*. Figure 6.9 identifies the various elements in the expanded PivotTable shown in Figure 6.8.

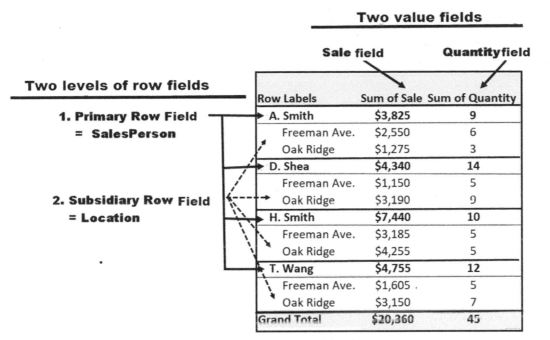

Figure 6.9 PivotTable elements

Although any number of subsidiary row field levels can be added to a PivotTable, as a practical matter and to keep a central focus on what is being summarized, generally no more than two subsidiary row label levels, in general, should be used. If more row labels are needed, it may at times be better to create a second PivotTable.

Finally, notice that while a Row Label field almost always contains text (or numeric labels like dates, for example), Summary columns generally contain numeric values (hence, the PivotTable terminology *value fields*). In addition to computing totals in a Summary/Value column, PivotTable options provide for calculating counts, averages, maximums, minimums, and other statistical values for the summarized data.

EXERCISES 6.1

1. What is the purpose of a PivotTable?

2. In addition to the row fields used in Tables 6.2 and 6.3, list two other sets of row fields that could have been used to summarize Total Sales shown in Figure 6.1.

3. In addition to summarizing the Total Sales of each product as shown in Tables 6.2 what additional value fields might be useful?

4. a. What is a Primary Row Field?

b. What is a Subsidiary Row Field level?

c. What type of data is summarized in the columns to the right of the row fields column?

5. Create the following spreadsheet on your computer.

Order No	Date	Sales Person	Mall Location	Product	Quantity	Unit Price	Sale
261-10010	1/7	A. Smith	Oak Ridge	Lounge Chair	3	$425	$1,275
322-10010	1/10	H. Smith	Oak Ridge	Sofa	4	$895	$3,580
265-10010	1/20	D. Shea	Oak Ridge	Straight Chair	8	$370	$2,960
282-10010	1/22	T. Wang	Oak Ridge	Tables	5	$580	$2,900
282-10011	2/4	T. Wang	Oak Ridge	Ottoman	2	$125	$250
322-10011	2/6	H. Smith	Oak Ridge	Recliner	1	$675	$675
261-10011	2/10	A. Smith	Freeman Ave.	Lounge Chair	6	$425	$2,550
265-10011	2/16	D. Shea	Freeman Ave.	Rocking Chair	5	$230	$1,150
322-10012	2/18	H. Smith	Freeman Ave.	Table	2	$580	$1,160
322-10013	2/22	H. Smith	Freeman Ave.	Recliner	3	$675	$2,025
265-10012	2/25	D. Shea	Oak Ridge	Rocking Chair	1	$230	$230
282-10012	2/25	T. Wang	Freeman Ave.	Ottoman	1	$125	$125
282-10012	2/25	T. Wang	Freeman Ave.	Straight Chair	4	$370	$1,480

6. Using the spreadsheet created in Exercise 5, produce a table, without using Excel's PivotTable option, that lists each salesperson and their individual total sales. When you are done, your spreadsheet should look like the one that follows. (In the next section, you will see how easily this list is produced using Excel's PivotTable feature.)

Row Labels	Sum of Sale
A. Smith	$3,825
D. Shea	$4,340
H. Smith	$7,440
T. Wang	$4,755
Grand Total	$20,360

7. Using the spreadsheet created in Exercise 6, produce a table, without using Excel's PivotTable options, that lists each product and the total sales for each product. When you are done, your spreadsheet should look like the one that follows. (In the next section, you will see how easily this list is produced using Excel's PivotTable feature.)

Row Labels	Sum of Sale
Lounge Chair	$3,825
Ottoman	$375
Recliner	$2,700
Rocking Chair	$1,380
Sofa	$3,580
Straight Chair	$4,440
Table	$4,060
Grand Total	$20,360

6.2   CREATING A BASIC PIVOTTABLE

All PivotTables are created using the same three-step procedure. Once these steps are completed, a specific PivotTable can be constructed. The initial three steps are as follows:

Step 1: Highlight the original spreadsheet (for large spreadsheets, click on any cell and press Ctrl-A).

Step 2: Select the PivotTable option from the Excel ribbon **Insert Tab – Table group – PivotTable**, as shown in Figure 6.10.

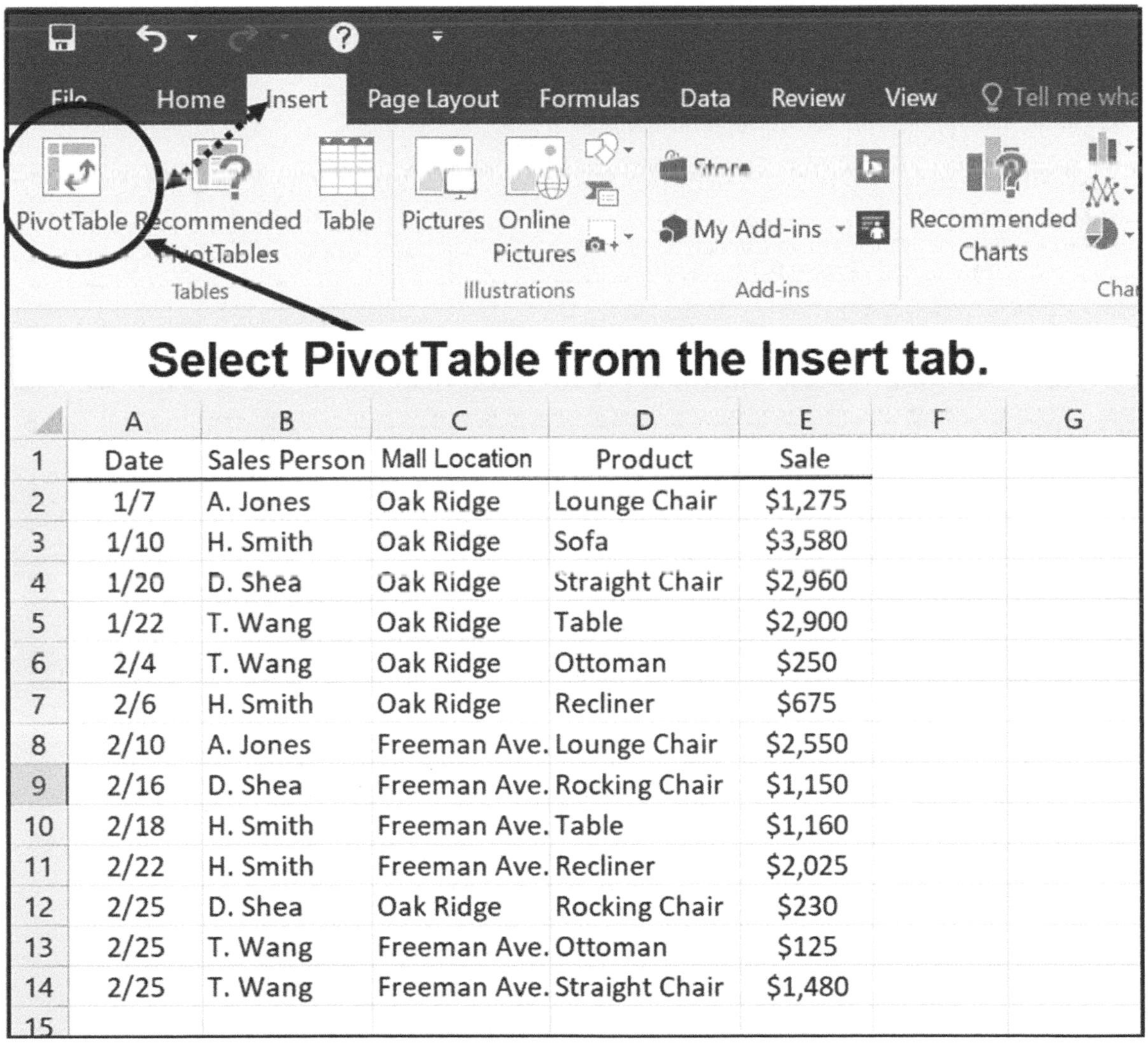

Figure 6.10 Starting to Create a PivotTable

Step 3: Fill in the PivotTable location in the Create PivotTable dialog box, as shown in Figure 6.11.

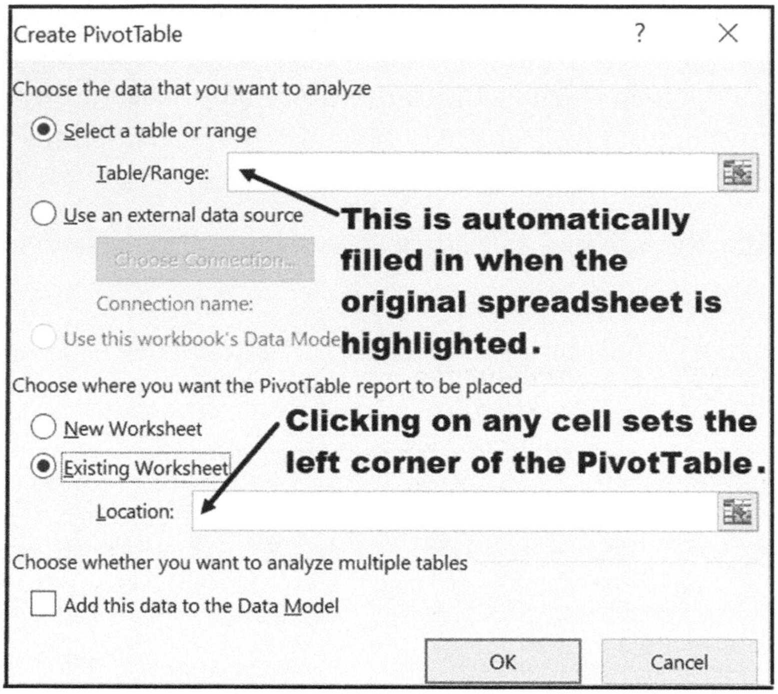

Figure 6.11 Selecting options for the PivotTable

Once the required locations are entered in the Create PivotTable dialog box shown in Figure 6.11 and the OK button is pressed, the displays shown in Figures 6.12 and 6.13 appear.

The display shown in Figure 6.12 is a blank PivotTable located at the address previously entered into the Create PivotTable dialog box. It is a placeholder showing you where your PivotTable will appear when completed. Except for noticing its position, you can safely move on to the next part of the PivotTable Fields dialog.

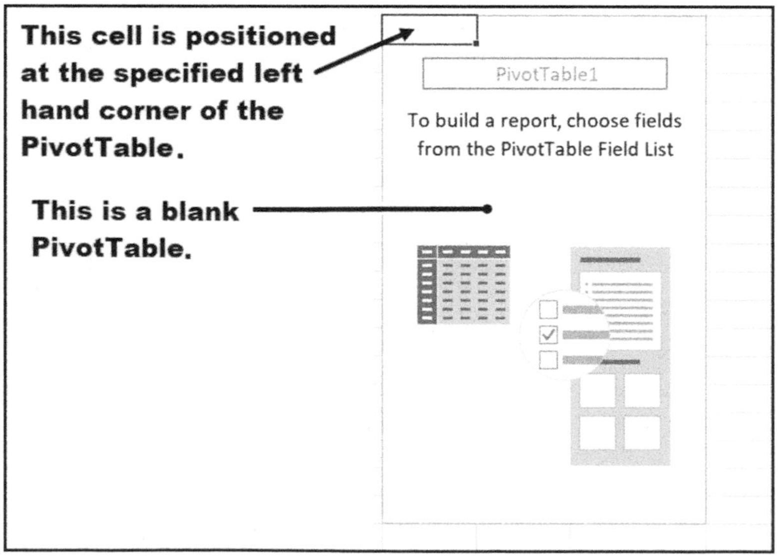

Figure 6.12 The blank PivotTable displayed on the left side of the screen

The PivotTable Fields dialog box shown in Figure 6.13, however, is extremely important. This dialog is where you select the fields that become your PivotTable's Row Labels, Summary/value columns, and Column Labels.

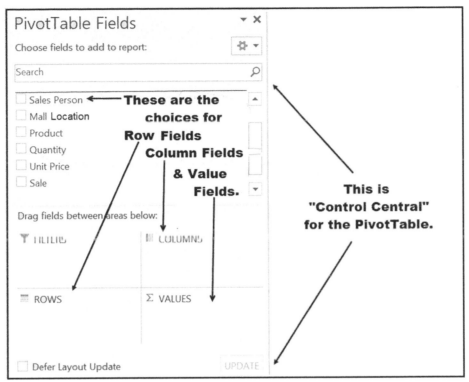

Figure 6.13 The PivotTable Fields selection dialog box displayed on the right side of the screen

To create a simple PivotTable, the only two field selection boxes required are those circled in Figure 6.14. A single field entry into each of these boxes is sufficient to create a simple, but meaningful PivotTable.

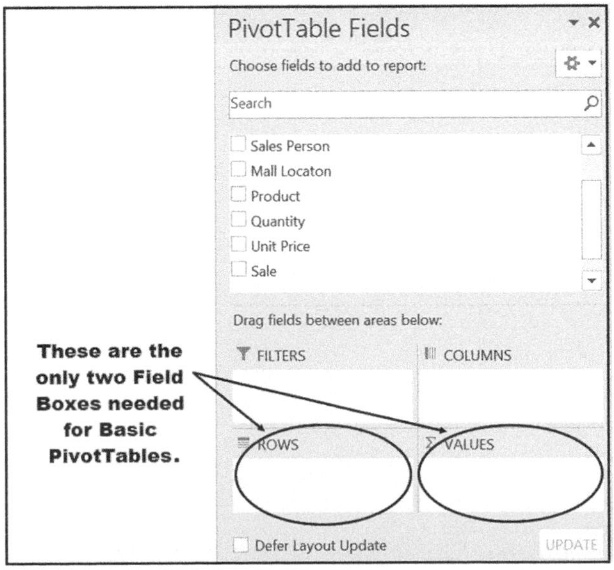

Figure 6.14 The two basic field selection boxes

Application Note
Deleting a PivotTable

There will be times when, rather than modifying an existing PivotTable, you may want to simply delete the entire table and start over. The steps necessary to do this are as follows:

a. Click on any cell within the PivotTable to bring up the PivotTable Tools menu – Analyze submenu.

b. Follow the four steps shown on the figure below.

c. Click the Delete key

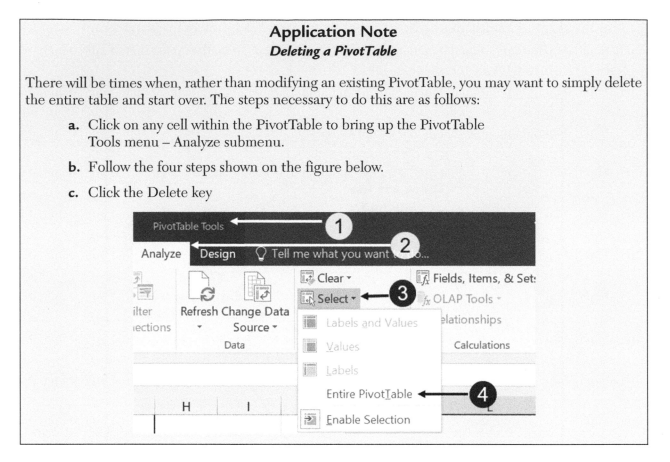

For example, the PivotTable in the left-hand corner of Figure 6.15 was created using only two mouse clicks. Clicking on the Product Field filled in the entry in the ROWS field selection box, while clicking in the Sale field filled in the VALUES selection box.

NOTE

The correct box is selected because Excel considers by default, all text categories as Row fields (and will place the clicked text field into the ROWS selection box) and numerical categories as Value Fields (which will place the clicked numeric field into the VALUES selections box). Alternatively, each of these fields could have been dragged and dropped into the desired selection box.

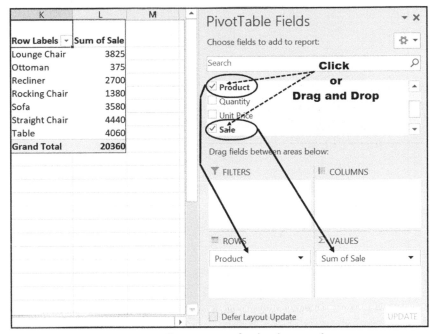

Figure 6.15 Summary of sales by product

Additional Row and Summary Column Examples

While many useful PivotTables can be produced using one or two row fields and one or more value fields, often it is necessary to employ additional column, row, report filter, and value fields.

Each row field is placed into a PivotTable either by clicking on a desired field or dragging and dropping it into the row selection box, as shown in Figure 6.15. Unless otherwise indicated, any clicked text field is considered by default to be a row field.

In the same manner as row fields, each value field is created by either clicking on a desired field or by dragging and dropping it into the Σ VALUES selection box, as shown in Figure 6.15. By default, any clicked numerical field is considered to be a value field, unless you specify otherwise.

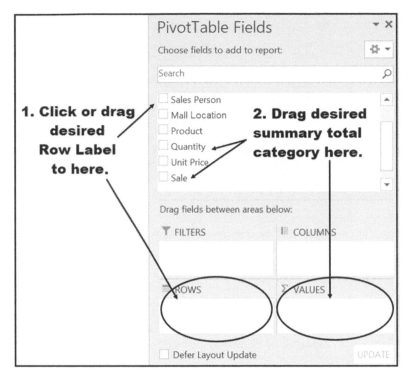

Figure 6.16 PivotTable row and value field inputs

The following are four examples of tables having differing numbers of row fields and value fields. The first example illustrates a PivotTable having a single row field and a single value field. The next two examples show how to add additional row fields and value fields independently of each other. Finally, the last example illustrates a Pivot-Table having both multiple row fields and multiple value fields.

All of the following examples summarize data from the following spreadsheet.

	A	B	C	D	E	F	G
1	Date	Sales Person	Mall Locaton	Product	Quantity	Unit Price	Sale
2	1/7	A. Smith	Oak Ridge	Lounge Chair	3	$425	$1,275
3	1/10	H. Smith	Oak Ridge	Sofa	4	$895	$3,580
4	1/20	D. Shea	Oak Ridge	Straight Chair	8	$370	$2,960
5	1/22	T. Wang	Oak Ridge	Table	5	$580	$2,900
6	2/4	T. Wang	Oak Ridge	Ottoman	2	$125	$250
7	2/6	H. Smith	Oak Ridge	Recliner	1	$675	$675
8	2/10	A. Smith	Freeman Ave.	Lounge Chair	6	$425	$2,550
9	2/16	D. Shea	Freeman Ave.	Rocking Chair	5	$230	$1,150
10	2/18	H. Smith	Freeman Ave.	Table	2	$580	$1,160
11	2/22	H. Smith	Freeman Ave.	Recliner	3	$675	$2,025
12	2/25	D. Shea	Oak Ridge	Rocking Chair	1	$230	$230
13	2/25	T. Wang	Freeman Ave.	Ottoman	1	$125	$125
14	2/25	T. Wang	Freeman Ave.	Straight Chair	4	$370	$1,480

Figure 6.17 Sales data

Example 1

Single Row Field and Single Value Field

The PivotTable shown in Figure 6.18a consists of one row field and one value field. Determine the options in the PivotTable Fields dialog box needed to produce this PivotTable.

Row Labels	Sum of Sale
Freeman Ave.	$8,490
Oak Ridge	$11,870
Grand Total	$20,360

Figure 6.18a Summary of sales by mall location

Solution: Figure 6.18b shows the PivotTable Fields dialog box used to produce Figure 6.18a. Note that the Currency format, within centered columns, was produced after creating the PivotTable, using the PivotTable Value Field Settings dialog box.

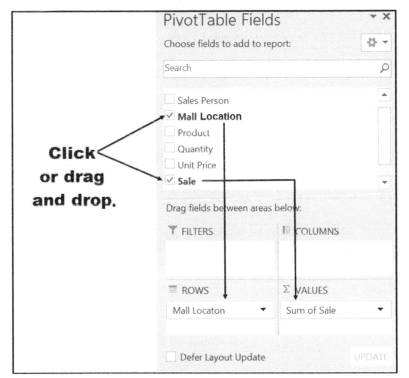

Figure 6.18b The PivotTable Fields dialog box used to create Figure 6.18a

Example 2

Multiple Row Fields and Single Value Fields

The PivotTable shown in Figure 6.19a consists of two row fields and one value field. Determine the options in the PivotTable Fields dialog box needed to produce this PivotTable.

Row Labels	Sum of Sale
Freeman Ave.	**$8,490**
Lounge Chair	$2,550
Ottoman	$125
Recliner	$2,025
Rocking Chair	$1,150
Straight Chair	$1,480
Table	$1,160
Oak Ridge	**$11,870**
Lounge Chair	$1,275
Ottoman	$250
Recliner	$675
Rocking Chair	$230
Sofa	$3,580
Straight Chair	$2,960
Table	$2,900
Grand Total	**$20,360**

Figure 6.19a Summary of sales by mall location and product

Solution: Figure 6.19b shows the PivotTable Fields dialog used to produce Figure 6.19a. Note that the Currency format, within centered columns, was produced after creating the PivotTable, using the PivotTable Fields dialog box.

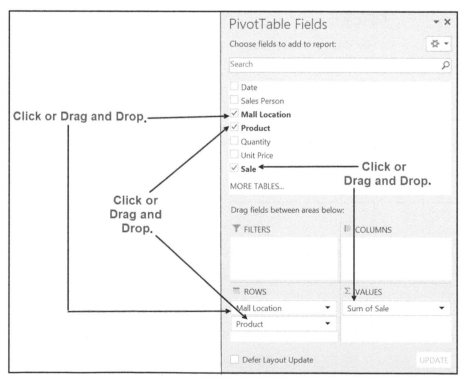

Figure 6.19b The PivotTable Fields dialog box to create Figure 6.19a

Example 3

Single Row Fields and Multiple Value Fields

The PivotTable shown in Figure 6.20a consists of one row field and two value fields. Determine the options in the PivotTable Fields dialog box needed to produce this PivotTable.

Row Labels	Sum of Sale	Sum of Quantity
Freeman Ave.	$8,490	21
Oak Ridge	$11,870	24
Grand Total	$20,360	45

Figure 6.20a Summary of sales and quantity by mall location

Solution: Figure 6.20b shows the PivotTable Fields dialog box used to produce Figure 6.20a. Note that the Currency format, within centered columns, was produced after creating the PivotTable, using the PivotTable Fields dialog.

While more of a PivotTable formatting issue, you will note the Σ **VALUES** entry in the Columns box below. This indicates that the two value fields are being displayed from the columns (vertically), rather than from the rows (horizontally).

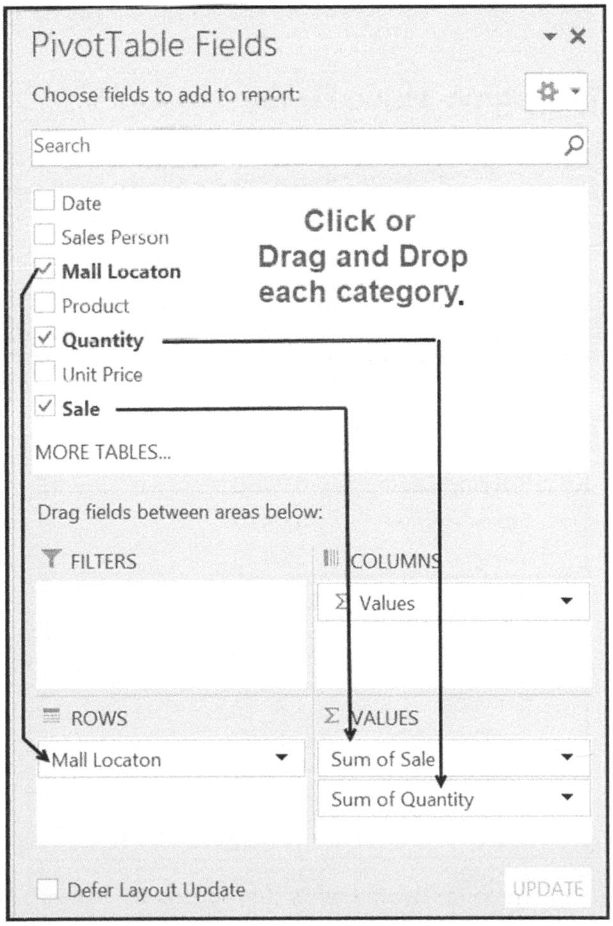

Figure 6.20b The PivotTable Fields dialog box used to create Figure 6.20a

---

Application Note
Changing Summary Field Calculations

In addition to calculating totals, other measures, such as averages, counts, maximums, and minimums, can be summarized using the value field. These other measures are obtained by ① clicking on the drop-down arrow to the right of a selected summary field in the Σ VALUES box, ② choosing the *Value Field Settings* option from the resulting drop-down menu, and ③ clicking on the desired summary measure, as shown in the Figure below.

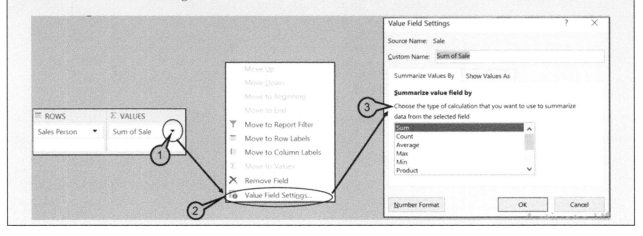

Example 4

Multiple Row Fields and Multiple Value Fields

The PivotTable shown in Figure 6.21a consists of two sets of row fields and two value fields. Determine the options in the PivotTable Fields dialog box needed to produce this PivotTable.

Row Labels	Sum of Sale	Sum of Quantity
Freeman Ave.	**$8,490**	**21**
Lounge Chair	$2,550	6
Ottoman	$125	1
Recliner	$2,025	3
Rocking Chair	$1,150	5
Straight Chair	$1,480	4
Table	$1,160	2
Oak Ridge	**$11,870**	**24**
Lounge Chair	$1,275	3
Ottoman	$250	2
Recliner	$675	1
Rocking Chair	$230	1
Sofa	$3,580	4
Straight Chair	$2,960	8
Table	$2,900	5
Grand Total	**$20,360**	**45**

Figure 6.21a Summary of sales and quantity by mall location and product

Solution: Figure 6.21b shows the PivotTable Fields dialog used to produce Table 6.21a. Note that the Currency format, within centered columns, was employed after creating the PivotTable using the illustrated PivotTable Fields dialog box.

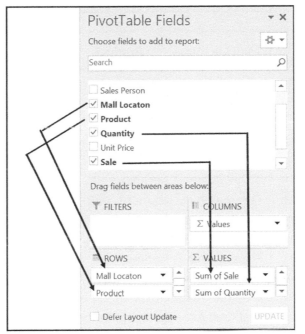

Figure 6.21b Using two row fields and two value fields

EXERCISES 6.2

1. List the three initial steps required to begin creating a PivotTable.

2. Complete parts a-b.

   a. What two displays/dialogs are presented on the screen once the steps in Exercise 1 have been completed?

   b. Which of the displays listed in Exercise 2a is primarily informational, and which one is essential in creating a PivotTable?

3. Complete parts a-b.

   a. List the four Selection boxes provided by a PivotTable Field selection dialog box.

   b. Describe the role that each of the boxes plays when constructing a PivotTable.

4. Using the following spreadsheet, place check marks in the appropriate boxes of the following PivotTable Fields dialog box to produce the PivotTable shown in the second image.

	A	B	C	D	E	F	G
1	Date	Sales Person	Mall Locaton	Product	Quantity	Unit Price	Sale
2	1/7	A. Smith	Oak Ridge	Lounge Chair	3	$425	$1,275
3	1/10	H. Smith	Oak Ridge	Sofa	4	$895	$3,580
4	1/20	D. Shea	Oak Ridge	Straight Chair	8	$370	$2,960
5	1/22	T. Wang	Oak Ridge	Table	5	$580	$2,900
6	2/4	T. Wang	Oak Ridge	Ottoman	2	$125	$250
7	2/6	H. Smith	Oak Ridge	Recliner	1	$675	$675
8	2/10	A. Smith	Freeman Ave.	Lounge Chair	6	$425	$2,550
9	2/16	D. Shea	Freeman Ave.	Rocking Chair	5	$230	$1,150
10	2/18	H. Smith	Freeman Ave.	Table	2	$580	$1,160
11	2/22	H. Smith	Freeman Ave.	Recliner	3	$675	$2,025
12	2/25	D. Shea	Oak Ridge	Rocking Chair	1	$230	$230
13	2/25	T. Wang	Freeman Ave.	Ottoman	1	$125	$125
14	2/25	T. Wang	Freeman Ave.	Straight Chair	4	$370	$1,480

	G	H	I
	Row Labels	Sum of Sale	
	A. Smith	$3,825	
	D. Shea	$4,340	
	H. Smith	$7,440	
	T. Wang	$4,755	
	Grand Total	$20,360	

PivotTable Fields ▾ ✕

Choose fields to add to report: ⚙ ▾

Search 🔍

☐ Sales Person
☐ Mall Locaton
☐ Product
☐ Quantity
☐ Unit Price
☐ Sale

5. Using the spreadsheet shown in Exercise 4, place check marks in the appropriate boxes of the following PivotTable Fields dialog box to produce the following PivotTable.

Row Labels	Sum of Quantity
Lounge Chair	9
Ottoman	3
Recliner	4
Rocking Chair	6
Sofa	4
Straight Chair	12
Table	7
Grand Total	45

PivotTable Fields

Choose fields to add to report:

Search

- Sales Person
- Mall Location
- Product
- Quantity
- Unit Price
- Sale

6. Use the following spreadsheet for Exercise 6.

	A	B	C	D	E	F
1	Department	Age	Gender	Degree	Years	Salary
2	Accounting	32	M	BA	7	$38,000
3	Accounting	28	F	BA	6	$34,000
4	Finance	42	F	MBA	15	$87,000
5	Finance	33	M	MBA	7	$55,000
6	Finance	26	F	MBA	3	$44,000
7	Management	29	F	MBA	4	$60,000
8	Management	28	F	MBA	5	$48,000
9	Marketing	20	F	MBA	1	$32,000
10	Production	35	M	BA	11	$45,000
11	Production	39	M	MA	14	$36,000
12	Production	27	F	MA	8	$37,000
13	Research	28	F	BS	5	$44,000
14	Research	24	M	BS	2	$36,000

Place check marks in the appropriate boxes of the PivotTable Fields dialog box to produce the given PivotTable.

K	L	M
Row Labels	**Sum of Salary**	
Accounting	$72,000	
Finance	$186,000	
Management	$108,000	
Marketing	$32,000	
Production	$118,000	
Research	$80,000	
Grand Total	**$596,000**	

PivotTable Fields   ▾ ✕

Choose fields to add to report: ⚙ ▾

Search   🔎

☐ Department
☐ Age
☐ Gender
☐ Degree
☐ Years
☐ Salary

7. Refer to the spreadsheet shown in Exercise 6. Place check marks in the appropriate boxes of the following PivotTable Fields dialog box to produce the PivotTable shown.

O	P	
Row Labels	**Sum of Years**	
Accounting	13	
Finance	25	
Management	9	
Marketing	1	
Production	33	
Research	7	
Grand Total	**88**	

PivotTable Fields   ▾ ✕

Choose fields to add to report: ⚙ ▾

Search   🔎

☐ Department
☐ Age
☐ Gender
☐ Degree
☐ Years
☐ Salary

8. Enter the following Sales data into a spreadsheet on your computer.

	A	B	C	D	E	F	G
1	Date	Sales Person	Mall Locaton	Product	Quantity	Unit Price	Sale
2	1/7	A. Smith	Oak Ridge	Lounge Chair	3	$425	$1,275
3	1/10	H. Smith	Oak Ridge	Sofa	4	$895	$3,580
4	1/20	D. Shea	Oak Ridge	Straight Chair	8	$370	$2,960
5	1/22	T. Wang	Oak Ridge	Table	5	$580	$2,900
6	2/4	T. Wang	Oak Ridge	Ottoman	2	$125	$250
7	2/6	H. Smith	Oak Ridge	Recliner	1	$675	$675
8	2/10	A. Smith	Freeman Ave.	Lounge Chair	6	$425	$2,550
9	2/16	D. Shea	Freeman Ave.	Rocking Chair	5	$230	$1,150
10	2/18	H. Smith	Freeman Ave.	Table	2	$580	$1,160
11	2/22	H. Smith	Freeman Ave.	Recliner	3	$675	$2,025
12	2/25	D. Shea	Oak Ridge	Rocking Chair	1	$230	$230
13	2/25	T. Wang	Freeman Ave.	Ottoman	1	$125	$125
14	2/25	T. Wang	Freeman Ave.	Straight Chair	4	$370	$1,480

9. Using the spreadsheet from Exercise 8, create the following PivotTable.

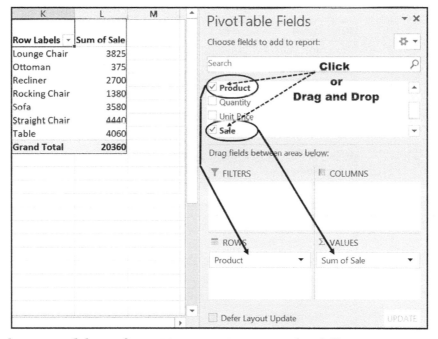

10. Using the spreadsheet from Exercise 8, create the following PivotTable.

Row Labels	Sum of Sale
Freeman Ave.	$8,490
Oak Ridge	$11,870
Grand Total	$20,360

11. Using the spreadsheet from Exercise 8, create the following PivotTable.

Row Labels	Sum of Sale
Freeman Ave.	$8,490
Lounge Chair	$2,550
Ottoman	$125
Recliner	$2,025
Rocking Chair	$1,150
Straight Chair	$1,480
Table	$1,160
Oak Ridge	$11,870
Lounge Chair	$1,275
Ottoman	$250
Recliner	$675
Rocking Chair	$230
Sofa	$3,580
Straight Chair	$2,960
Table	$2,900
Grand Total	$20,360

12. Using the spreadsheet from Exercise 8, create the following PivotTable.

Row Labels	Sum of Sale	Sum of Quantity
Freeman Ave.	$8,490	21
Oak Ridge	$11,870	24
Grand Total	$20,360	45

13. Using the spreadsheet from Exercise 8, create the following PivotTable.

Row Labels	Sum of Sale	Sum of Quantity
Freeman Ave.	$8,490	21
Lounge Chair	$2,550	6
Ottoman	$125	1
Recliner	$2,025	3
Rocking Chair	$1,150	5
Straight Chair	$1,480	4
Table	$1,160	2
Oak Ridge	$11,870	24
Lounge Chair	$1,275	3
Ottoman	$250	2
Recliner	$675	1
Rocking Chair	$230	1
Sofa	$3,580	4
Straight Chair	$2,960	8
Table	$2,900	5
Grand Total	$20,360	45

6.3 ADDING COLUMN FIELDS

Both Figures 6.22a and 6.22b provide the same information; the difference is in the presentation. In both figures, the primary Row Field is Sales Person. However, in Figure 6.22a Mall Location is presented as an indented (that is, subsidiary) Row field, while Figure 6.21b Mall Location is used a Column Field. It is a matter of preference as to which is the better presentation.

Column Fields are added into a PivotTable in a similar manner as Row Fields, except that *they must always be dragged and dropped*; they cannot be clicked in the PivotTable Field dialog.

Row Labels	▾	Sum of Sale
⊟A. Smith		$3,825
Freeman Ave.		$2,550
Oak Ridge		$1,275
⊟D. Shea		$4,340
Freeman Ave.		$1,150
Oak Ridge		$3,190
⊟H. Smith		$7,440
Freeman Ave.		$3,185
Oak Ridge		$4,255
⊟T. Wang		$4,755
Freeman Ave.		$1,605
Oak Ridge		$3,150
Grand Total		$20,360

(a)

Sum of Sale	Column Labels ▾		
Row Labels ▾	Freeman Ave.	Oak Ridge	Grand Total
A. Smith	$2,550	$1,275	$3,825
D. Shea	$1,150	$3,190	$4,340
H. Smith	$3,185	$4,255	$7,440
T. Wang	$1,605	$3,150	$4,755
Grand Total	$8,490	$11,870	$20,360

(b)

Figure 6.22 Equivalent row and column PivotTables

As an example of including a set of column fields (which are distinct from Summary columns) consider Figure 6.23.

Sum of Quantity	Column Labels							
Row Labels	Lounge Chair	Ottoman	Recliner	Rocking Chair	Sofa	Straight Chair	Table	Grand Total
Freeman Ave.	6	1	3	5		4	2	21
Oak Ridge	3	2	1	1	4	8	5	24
Grand Total	9	3	4	6	4	12	7	45

Figure 6.23 A PivotTable with one set of row fields and one set of column fields

Figure 6.23 illustrates a PivotTable having one set of row fields and one set of column fields. In this figure, the row fields provide the Mall Location and the column fields provide the product name. Each entry in the table lists the number of each product sold at each Mall Location. The last column, which is a value field column, provides the total number of items sold at each Mall Location. Because there is now a set of column fields, a Grand Total row is also provided, which is the last row in the table. This row provides a total for each product sold in both stores together.

Application Note
Sorting and Selecting Row and Column Labels

Row and column labels can be sorted and/or selected by clicking on the arrows to the right of each label designation, as shown in the figure below.

Each arrow, as shown, provides its own drop-down menu. These sort and search options, however, are available during PivotTable development process.

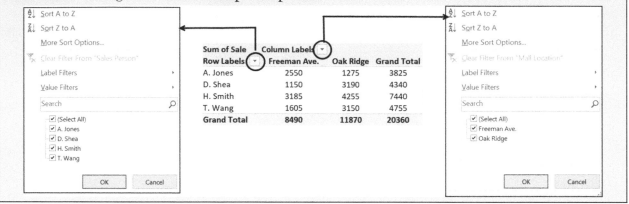

Figure 6.24 shows the PivotTable Fields dialog box used to created Figure 6.23. The only new feature shown in Figure 6.24 is that creating a set of column fields, unlike row fields, requires that the desired field *must be* dragged and dropped into the COLUMNS field's selection box. Simply clicking on the desired field will create it as a ROWS field.

Figure 6.24 Creating a set of column labels (fields)

Additional Column Field Examples

Each set of column fields (remember, these are different from Summary columns) is placed into a PivotTable by dragging and dropping the desired label field into the COLUMNS selection box, as shown in Figure 6.25.

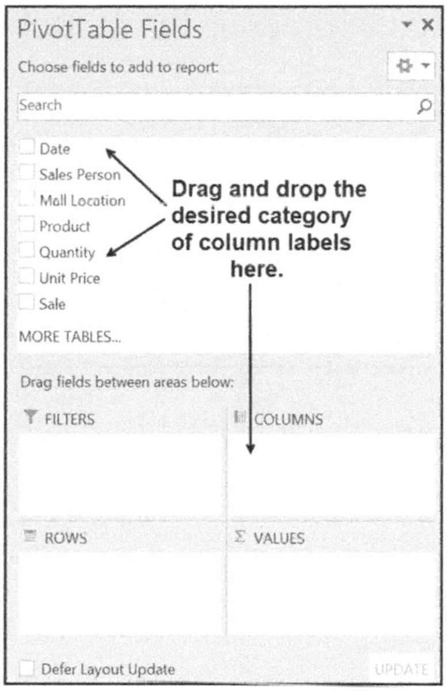

Figure 6.25 PivotTable fields

Here are two examples of creating a PivotTable with each one having a single set of column fields. The first example illustrates a PivotTable having a single row field, a single column field, and a single value field. The second example illustrates a table with two row fields, a single column field, and a single value field. Both examples summarize data from the spreadsheet shown in Figure 6.26.

	A	B	C	D	E	F	G
1	Date	Sales Person	Mall Locaton	Product	Quantity	Unit Price	Sale
2	1/7	A. Smith	Oak Ridge	Lounge Chair	3	$425	$1,275
3	1/10	H. Smith	Oak Ridge	Sofa	4	$895	$3,580
4	1/20	D. Shea	Oak Ridge	Straight Chair	8	$370	$2,960
5	1/22	T. Wang	Oak Ridge	Table	5	$580	$2,900
6	2/4	T. Wang	Oak Ridge	Ottoman	2	$125	$250
7	2/6	H. Smith	Oak Ridge	Recliner	1	$675	$675
8	2/10	A. Smith	Freeman Ave.	Lounge Chair	6	$425	$2,550
9	2/16	D. Shea	Freeman Ave.	Rocking Chair	5	$230	$1,150
10	2/18	H. Smith	Freeman Ave.	Table	2	$580	$1,160
11	2/22	H. Smith	Freeman Ave.	Recliner	3	$675	$2,025
12	2/25	D. Shea	Oak Ridge	Rocking Chair	1	$230	$230
13	2/25	T. Wang	Freeman Ave.	Ottoman	1	$125	$125
14	2/25	T. Wang	Freeman Ave.	Straight Chair	4	$370	$1,480

Figure 6.26 Sales data

Example 1

A Single Set of ROW and COLUMN Fields

The PivotTable shown in Figure 6.27a consists of one set of row fields and one set of column fields. Also included is a single value field. Determine options in the Pivot-Table Fields dialog box needed to produce this PivotTable.

Sum of Quantity	Column Labels							
Row Labels	Lounge Chair	Ottoman	Recliner	Rocking Chair	Sofa	Straight Chair	Table	Grand Total
A. Smith	9							9
D. Shea				6		8		14
H. Smith			4		4		2	10
T. Wang		3				4	5	12
Grand Total	9	3	4	6	4	12	7	45

Figure 6.27a Quantity sold by product and salesperson

Solution: Figure 6.27b shows the PivotTable Fields dialog box used to produce Figure 6.27a.

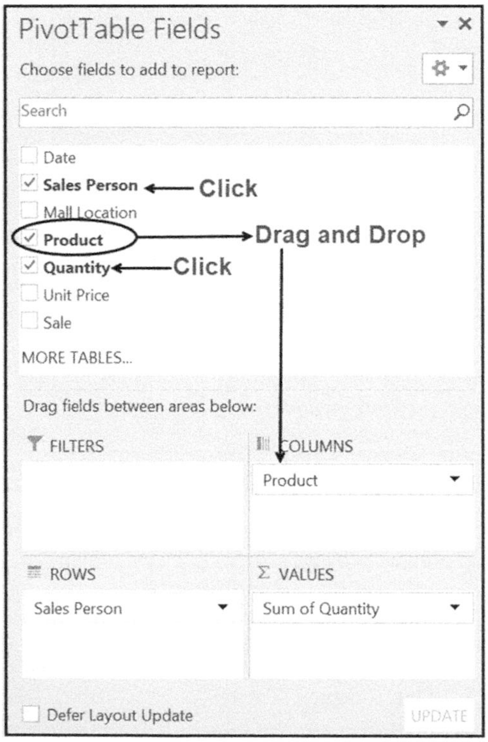

Figure 6.27b The PivotTable Fields dialog box used to create Figure 6.27a

Your initial PivotTables may contain just a single set of row and column fields. The reason is that each additional set of column fields extends the table horizontally, which can create a table that may not fit on a single sheet of paper.[1] If two sets of column fields are required, and printed output size is critical, one option is to create two pivot tables, with each pivot table including one of the desired column fields.

---

[1] Clearly, if the column labels contain two or three labels, more sets can be included in the table.

At times, you may create a PivotTable with two row fields, and a single column field. An example of constructing this type of PivotTable is shown in the following example.

Example 2

Two Sets of Row Fields and a Single Set of Column Fields

The PivotTable shown in Figure 6.28a consists of two sets of row fields and one set of column fields. Also included is a single value field. Determine the options in the PivotTable Fields dialog box needed to produce this PivotTable.

Row Labels	Lounge Chair	Ottoman	Recliner	Rocking Chair	Sofa	Straight Chair	Table	Grand Total
A. Smith	9							9
Freeman Ave.	6							6
Oak Ridge	3							3
D. Shea				6		8		14
Freeman Ave.				5				5
Oak Ridge				1		8		9
H. Smith			4		4		2	10
Freeman Ave.			3				2	5
Oak Ridge			1		4			5
T. Wang		3				4	5	12
Freeman Ave.		1				4		5
Oak Ridge		2					5	7
Grand Total	9	3	4	6	4	12	7	45

Figure 6.28a Quantity of product sold by salesperson and mall location

Solution: Figure 6.28b shows the PivotTable Fields dialog box options used to produce Figure 6.28a.

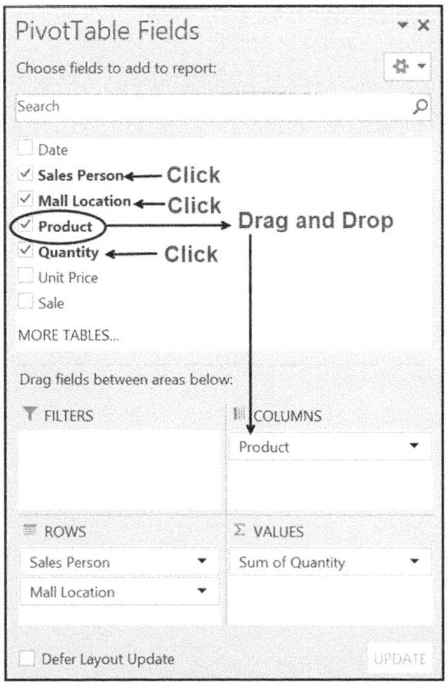

Figure 6.28b PivotTable Fields dialog box options used to create Figure 6.28a

Application Note
Refreshing PivotTables

PivotTables are *static*, which means that they summarize the data that exists when the table was created. As such, they are not automatically updated when changes are made to the original data. To keep them current for such changes requires *refreshing*. This is accomplished by either

1. Pressing the Alt-F5 key combination, or

2. Selecting the Excel ribbon's Data Tab - Queries & Connections Group - Refresh All option, shown below (or using the menu command PivotTable Tools – Analyze – Data Group – Refresh – Refresh All)

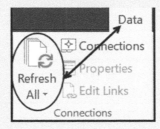

Alternatively, all PivotTables can be automatically refreshed when a spreadsheet is opened by right-clicking within any PivotTable, selecting the *PivotTable Options*, choosing the Data tab, selecting the *Refresh data when opening the file* option, and clicking "OK."

Since the purpose of this chapter was to provide a general and basic introduction to PivotTables, it is important to note that there is much more to what PivotTables can offer. While it was mentioned that it is best to start simple and build your way up in terms of complexity, there are many other features that you can explore after you understand and have mastered the basics.

Some of the options include more complex PivotTables using multiple columns, rows, report filters, and value fields. There is the ability to create PivotCharts, which are based on your PivotTable data, and the charts themselves can be "pivoted." It is possible to filter your PivotTable using slicers and timelines. Custom fields can be derived from the original fields in your spreadsheets, known as *calculated fields*. It is also possible to establish relationships between multiple lists/tables, simulating a capability found in relational databases.

There are many resources available for you to explore PivotTables in more depth, once you have grasped the basics.

EXERCISES 6.3

1. Enter the following spreadsheet into your computer.

	B	C	D	E	F	G
1	Sales Person	Mall Locaton	Product	Quantity	Unit Price	Sale
2	A. Smith	Oak Ridge	Lounge Chair	3	$425	$1,275
3	H. Smith	Oak Ridge	Sofa	4	$895	$3,580
4	D. Shea	Oak Ridge	Straight Chair	8	$370	$2,960
5	T. Wang	Oak Ridge	Table	5	$580	$2,900
6	T. Wang	Oak Ridge	Ottoman	2	$125	$250
7	H. Smith	Oak Ridge	Recliner	1	$675	$675
8	A. Smith	Freeman Ave.	Lounge Chair	6	$425	$2,550
9	D. Shea	Freeman Ave.	Rocking Chair	5	$230	$1,150
10	H. Smith	Freeman Ave.	Table	2	$580	$1,160
11	H. Smith	Freeman Ave.	Recliner	3	$675	$2,025
12	D. Shea	Oak Ridge	Rocking Chair	1	$230	$230
13	T. Wang	Freeman Ave.	Ottoman	1	$125	$125
14	T. Wang	Freeman Ave.	Straight Chair	4	$370	$1,480

2. Using the spreadsheet created in Exercise 1, create the following PivotTable.

Sum of Quantity	Column Labels							
Row Labels	Lounge Chair	Ottoman	Recliner	Rocking Chair	Sofa	Straight Chair	Table	Grand Total
Freeman Ave.	6	1	3	5		4	2	21
Oak Ridge	3	2	1	1	4	8	5	24
Grand Total	9	3	4	6	4	12	7	45

3. Using the spreadsheet created in Exercise 1, create the following PivotTable.

Sum of Quantity	Column Labels							
Row Labels	Lounge Chair	Ottoman	Recliner	Rocking Chair	Sofa	Straight Chair	Table	Grand Total
A. Smith	9							9
D. Shea				6		8		14
H. Smith			4		4		2	10
T. Wang		3				4	5	12
Grand Total	9	3	4	6	4	12	7	45

4. Using the spreadsheet created in Exercise 1, create the PivotTable shown below.

Row Labels	Lounge Chair	Ottoman	Recliner	Rocking Chair	Sofa	Straight Chair	Table	Grand Total
A. Smith	9							9
Freeman Ave.	6							6
Oak Ridge	3							3
D. Shea				6		8		14
Freeman Ave.				5				5
Oak Ridge				1		8		9
H. Smith			4		4		2	10
Freeman Ave.			3				2	5
Oak Ridge			1		4			5
T. Wang		3				4	5	12
Freeman Ave.		1				4		5
Oak Ridge		2					5	7
Grand Total	9	3	4	6	4	12	7	45

5. Using the spreadsheet created in Exercise 1, create the following PivotTable.

Sum of Sale	Column Labels		
Row Labels	Freeman Ave.	Oak Ridge	Grand Total
A. Smith	$2,550	$1,275	$3,825
D. Shea	$1,150	$3,190	$4,340
H. Smith	$3,185	$4,255	$7,440
T. Wang	$1,605	$3,150	$4,755
Grand Total	$8,490	$11,870	$20,360

6. Using the spreadsheet created in Exercise 1, create the following PivotTable.

Sum of Sale								
	Lounge Chair	Ottoman	Recliner	Rocking Chair	Sofa	Straight Chair	Table	Grand Total
Freeman Ave.	$2,550	$125	$2,025	$1,150		$1,480	$1,160	$8,490
Oak Ridge	$1,275	$250	$675	$230	$3,580	$2,960	$2,900	$11,870
Grand Total	$3,825	$375	$2,700	$1,380	$3,580	$4,440	$4,060	$20,360

7. Using the spreadsheet created in Exercise 1, create the following PivotTable.

Sum of Sale								
	Lounge Chair	Ottoman	Recliner	Rocking Chair	Sofa	Straight Chair	Table	Grand Total
A. Smith	$3,825							$3,825
D. Shea				$1,380		$2,960		$4,340
H. Smith			$2,700		$3,580		$1,160	$7,440
T. Wang		$375				$1,480	$2,900	$4,755
Grand Total	$3,825	$375	$2,700	$1,380	$3,580	$4,440	$4,060	$20,360

6.4   COMMON EXCEL ERRORS

The most common errors associated with PivotTables are the following:

1. Not using PivotTables at all because you think they are difficult to create. It helps to realize that a PivotTable is simply a summary table. With a minimum of two clicks of a mouse, a PivotTable can be created. A more complex PivotTable beyond this can also be created relatively easily.

2. Making PivotTables too complicated. It is best to create a PivotTable as simple as possible, considering the data being analyzed, as well as the intended goal and purpose of creating it.

3. Not activating the PivotTable Tools menu to either refresh a PivotTable, change the row and column label headings, or change the calculation method in a Pivot-Table Fields dialog box. Clicking on any PivotTable cell activates the Tools menu (see Application Notes included throughout this chapter).

6.5   CHAPTER APPENDIX: PIVOTTABLE DESIGN CRITERIA

The purpose of a PivotTable is to summarize specific aspects of a larger spreadsheet. As such, a PivotTable should not be too large and force the viewer to focus on the items you wish to emphasize. The following guidelines will help you achieve this goal.

There is no reason not to start with the simplest structure of a single set of row field, and one or two value fields, as shown in Figure 6.29.

Row Labels	Sum of Quantity	Sum of Sale
Lounge Chair	9	$3,825
Ottoman	3	$375
Recliner	4	$2,700
Rocking Chair	6	$1,380
Sofa	4	$3,580
Straight Chair	12	$4,440
Table	7	$4,060
Grand Total	45	$20,360

Figure 6.29 A single set of row fields and two summary columns (value fields)

PivotTables with either two sets of row fields or a single set of row and column fields are also generally concise enough to focus a user's attention. For example, consider Figure 6.30, which presents sales data, classified by Sales Person and Mall Location. Including one or more value fields to either of these figures is acceptable because each summary column can be viewed individually and does not detract from the overall presentation.

Application Note
Using the PivotTable's Analyze Tab

In addition to refreshing a PivotTable and deleting one, there are a number of other useful options for changing and manipulating a table under development. The most useful of these are provided as options in the Analyze Tab under the PivotTable's Tools menu, as shown below. Clicking on any PivotTable cell activates the PivotTable Tools menu.

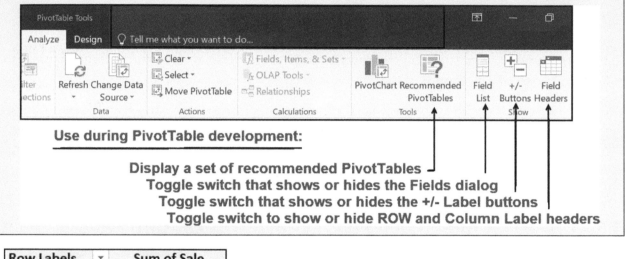

Use during PivotTable development:

Display a set of recommended PivotTables
Toggle switch that shows or hides the Fields dialog
Toggle switch that shows or hides the +/- Label buttons
Toggle switch to show or hide ROW and Column Label headers

Row Labels ▾	Sum of Sale
⊟ Freeman Ave.	$8,490
A. Smith	$2,550
D. Shea	$1,150
H. Smith	$3,185
T. Wang	$1,605
⊟ Oak Ridge	$11,870
A. Smith	$1,275
D. Shea	$3,190
H. Smith	$4,255
T. Wang	$3,150
Grand Total	$20,360

(a)

Sum of Sale	Column Labels ▾		
Row Labels ▾	Freeman Ave.	Oak Ridge	Grand Total
A. Smith	$2,550	$1,275	$3,825
D. Shea	$1,150	$3,190	$4,340
H. Smith	$3,185	$4,255	$7,440
T. Wang	$1,605	$3,150	$4,755
Grand Total	$8,490	$11,870	$20,360

(b)

Figure 6.30 Presenting the same data in different ways

As seen in Figure 6.30a, two row label categories are used, while in Figure 6.30b, the two row label categories are replaced by a single row and column set of fields. The choice as to which structure is better in any given situation, is one you must make based on your own sense of which is more appropriate for what you are intending to present. Figures 6.31 and 6.32 illustrate two additional PivotTables using this arrangement.

Sum of Sale								
	Lounge Chair	Ottoman	Recliner	Rocking Chair	Sofa	Straight Chair	Table	Grand Total
Freeman Ave.	$2,550	$125	$2,025	$1,150		$1,480	$1,160	$8,490
Oak Ridge	$1,275	$250	$675	$230	$3,580	$2,960	$2,900	$11,870
Grand Total	$3,825	$375	$2,700	$1,380	$3,580	$4,440	$4,060	$20,360

Figure 6.31 A single row field, column field, and values field PivotTable

Sum of Sale								
	Lounge Chair	Ottoman	Recliner	Rocking Chair	Sofa	Straight Chair	Table	Grand Total
A. Smith	$3,825							$3,825
D. Shea				$1,380		$2,960		$4,340
H. Smith			$2,700		$3,580		$1,160	$7,440
T. Wang		$375				$1,480	$2,900	$4,755
Grand Total	$3,825	$375	$2,700	$1,380	$3,580	$4,440	$4,060	$20,360

Figure 6.32 A Different single row field, column field, and value field PivotTable

More than two sets of column fields tend to produce tables that are too wide to fit on a standard sheet of paper. Thus, in general, a basic PivotTable could comfortably contain two sets of row fields and one set of column fields, with as many summary columns (value fields) as needed. Figure 6.33 provides an example of such a PivotTable. More complex PivotTables are of course possible, but added complexity should only be added if the data analysis requires it.

Sum of Sale								
	Lounge Chair	Ottoman	Recliner	Rocking Chair	Sofa	Straight Chair	Table	Grand Total
A. Smith	**$3,825**							**$3,825**
Freeman Ave.	$2,550							$2,550
Oak Ridge	$1,275							$1,275
D. Shea				**$1,380**		**$2,960**		**$4,340**
Freeman Ave.				$1,150				$1,150
Oak Ridge				$230		$2,960		$3,190
H. Smith			**$2,700**		**$3,580**		**$1,160**	**$7,440**
Freeman Ave.			$2,025				$1,160	$3,185
Oak Ridge			$675		$3,580			$4,255
T. Wang		**$375**				**$1,480**	**$2,900**	**$4,755**
Freeman Ave.		$125				$1,480		$1,605
Oak Ridge		$250					$2,900	$3,150
Grand Total	**$3,825**	**$375**	**$2,700**	**$1,380**	**$3,580**	**$4,440**	**$4,060**	**$20,360**

Figure 6.33 Two row fields, a column field, and a summary column (value field)

Notice in Figures 6.31 through 6.33 that the PivotTables have been formatted as Currency, with the data in each column centered, and that the headings *Row Labels* and *Column Labels* do not appear (because the output shown is how the display is printed and is not the development display).

Part 3 *INTERMEDIATE SKILLS*

SORTING AND SEARCHING

Most Excel users encounter the need to both sort and search a list of data items at some time in their professional careers. For example, employee identification codes might have to be arranged in either increasing (ascending) or decreasing (descending) order. Similarly, a list of dates may have to be rearranged in ascending date order or a list of names sorted in alphabetical (ascending) order. Similarly, a list of names may have to be searched to find a particular name or a list of dates searched to locate a particular date. In this chapter, the fundamentals of Excel's sorting and searching capabilities are presented.

7.1 RECORDS AS ROWS

Excel spreadsheets can be set up in many different ways, such as financial statements, sets of calculations, or as organized lists and tables. In the case of Excel lists (and tables), an example of which is in Figure 7.1, there is a set structure and organization which guides the spreadsheet setup and the entry of data. It could be termed as a kind of *database* structure in that it is an "organized collection of information" and has both specific data items, known as *fields*, and collections of these fields, which makes up what are known as *records*. You can take as an example an address list of customers as the "database" with various data elements such as name, address, city, state, zip, and phone as fields. These data elements generally have an expected data type, such as text, number, or something else. When you have a collection of associated fields, this forms a record, which in this example would be the data for one customer. It should be noted that Excel lists and tables are technically not databases, although they are set up to resemble and can operate as one.

The distinction was made between lists and tables. *Lists* are collections of fields and records. *Tables* are lists to which the Excel Table structure has been applied, which provides additional tools for working with list data (such as sorting and filtering). The term *Excel Table* should not be confused with the concept of a table in a relational database, although if set up properly, an Excel Table can be made to resemble, and in some aspects, simulate the workings of, a relational database. However, if an Excel list or table can loosely be termed a "database," then it would be best characterized as a flat-file database, rather than a relational database, since there are normally no relationships between the various data items.

In an organization, such as a company, university, or governmental agency, a *record* typically contains two or more related fields. For example, consider Figure 7.1, which provides information on employees in a small company, where an employee is assigned to one of two offices, Home (coded as HM) or Field (coded as FLD). In Figure 7.1, each record is listed in a single row, with the record containing information related to an individual employee.

ID	Office	Last Name	First Name	Address	City	State	Zip
10010	HM	Bottle	Bill	614 Tremont Ave.	Hoboken	NJ	07030
10015	HM	Deiter	Alan	892 Freeman St.	Orange	NJ	07050
10020	FLD	Dreskin	Mary	56 Lyons Ave, Apt 12	Bloomfield	NJ	07112
10025	FLD	Farrel	Jayne	78 Barnstable Rd.	Berkeley Hgts.	NJ	07922
10030	HM	Grill	Mellisa	643 Schuller Dr.	Orange	NJ	07050
10035	HM	Jones	Helen	932 Coleridge Rd.	Camden	NJ	08030
10040	HM	Jones	Mark	93 Fairmount Ter.	Maplewood	NJ	07040
10045	FLD	Miller	Scott	745 Skyline Dr.	Chatham	NJ	07928
10050	FLD	O'Neil	Pat	17 Tuney St.	Madison	NJ	07940
10055	HM	Somers	Ann	2 Travers Way	Trenton	NJ	08601
10060	FLD	Swan	Kurt	16 Rollinson Rd.	Orange	NJ	07050
10065	HM	Thomas	Harriet	192 Oakridge St.	Summit	NJ	07901
10070	HM	Timers	John	849 Birchwood Dr.	Hoboken	NJ	07030
10075	FLD	Ward	Kay	2 Pine Ter.	Chatham	NJ	07928
10080	FLD	Williams	Blake	85 Wellforest Ave.	Madison	NJ	07940

Figure 7.1 Employee data (Excel list structure)

Records can be created and stored in a number of formats, from paper to computer files to spreadsheets. When a record (complete or partial) is stored using a spreadsheet, it is always stored as a row. Thus, with respect to spreadsheets, the terms *row* and *record* are frequently used interchangeably, as they will be in this chapter. From an applications viewpoint, the term *record* emphasizes the data's usage as an organized structure of related data; from a spreadsheet viewpoint, the word *row* emphasizes the data's physical organization within the spreadsheet.

Once records are stored as rows within a spreadsheet, two operations that are frequently done include

1. Sorting the records in a specific order, perhaps by name, location, or zip code (or on a sequence of different fields)

2. Search for and select ("filter") records meeting specific criteria.

Each of these operations involves either sorting or selecting (filtering) records based on specific item values. As an example, in Figure 7.1, a list of employees sorted by office location might be required. Similarly, in a list of student records, we might want to know how many students are Liberal Arts majors, or how many students have a Grade Pt. Average (GPA) above 3.4, or how many students have earned more than 80 credits and have a GPA above 3.4.

Sections 7.3 through 7.5 present Excel methods for sorting, counting, and searching spreadsheets for records that meet the desired criteria.

EXERCISES 7.1

1. Complete parts a-h.

   a. What is a database?

   b. What is a field?

   c. What is a record?

   d. How are fields and records stored in spreadsheets?

   e. What is an Excel list?

   f. What is an Excel table?

   g. What is the best term to describe the physical structure of an Excel "database?"

   h. What kind of database can an Excel list/table be made to simulate?

2. Although a spreadsheet row can almost always be considered a record, is a record always a spreadsheet row?

3. List two operations that can be used on Excel "database" structures.

7.2   SORTING SPREADSHEET ROWS

There are times when you will need to reorganize the rows in your spreadsheet in either ascending (from lowest to highest) or descending (highest to lowest) order based on one or more column's data.[1] The sorting procedure based on a single criterion includes the following steps:

Step 1: Click on any cell in the column that you want to be sorted

Step 2: Select the desired sort, ascending or descending, on the Excel ribbon Data Tab, Sort & Filter Group.

When this is done, all of the rows on the spreadsheet will be reordered, based on the item chosen for the sort. As a specific example, consider that the spreadsheet shown in Figure 7.2 must be sorted by Department, from Accounting to Research (ascending order, alphabetical).

	A	B	C	D	E	F
	Department	**Age**	**Gender**	**Degree**	**Years**	**Salary**
1						
2	Finance	42	F	MBA	15	$87,000
3	Management	29	F	MBA	4	$60,000
4	Production	35	M	BA	11	$45,000
5	Research	28	F	BS	5	$44,000
6	Production	39	M	MA	14	$36,000
7	Management	28	F	MBA	5	$48,000
8	Finance	33	M	MBA	7	$55,000
9	Marketing	20	F	MBA	1	$32,000
10	Research	28	M	BS	5	$38,000
11	Production	27	F	MA	8	$37,000
12	Research	24	M	BS	2	$36,000
13	Finance	26	F	MBA	3	$44,000
14	Accounting	32	M	BA	7	$38,000
15	Accounting	28	F	BA	6	$34,000
16	Production	25	M	BA	3	$29,000
17	Production	26	F	BA	3	$29,000
18	Research	32	M	Ph.D.	2	$54,000
19	Administration	45	F	MBA	14	$58,000
20	Production	27	M	MA	3	$29,000

Figure 7.2 The initial spreadsheet data

---

[1] A spreadsheet operating as a database is described more fully in the chapter appendix. In this context, a spreadsheet's rows (records) correspond to the database's records, and its columns (fields) correspond to the categories of items stored within a record. When viewed this way, the sorting and searching of rows (filtering) in a spreadsheet become the sorting and searching of records within a database.

The first step in performing the sort is to *click on any* cell within the Department column (Step 1).

Next, select either an ascending (lowest to highest) or descending sort (highest to lowest), from the ribbon's Data tab (Step 2), as shown in Figure 7.3.

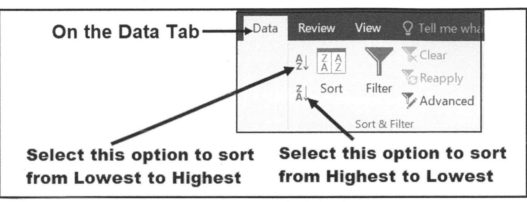

Figure 7.3 Creating a single-level sort

In this case, we want the sort of Departments in ascending order (lowest to highest). When the A to Z option is selected, the spreadsheet will be sorted in Department order, as shown in Figure 7.4.

	A	B	C	D	E	F
1	**Department**	**Age**	**Gender**	**Degree**	**Years**	**Salary**
2	Accounting	32	M	BA	7	$38,000
3	Accounting	28	F	BA	6	$34,000
4	Finance	42	F	MBA	15	$87,000
5	Finance	33	M	MBA	7	$55,000
6	Finance	26	F	MBA	3	$44,000
7	Management	29	F	MBA	4	$60,000
8	Management	28	F	MBA	5	$48,000
9	Marketing	20	F	MBA	1	$32,000
10	Production	35	M	BA	11	$45,000
11	Production	39	M	MA	14	$36,000
12	Production	27	F	MA	8	$37,000
13	Production	27	M	MA	3	$29,000
14	Research	28	F	BS	5	$44,000
15	Research	28	M	BS	5	$38,000
16	Research	24	M	BS	2	$36,000

Figure 7.4 The data sorted in ascending Department order

In reviewing Figure 7.4, notice that the complete spreadsheet has been reordered. That is, while the departments were being sorted, the remaining data in each row "follows" the new Department ordering. Thus, the data within each row remains the same as the original data, but simply moves up or down to correspond to the ordering of its Department value. This is known as a "single level" or "single field" sort because it sorts all of the values in the Department field in ascending order. This kind of sort is most useful when you only want to sort a single field. In essence, if you do a single field sort followed by another single-field sort on another field, then the entire list will be re-sorted based on second field specified, and so in many ways, the earlier sort is lost and replaced by the new sorted list. If you would like to do multiple levels of sorting without losing the results of other sorts, you need to do multi-level sorting.

Multi-Level Sorting

In many cases, you want to do a multi-level (or multi-field sort), which does not discard the previous sorts when you do several in a sequence. As such, a multi-level sort is a sort within a sort. For example, consider the spreadsheet shown in Figure 7.4. For example, a three-level sort of this data could be first by Department (in Ascending order, that is, A to Z order), then by Degree (again in Ascending order, or A to Z order), and then finally by Salary (in Descending, or highest-to-lowest order). In effect, when you finish sorting one field and move on to the next, the earlier sorts are kept, and the new one is "added on" to the previous ones. In this example, what we have is a Salary sort within a Degree sort within a Department sort.

To create a multilevel sort, first click on any cell within the spreadsheet and then click the Excel ribbon's Data tab's Sort icon, as shown in Figure 7.5. (You should note that the icons beside it to the left, with the arrows and letters, are the icons for the single level sorts, so be sure you select the main Sort icon).

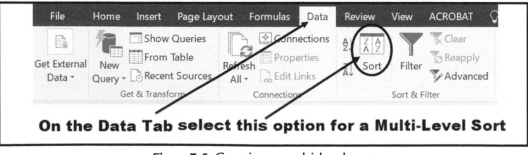

Figure 7.5 Creating a multi-level sort

After clicking on the Sort icon, the sort dialog box shown in Figure 7.6 appears. Within this box, click on the **Sort by** arrow (labelled as item 1 in the figure), and then select

Department (labeled as item 2). This sets the first, or *primary sort*, based on Department. (Note, at this stage, if you pressed the OK button, the single sort shown in Figure 7.4 is produced, and you would have to click on any cell within the spreadsheet and then click on the Sort icon to have the Sort dialog box reappear.)

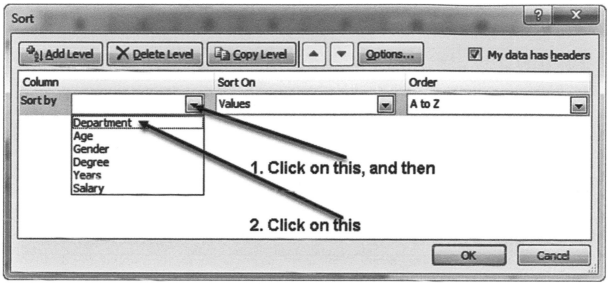

Figure 7.6 Selecting the primary sort within the Sort dialog box

To create the desired three-level sort, you will now have to add two additional sort columns to the sort. Figure 7.6 illustrates how to add the second sort column using the sort dialog box. After you have added the Degree column, you still have to add the Salary column, making sure to change the sort order to Z to A.

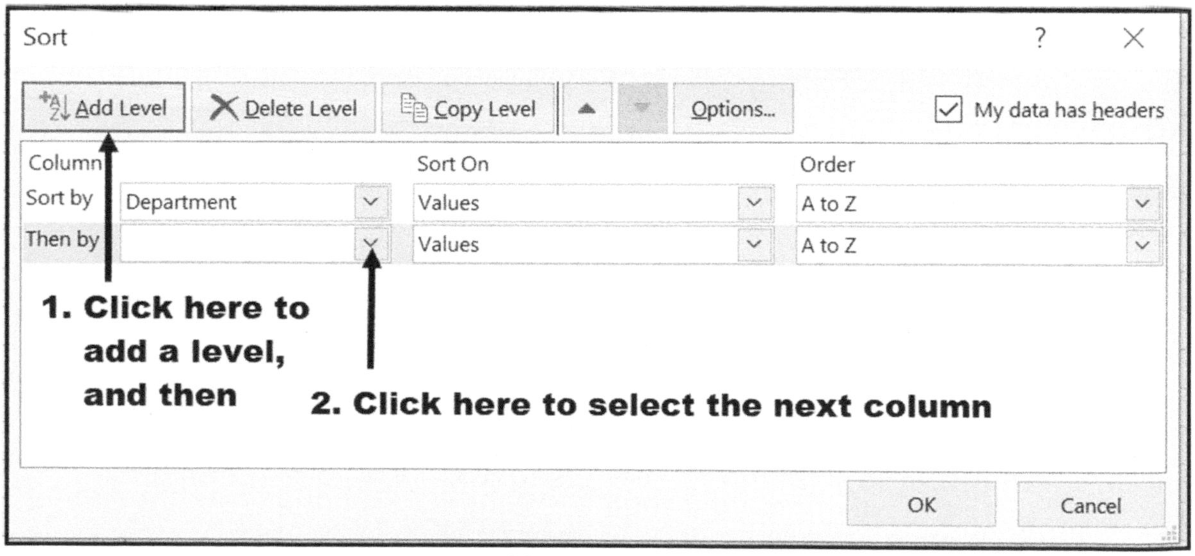

Figure 7.7 Adding a second sort column

Once all three sort columns have been selected (Department, Degree, and Salary), pressing the OK button reorganizes the spreadsheet to appear in the selected sort order, as shown in Figure 7.8. Note, that if you wanted additional sorts within the existing three sorts, all you have to do is repeat Steps 1 and 2 shown in Figure 7.7.

	A	B	C	D	E	F
1	Department	Age	Gender	Degree	Years	Salary
2	Accounting	32	M	BA	7	$38,000
3	Accounting	28	F	BA	6	$34,000
4	Administration	45	F	MBA	14	$58,000
5	Finance	42	F	MBA	15	$87,000
6	Finance	33	M	MBA	7	$55,000
7	Finance	26	F	MBA	3	$44,000
8	Management	29	F	MBA	4	$60,000
9	Management	28	F	MBA	5	$48,000
10	Marketing	20	F	MBA	1	$32,000
11	Production	35	M	BA	11	$45,000
12	Production	25	M	BA	3	$29,000
13	Production	26	F	BA	3	$29,000
14	Production	27	F	MA	8	$37,000
15	Production	39	M	MA	14	$36,000
16	Production	27	M	MA	3	$29,000
17	Research	28	F	BS	5	$44,000
18	Research	28	M	BS	5	$38,000
19	Research	24	M	BS	2	$36,000
20	Research	32	M	Ph.D.	2	$54,000

Figure 7.8 The data sorted in Department, Degree, and Salary order

In reviewing Figure 7.7, notice that the spreadsheet is sorted by Department (first level sort, ascending), and that within each Department the rows are arranged by Degree (second level sort, ascending). Finally, notice that within each degree category, Salary is ordered from highest to lowest (the third level sort, descending). Again, to continue adding additional selections, simply repeat adding sort levels, as shown in Figure 7.7.

EXERCISES 7.2

1. Create the following spreadsheet in Excel, and sort the data by city in ascending (A to Z) order.

	A	B	C	D	E	F	G	H
1	ID	Office	Last Name	First Name	Address	City	State	Zip
2	10010	HM	Bottle	Bill	614 Tremont Ave.	Hoboken	NJ	07030
3	10015	HM	Dieter	Alan	892 Freeman St.	Orange	NJ	07050
4	10020	FLD	Dreskin	Mary	56 Lyons Ave, Apt 12	Bloomfiled	NJ	07060
5	10025	FLD	Farrel	Jayne	78 Barstable Rd.	Summit	NJ	07045
6	10030	HM	Grill	Mellisa	643 Schluller Dr.	Orange	NJ	07050
7	10035	HM	Jones	Helen	932 Coleridge Rd.	Camden	NJ	07920

2. Using the spreadsheet entered for Exercise 1, sort the data by Office so that the home office (HM) employees are listed before the field office (FLD) employees (descending order).

3. Create the following spreadsheet, then sort the data by Department, ascending order.

	A	B	C	D	E	F
1	Department	Age	Gender	Degree	Years	Salary
2	Finance	42	F	MBA	15	$87,000
3	Management	29	F	MBA	4	$60,000
4	Production	35	M	BA	11	$45,000
5	Research	28	F	BS	5	$44,000
6	Production	39	M	MA	14	$36,000
7	Management	28	F	MBA	5	$48,000
8	Finance	33	M	MBA	7	$55,000
9	Marketing	20	F	MBA	1	$32,000
10	Research	28	M	BS	5	$38,000
11	Production	27	F	MA	8	$37,000
12	Research	24	M	BS	2	$36,000
13	Finance	26	F	MBA	3	$44,000
14	Accounting	32	M	BA	7	$38,000
15	Accounting	28	F	BA	6	$34,000
16	Production	25	M	BA	3	$29,000
17	Production	26	F	BA	3	$29,000
18	Research	32	M	Ph.D.	2	$54,000
19	Administration	45	F	MBA	14	$58,000
20	Production	27	M	MA	3	$29,000

4. Use the same spreadsheet you created in Exercise 3 to sort the Salary from lowest to highest.

5. Sort the spreadsheet shown in Exercise 1 by Office and then alphabetically by Last Name within each office. The home (HM) office employees should be listed before field office (FLD) employees (descending order).

6. Sort the spreadsheet shown in Figure 7.2 so that the final sorted spreadsheet appears as shown in the following spreadsheet (that is, the sorted list is in ascending order by Department, in ascending order by Degree within each department, and finally in Descending order by Salary within each degree).

	A	B	C	D	E	F
1	**Department**	**Age**	**Gender**	**Degree**	**Years**	**Salary**
2	Accounting	32	M	BA	7	$38,000
3	Accounting	28	F	BA	6	$34,000
4	Administration	45	F	MBA	14	$58,000
5	Finance	42	F	MBA	15	$87,000
6	Finance	33	M	MBA	7	$55,000
7	Finance	26	F	MBA	3	$44,000
8	Management	29	F	MBA	4	$60,000
9	Management	28	F	MBA	5	$48,000
10	Marketing	20	F	MBA	1	$32,000
11	Production	35	M	BA	11	$45,000
12	Production	25	M	BA	3	$29,000
13	Production	26	F	BA	3	$29,000
14	Production	27	F	MA	8	$37,000
15	Production	39	M	MA	14	$36,000
16	Production	27	M	MA	3	$29,000
17	Research	28	F	BS	5	$44,000
18	Research	28	M	BS	5	$38,000
19	Research	24	M	BS	2	$36,000
20	Research	32	M	Ph.D.	2	$54,000

7. Create the following spreadsheet and sort the data by Sales Company, ascending order.

Year Sold	Prop. Style	Price	Sales Company
2016	Lower	$180,000	Berkshire
2016	Lower	$180,000	Olney
2016	Middle	$179,000	Olney
2016	Middle	$235,000	Olney
2016	Upper	$235,000	Lenox
2017	Lower	$195,000	Lenox
2017	Lower	$219,000	Berkshire
2017	Lower	$225,000	Berkshire
2017	Middle	$225,000	Olney
2017	Middle	$245,000	Lenox
2017	Upper	$240,000	Berkshire
2018	Lower	$285,000	Lenox
2018	Lower	$216,000	Lenox
2018	Middle	$188,000	Lenox
2018	Middle	$198,000	Berkshire
2018	Upper	$224,000	Olney

8. Use the spreadsheet created for Exercise 7. Sort the data by Price, from lowest to highest (ascending order).

9. Use the spreadsheet created for Exercise 7. Sort the data by Prop. Style, from Lower to Middle to Upper (ascending order).

10. Use the spreadsheet created for Exercise 7. First, sort the data by Sales Company and then have the data, within each Company, sorted by Prop. Style. Both sort fields are in ascending order.

7.3 CREATING GROUP SUBTOTALS[2]

Frequently, after a spreadsheet's data is sorted by a desired field, such as year or sales office, subtotals of the sales or profits for each field are required. For example, consider Figure 7.9, which lists the sales of three real estate companies.

---

[2] This topic may be omitted without loss of subject continuity.

	A	B	C	D
1	**Year Sold**	**Company**	**Type**	**Sale**
2	2018	Berkshire	Lower	$180,000
3	2018	Olney	Lower	$180,000
4	2018	Olney	Middle	$179,000
5	2018	Olney	Middle	$235,000
6	2018	Lenox	Upper	$235,000
7	2019	Lenox	Lower	$195,000
8	2019	Berkshire	Lower	$219,000
9	2019	Berkshire	Lower	$225,000
10	2019	Olney	Middle	$225,000
11	2019	Lenox	Middle	$245,000
12	2019	Berkshire	Upper	$240,000
13	2020	Lenox	Lower	$285,000
14	2020	Lenox	Lower	$216,000
15	2020	Lenox	Middle	$188,000
16	2020	Berkshire	Middle	$198,000
17	2020	Olney	Upper	$224,000

Figure 7.9 Property sales data

For this data, a logical question would be "What is the total sales from 2018 through 2020 for each of the listed companies?" To answer this question, the data must first be sorted by company. When this is accomplished, Excel's Subtotal option can then be used to subtotal the sales values for each company.

The steps necessary to produce a sort of the companies, whose sales will then be subtotaled, follow the sort procedure presented in Section 7.2, and are as shown in Figure 7.10.

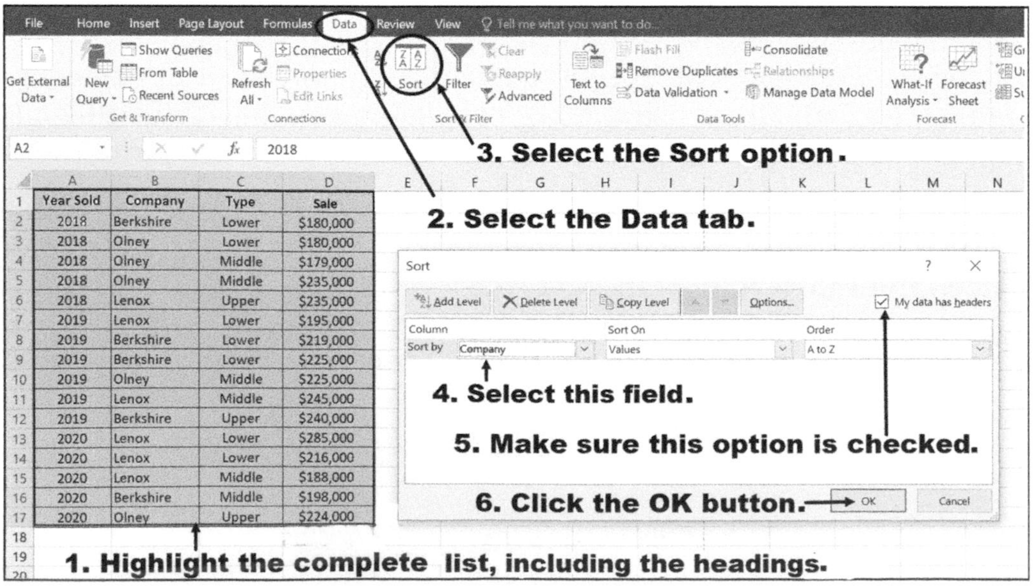

Figure 7.10 Sorting the original data by Company

Once the data has been sorted following the steps shown in Figure 7.10, the data will appear as shown in Figure 7.11. When the data is in this sorted order, it is ready to have the subtotals for the sales of each company computed.

It should be mentioned that Excel Subtotals can be made from Excel lists, but Excel Subtotals cannot be made from Excel Tables. If an attempt is made to create a Subtotal from a table, then the option would be grayed out and the operation cannot be completed.

	A	B	C	D
1	**Year Sold**	**Company**	**Type**	**Sale**
2	2018	Berkshire	Lower	$180,000
3	2019	Berkshire	Lower	$219,000
4	2019	Berkshire	Lower	$225,000
5	2019	Berkshire	Upper	$240,000
6	2020	Berkshire	Middle	$198,000
7	2018	Lenox	Upper	$235,000
8	2019	Lenox	Lower	$195,000
9	2019	Lenox	Middle	$245,000
10	2020	Lenox	Lower	$285,000
11	2020	Lenox	Lower	$216,000
12	2020	Lenox	Middle	$188,000
13	2018	Olney	Lower	$180,000
14	2018	Olney	Middle	$179,000
15	2018	Olney	Middle	$235,000
16	2019	Olney	Middle	$225,000
17	2020	Olney	Upper	$224,000

Figure 7.11 The initial data in sorted order by Company

To create sales subtotals for each company, the complete spreadsheet must be highlighted (clicking on a cell within the table and then pressing the Ctrl and A keys at the same time will highlight the complete sheet). Once the data is highlighted, clicking on the Excel ribbon Data tab-Outline group-Subtotal icon in the Data ribbon, as shown in Figure 7.12, brings up the Subtotal dialog box shown in Figure 7.13.

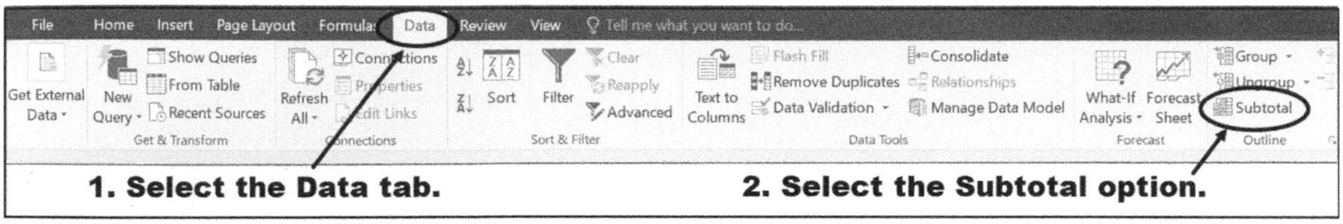

Figure 7.12 Selecting the Subtotal option

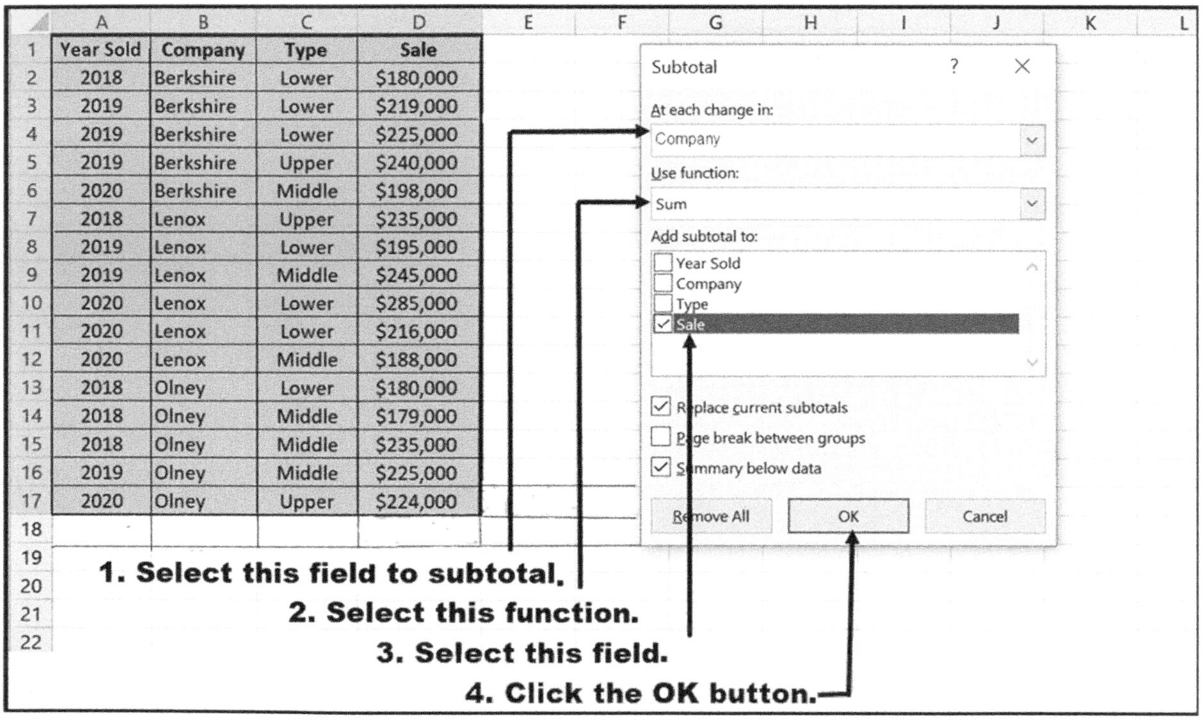

Figure 7.13 The Subtotal dialog box

Selecting the choices shown in Figure 7.13 causes the desired subtotals, by Company, to appear, as shown in Figure 7.14. Notice that in Figure 7.14, Types are not grouped together for each Company (see the Type listing for the Lenox subtotal, for example), but remain in the order they appear in the original list. Although this is not a problem, it would be preferable to have these grouped together for each Company (this can be accomplished by initially sorting the data by Company and then by Type in the original sort, before any subtotals are taken).

	A	B	C	D
1	Year Sold	Company	Type	Sale
2	2018	Berkshire	Lower	$180,000
3	2019	Berkshire	Lower	$219,000
4	2019	Berkshire	Lower	$225,000
5	2019	Berkshire	Upper	$240,000
6	2020	Berkshire	Middle	$198,000
7	**Berkshire Total**			$1,062,000
8	2018	Lenox	Upper	$235,000
9	2019	Lenox	Lower	$195,000
10	2019	Lenox	Middle	$245,000
11	2020	Lenox	Lower	$285,000
12	2020	Lenox	Lower	$216,000
13	2020	Lenox	Middle	$188,000
14	**Lenox Total**			$1,364,000
15	2018	Olney	Lower	$180,000
16	2018	Olney	Middle	$179,000
17	2018	Olney	Middle	$235,000
18	2019	Olney	Middle	$225,000
19	2020	Olney	Upper	$224,000
20	**Olney Total**			$1,043,000
21	**Grand Total**			$3,469,000

Figure 7.14 The sorted data subtotaled by Company

At this point, you will see the results of the Subtotal feature applied to the spreadsheet. By employing features from Excel's Outline Group feature, not only are the requested subtotals added with new row subtotals and a Grand Total, but a new structure has been applied to the spreadsheet. The "group" feature allows you to select different "levels" of summary data to be displayed. The lower the number, the higher level it is in terms of summarization, and therefore a higher number would bring about a greater level of detail (meaning it is a higher level in terms of summary). There are also buttons to click to contract (-) or expand (+) a specific level and the detail being displayed. In the example shown in Figure 7.14, clicking on these allows you to contract and expand the individual subtotal groups. For example, if you click on the 2 box, the spreadsheet will appear as in Figure 7.15. Notice that you can expand individual groups by clicking on the + icons in the 2 column or the complete spreadsheet by clicking on the 3 box itself.

	A	B	C	D
1	Year Sold	Company	Type	Sale
7	Berkshire Total			$1,062,000
14	Lenox Total			$1,364,000
20	Olney Total			$1,043,000
21	Grand Total			$3,469,000

Figure 7.15 The data summarized by Company and Sale subtotals

Although it is easy to visually determine that Lenox had the highest sales for the three companies listed in Figure 7.15, for larger data sets, a final sort (in this case, based on Sale) is frequently useful. This is accomplished by sorting the summarized spreadsheet shown in Figure 7.15 from highest to lowest (or from lowest to highest) sales. (see Exercise 3b).

Notice that the general rule for calculating subtotals of individual items within a field requires that the data must first be sorted by the field under consideration. Thus, if the subtotals of sales by salesperson is required, the data must first be sorted by Salesperson. Similarly, as shown in Figures 7.14 and 7.15, the subtotals by company required that the data was first sorted in Company order.

Nested Subtotals

In addition to subtotals for individual categories, or groups of data, such as the subtotals for Department, Salesperson, or Company, it is often necessary to have a nested set of subtotals – that is, subtotals *within* subtotals. You can consider this as adding an additional level of subtotals within a current one. For example, while Figure 7.15 provides subtotals by Company, Figure 7.16 provides subtotals for each property Type *within* each Company subtotal.

	A	B	C	D
1	Year Sold	Company	Type	Sale
5	.		Lower Total	$624,000
7			Middle Total	$198,000
9			Upper Total	$240,000
10		Berkshire Total		$1,062,000
14			Lower Total	$696,000
17			Middle Total	$433,000
19			Upper Total	$235,000
20		Lenox Total		$1,364,000
22			Lower Total	$180,000
26			Middle Total	$639,000
28			Upper Total	$224,000
29		Olney Total		$1,043,000
30		Grand Total		$3,469,000
31				

Figure 7.16 Nested subtotals of Sale by Type within each Company

Creating subtotals for individual groups (or categories) of data always requires that the data first be sorted by the field for which subtotals are desired, and the general rule for creating subtotals within subtotals, such as that shown in Figure 7.16 is as follows:

General Rule for Data Sorting Prior to Creating Nested Subtotals: *The data must be sorted, using a multi-level sort, in the same order as each level of desired subtotals. That is, the first-level sort corresponds to the highest level desired subtotal field (outside level) and continues to the lowest (inside level) desired subtotal field.*

For example, if subtotals of Sales by Type *within* subtotals by Company are required, as shown in Figure 7.16, the highest, or outside level, is Company, and the next, or interior level, is Type. Thus, the data must first be sorted by Company and then by Type.

Example

A nested subtotal of Salary by Job Title *within* a Department subtotal group is desired. What order must the data be sorted so that the desired nested subtotals can be determined?

Solution: Because the nesting is subtotals of Salary by Job Title *within* Departments, the data must first be sorted by Department and then by Job Title. That is, the outside field (i.e., group) is department and the interior, or inside group, is Job Title.

Example

A nested subtotal of Sales Calls by Salesperson ***within*** each Office Location is desired. What order must the data be sorted so that the desired nested subtotals can be determined?

Solution: Because the nesting is subtotals of Sales Calls by Salesperson ***within*** each Office Location, the data must first be sorted by Office Location, and then by Salesperson. That is, the outside field (i.e., group) is Office Location and the interior, or inside group, is Salesperson.

Creating Nested Subtotals

Once the required multi-level data sorting is complete, nested subtotals can be created.[3] These subtotals are created, one-at-a-time, in the same order that the data was sorted.

As an example of creating a nested group of subtotals, we will use the data shown in Figure 7.17 to create subtotals of sales by property Type within each Company.

---

[3] The sorts must be completed prior to creating subtotals.

	A	B	C	D
1	**Year Sold**	**Company**	**Type**	**Sale**
2	2018	Berkshire	Lower	$180,000
3	2018	Olney	Lower	$180,000
4	2018	Olney	Middle	$179,000
5	2018	Olney	Middle	$235,000
6	2018	Lenox	Upper	$235,000
7	2019	Lenox	Lower	$195,000
8	2019	Berkshire	Lower	$219,000
9	2019	Berkshire	Lower	$225,000
10	2019	Olney	Middle	$225,000
11	2019	Lenox	Middle	$245,000
12	2019	Berkshire	Upper	$240,000
13	2020	Lenox	Lower	$285,000
14	2020	Lenox	Lower	$216,000
15	2020	Lenox	Middle	$188,000
16	2020	Berkshire	Middle	$198,000
17	2020	Olney	Upper	$224,000

Figure 7.17 Property sales data

Because we want nested sales subtotals of property Type *within* each Company, the required multi-level sort is first by Company, with the second-level by property Type. This is accomplished using the multi-sort procedure presented in the prior section and applied as shown in Figure 7.18.[4]

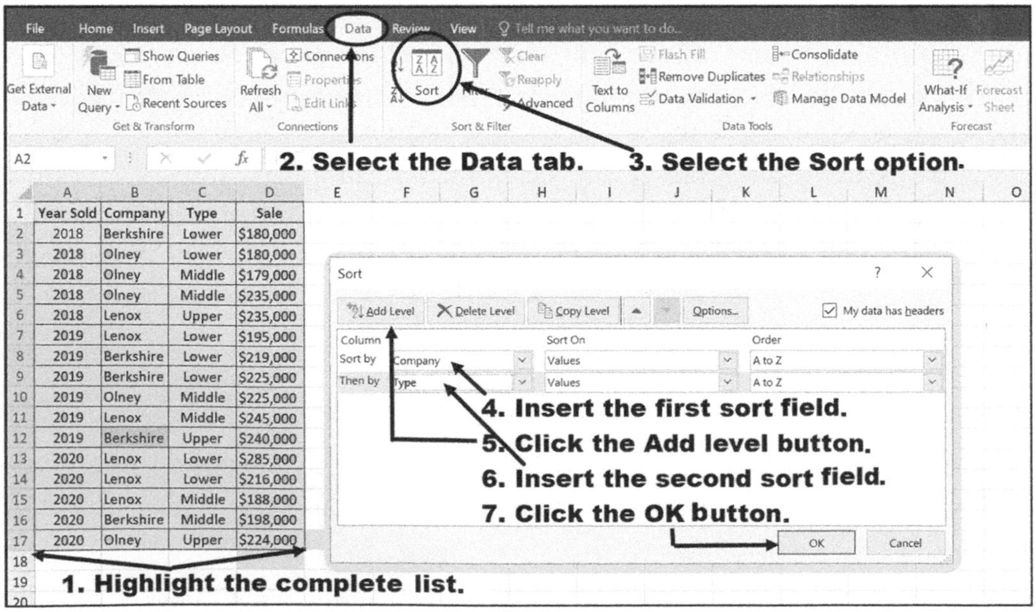

Figure 7.18 Creating the two-level sort

---

[4] The multi-level sort can be made with any list that contains the original data; it need not be in the original list, but must contain the desired categories for which subtotals are desired.

Figure 7.19 shows the sorted list produced by following the steps listed in Figure 7.18.

	A	B	C	D
1	Year Sold	Company	Type	Sale
2	2018	Berkshire	Lower	$180,000
3	2019	Berkshire	Lower	$219,000
4	2019	Berkshire	Lower	$225,000
5	2020	Berkshire	Middle	$198,000
6	2019	Berkshire	Upper	$240,000
7	2019	Lenox	Lower	$195,000
8	2020	Lenox	Lower	$285,000
9	2020	Lenox	Lower	$216,000
10	2019	Lenox	Middle	$245,000
11	2020	Lenox	Middle	$188,000
12	2018	Lenox	Upper	$235,000
13	2018	Olney	Lower	$180,000
14	2018	Olney	Middle	$179,000
15	2018	Olney	Middle	$235,000
16	2019	Olney	Middle	$225,000
17	2020	Olney	Upper	$224,000

Figure 7.19 The list sorted by Company and then by Type

Once the list is in the order that corresponds to the desired subtotals, the actual nested subtotals can be created. This is done as shown in Figure 7.20 by first highlighting the complete worksheet (clicking within the table and then pressing the Ctrl and A keys at the same time does this; ⌘-A for Mac Excel), and then using the information shown in Figure 7.20 to create the first set of subtotals. Pressing the OK button, once the Subtotal dialog box shown in the figure is filled in correctly, creates the list shown in Figure 7.21.

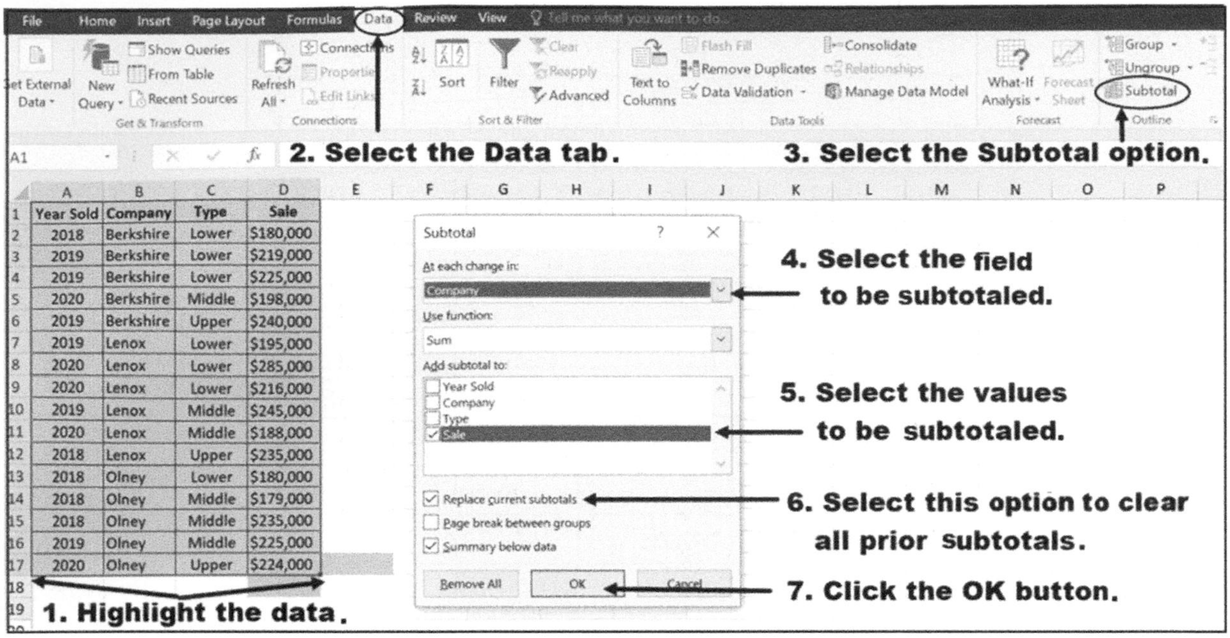

Figure 7.20 Creating the first set of subtotals by Company

Notice in Figure 7.21 that the property Types within each Company are also in sorted order. This is the result of the original multi-level sort performed before Company subtotals were taken. Because of this, we can now create subtotals for each property Type while still retaining the Sales by Company subtotals.

To create the second set of subtotals, click on the Excel ribbon's Data tab's Sub-total option once again and fill in the dialog box shown in Figure 7.22. Make sure to uncheck the box labeled ***Replace current subtotals***, so that the earlier subtotals are not erased. When the dialog box has been completed and the OK button is pressed, the nested list of subtotals for each property Type within each Company is produced, as shown in Figure 7.23. The summarized, subtotaled list displaying just the subtotals is shown in Figure 7.24. This last figure is the same as that initially shown as Figure 7.14, and is produced by clicking on the box labeled 3 at the top left corner of the spreadsheet.

	A	B	C	D
1	**Year Sold**	**Company**	**Type**	**Sale**
2	2018	Berkshire	Lower	$180,000
3	2019	Berkshire	Lower	$219,000
4	2019	Berkshire	Lower	$225,000
5	2020	Berkshire	Middle	$198,000
6	2019	Berkshire	Upper	$240,000
7		**Berkshire Total**		$1,062,000
8	2019	Lenox	Lower	$195,000
9	2020	Lenox	Lower	$285,000
10	2020	Lenox	Lower	$216,000
11	2019	Lenox	Middle	$245,000
12	2020	Lenox	Middle	$188,000
13	2018	Lenox	Upper	$235,000
14		**Lenox Total**		$1,364,000
15	2018	Olney	Lower	$180,000
16	2018	Olney	Middle	$179,000
17	2018	Olney	Middle	$235,000
18	2019	Olney	MIddle	$225,000
19	2020	Olney	Upper	$224,000
20		**Olney Total**		$1,043,000
21		**Grand Total**		$3,469,000

Figure 7.21 Sales data subtotaled by Company

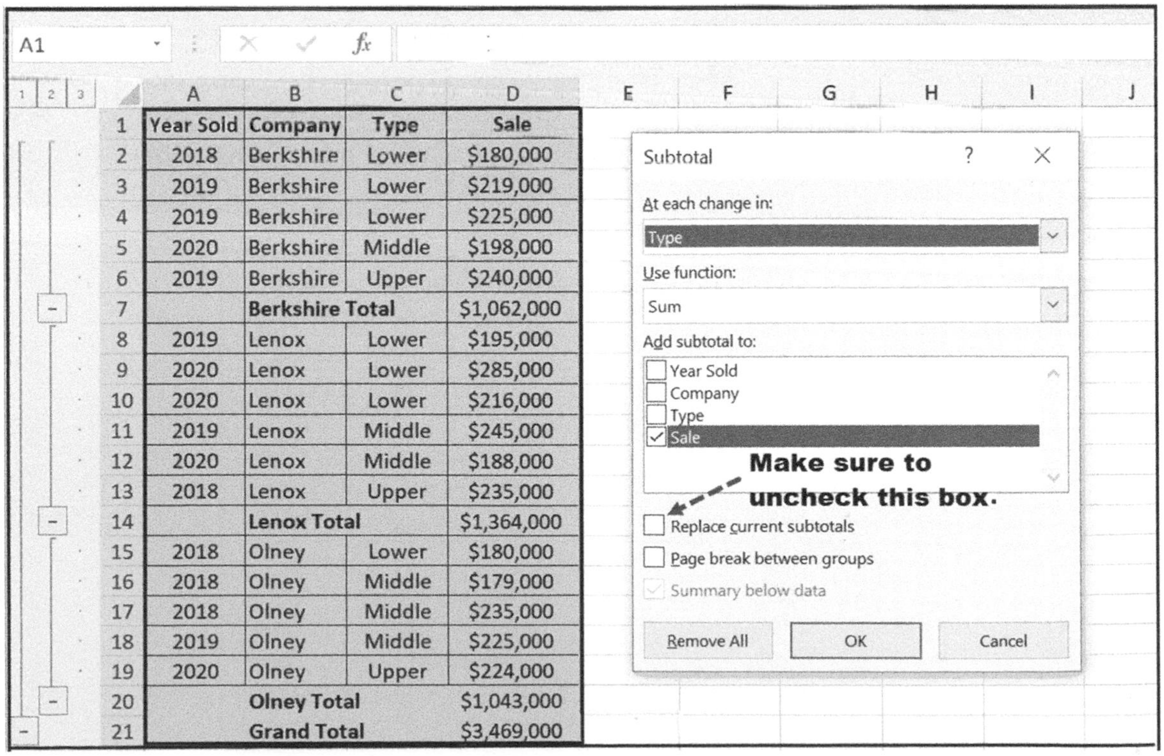

Figure 7.22 Creating the second (nested) set of subtotals

Year Sold	Company	Type	Sale
2018	Berkshire	Lower	$180,000
2019	Berkshire	Lower	$219,000
2019	Berkshire	Lower	$225,000
		Lower Total	**$624,000**
2020	Berkshire	Middle	$198,000
		Middle Total	**$198,000**
2019	Berkshire	Upper	$240,000
		Upper Total	**$240,000**
	Berkshire Total		**$1,062,000**
2019	Lenox	Lower	$195,000
2020	Lenox	Lower	$285,000
2020	Lenox	Lower	$216,000
		Lower Total	**$696,000**
2019	Lenox	Middle	$245,000
2020	Lenox	Middle	$188,000
		Middle Total	**$433,000**
2018	Lenox	Upper	$235,000
		Upper Total	**$235,000**
	Lenox Total		**$1,364,000**
2018	Olney	Lower	$180,000
		Lower Total	**$180,000**
2018	Olney	Middle	$179,000
2018	Olney	Middle	$235,000
2019	Olney	Middle	$225,000
		Middle Total	**$639,000**
2020	Olney	Upper	$224,000
		Upper Total	**$224,000**
	Olney Total		**$1,043,000**
	Grand Total		**$3,469,000**

Figure 7.23 The list with Type subtotals nested within Company subtotals

	A	B	C	D
1	Year Sold	Company	Type	Sale
5			**Lower Total**	$624,000
7			**Middle Total**	$198,000
9			**Upper Total**	$240,000
10		**Berkshire Total**		$1,062,000
14			**Lower Total**	$696,000
17			**Middle Total**	$433,000
19			**Upper Total**	$235,000
20		**Lenox Total**		$1,364,000
22			**Lower Total**	$180,000
26			**Middle Total**	$639,000
28			**Upper Total**	$224,000
29		**Olney Total**		$1,043,000
30		**Grand Total**		$3,469,000

Figure 7.24 Nested subtotals of Sales by Type within each Company

EXERCISES 7.3

1. What must be done to the spreadsheet data before a subtotal can be generated?

2. For the following, identify the sort that is required before the desired subtotals are determined.

    a. Profit totals by office, for a company with multiple offices.

    b. Sales totals by salesperson, for a company with multiple salespeople.

    c. Number of products sold, by product type, for a company selling multiple products.

3. Complete parts a-b.

    a. Create a spreadsheet with the following data, and sort the data by company (ascending). After your spreadsheet has been sorted, create the subtotals shown in the second figure.

	A	B	C	D
1	**Year Sold**	**Company**	**Type**	**Sale**
2	2018	Berkshire	Lower	$180,000
3	2018	Olney	Lower	$180,000
4	2018	Olney	Middle	$179,000
5	2018	Olney	Middle	$235,000
6	2018	Lenox	Upper	$235,000
7	2019	Lenox	Lower	$195,000
8	2019	Berkshire	Lower	$219,000
9	2019	Berkshire	Lower	$225,000
10	2019	Olney	Middle	$225,000
11	2019	Lenox	Middle	$245,000
12	2019	Berkshire	Upper	$240,000
13	2020	Lenox	Lower	$285,000
14	2020	Lenox	Lower	$216,000
15	2020	Lenox	Middle	$188,000
16	2020	Berkshire	Middle	$198,000
17	2020	Olney	Upper	$224,000

				A	B	C	D
1	2	3					
			1	Year Sold	Company	Type	Sale
			2	2018	Berkshire	Lower	$180,000
			3	2019	Berkshire	Lower	$219,000
			4	2019	Berkshire	Lower	$225,000
			5	2019	Berkshire	Upper	$240,000
			6	2020	Berkshire	Middle	$198,000
	−		7	Berkshire Total			$1,062,000
			8	2018	Lenox	Upper	$235,000
			9	2019	Lenox	Lower	$195,000
			10	2019	Lenox	Middle	$245,000
			11	2020	Lenox	Lower	$285,000
			12	2020	Lenox	Lower	$216,000
			13	2020	Lenox	Middle	$188,000
	−		14	Lenox Total			$1,364,000
			15	2018	Olney	Lower	$180,000
			16	2018	Olney	Middle	$179,000
			17	2018	Olney	Middle	$235,000
			18	2019	Olney	Middle	$225,000
			19	2020	Olney	Upper	$224,000
	−		20	Olney Total			$1,043,000
−			21	Grand Total			$3,469,000

b. For the spreadsheet in Exercise 3a, produce another spreadsheet that summarizes the sales, from the lowest to the highest values, as shown in the following spreadsheet.

				A	B	C	D
1	2	3					
			1	Year Sold	Company	Type	Sale
+			7	Berkshire Total			$1,062,000
+			14	Lenox Total			$1,364,000
+			20	Olney Total		'	$1,043,000
−			21	Grand Total			$3,469,000

4. Complete parts a-b.

    a. Using the spreadsheet created in Exercise 3a, produce a spreadsheet that provides the sales subtotals for each year, from 2018 to 2020. (**Hint:** First sort the spreadsheet by Year Sold.)

    b. For the spreadsheet prepared for Exercise 4a, produce a spreadsheet that summarizes the Sale values from lowest to highest values. (**Hint:** See Figures 7.15 and 7.16.)

5. Complete parts a-b.

    a. Using the sales data spreadsheet created in Exercise 3a, produce another spreadsheet that provides sales subtotals for each property type. (**Hint:** First sort the spreadsheet by Type.)

b. For the spreadsheet prepared for Exercise 5a, produce a spreadsheet that summarizes the Sales from the lowest to the highest values. (***Hint:*** see Figures 7.15 and 7.16.)

6. For the following spreadsheet, shown in Figure 7.25, create the salary subtotals for each Department. Your completed spreadsheet should appear as shown in Figure 7.26.

	A	B	C	D	E
1	**Department**	**Gender**	**Degree**	**Years**	**Salary**
2	Management	F	MBA	10	$70,250
3	Marketing	M	MBA	12	$74,150
4	Production	M	BA	5	$58,500
5	Production	M	BA	5	$56,195
6	Production	F	BA	4	$48,527
7	Production	M	MA	12	$71,648
8	Production	M	MA	7	$66,251
9	Production	F	MA	13	$64,225
10	Research	F	BS	5	$73,485
11	Research	M	BS	7	$79,350
12	Research	M	BS	5	$54,527
13	Research	M	Ph.D.	12	$84,250

Figure 7.25 Orignal data for Exercise 6

	A	B	C	D	E
1	**Department**	**Gender**	**Degree**	**Years**	**Salary**
2	Management	F	MBA	10	$70,250
3	**Management Total**				$70,250
4	Marketing	M	MBA	12	$74,150
5	**Marketing Total**				$74,150
6	Production	M	BA	5	$58,500
7	Production	M	BA	5	$56,195
8	Production	F	BA	4	$48,527
9	Production	M	MA	12	$71,648
10	Production	M	MA	7	$66,251
11	Production	F	MA	13	$64,225
12	**Production Total**				$365,346
13	Research	F	BS	5	$73,485
14	Research	M	BS	7	$79,350
15	Research	M	BS	5	$54,527
16	Research	M	Ph.D.	12	$84,250
17	**Research Total**				$291,612
18	**Grand Total**				$801,358

Figure 7.26 Subtotals of Salary by Department

7. Figure 7.14 provides subtotals for each company. Before creating these subtotals, perform a second sort for the Type (ascending) within each company. Your completed spreadsheet should then appear as follows:

	A	B	C	D
1	**Year Sold**	**Company**	**Type**	**Sale**
2	2018	Berkshire	Lower	$180,000
3	2019	Berkshire	Lower	$219,000
4	2019	Berkshire	Lower	$225,000
5	2020	Berkshire	Middle	$198,000
6	2019	Berkshire	Upper	$240,000
7		**Berkshire Total**		**$1,062,000**
8	2019	Lenox	Lower	$195,000
9	2020	Lenox	Lower	$285,000
10	2020	Lenox	Lower	$216,000
11	2019	Lenox	Middle	$245,000
12	2020	Lenox	Middle	$188,000
13	2018	Lenox	Upper	$235,000
14		**Lenox Total**		**$1,364,000**
15	2018	Olney	Lower	$180,000
16	2018	Olney	Middle	$179,000
17	2018	Olney	Middle	$235,000
18	2019	Olney	Middle	$225,000
19	2020	Olney	Upper	$224,000
20		**Olney Total**		**$1,043,000**
21		**Grand Total**		**$3,469,000**

8. Complete parts a-b.

a. If a nested subtotal of salaries by profession within a Department subtotal group is desired, what order should salary data be sorted before subtotals are determined?

b. If a nested subtotal of sales calls by salesperson within an office subtotal group is desired, what order should the sales calls be sorted before subtotals are determined?

9. Starting with the spreadsheet shown in Exercise 3a, follow the steps shown in Figures 7.18 through 7.23 and reproduce the nested subtotals shown in the following spreadsheet.

		A	B	C	D
	1	Year Sold	Company	Type	Sale
+	5			Lower Total	$624,000
+	7			Middle Total	$198,000
+	9			Upper Total	$240,000
−	10		Berkshire Total		$1,062,000
+	14			Lower Total	$696,000
+	17			Middle Total	$433,000
+	19			Upper Total	$235,000
−	20		Lenox Total		$1,364,000
+	22			Lower Total	$180,000
+	26			Middle Total	$639,000
+	28			Upper Total	$224,000
−	29		Olney Total		$1,043,000
−	30		Grand Total		$3,469,000

10. For the spreadsheet shown in Exercise 3a, create a spreadsheet that shows Sale subtotals for each Type, where the Sale prices are in increasing order. When you have completed this, your spreadsheet should look like the example. (**Hint:** To create the summarized and sorted spreadsheet shown, you will first have to sort the original data by Type, then determine Sale subtotals for each type, and finally sort, from lowest to highest, the summarized data by Sale price.)

		A	B	C	D
	1	Year Sold	Company	Type	Sale
+	5			Upper Total	$699,000
+	12			Middle Total	$1,270,000
+	20			Lower Total	$1,500,000
−	21			Grand Total	$3,469,000

11. For the spreadsheet shown in Figure 7.27, create a summary consisting of nested salaries by Degree, within Gender, within each Department. Your completed spreadsheet should appear as shown in Figure 7.28.

	A	B	C	D	E
1	**Department**	**Gender**	**Degree**	**Years**	**Salary**
2	Management	F	MBA	10	$70,250
3	Marketing	M	MBA	12	$74,150
4	Production	M	BA	5	$58,500
5	Production	M	BA	5	$56,195
6	Production	F	BA	4	$48,527
7	Production	M	MA	12	$71,648
8	Production	M	MA	7	$66,251
9	Production	F	MA	13	$64,225
10	Research	F	BS	5	$73,485
11	Research	M	BS	7	$79,350
12	Research	M	BS	5	$54,527
13	Research	M	Ph.D.	12	$84,250

Figure 7.27 Spreadsheet for Exercise 11

	A	B	C	D	E
1	**Department**	**Gender**	**Degree**	**Years**	**Salary**
2	Management	F	MBA	10	$70,250
3		**F Total**			$70,250
4	**Management Total**				$70,250
5	Marketing	M	MBA	12	$74,150
6		**M Total**			$74,150
7	**Marketing Total**				$74,150
8	Production	F	BA	4	$48,527
9	Production	F	MA	13	$64,225
10		**F Total**			$112,752
11	Production	M	BA	5	$58,500
12	Production	M	BA	5	$56,195
13	Production	M	MA	12	$71,648
14	Production	M	MA	7	$66,251
15		**M Total**			$252,594
16	**Production Total**				$365,346
17	Research	F	BS	5	$73,485
18		**F Total**			$73,485
19	Research	M	BS	7	$79,350
20	Research	M	BS	5	$54,527
21	Research	M	Ph.D.	12	$84,250
22		**M Total**			$218,127
23	**Research Total**				$291,612
24	**Grand Total**				$801,358

Figure 7.28 Subtotals of Salary by Gender within Department

7.4   SEARCHING (FILTERING) FOR SELECTED RECORDS

Searching a spreadsheet and displaying (also known as *filtering*) either the complete row or selected items from each row containing the searched for item is accomplished using the Excel ribbon's Data tab's **Advanced Filter** option. Essentially, each row in the spreadsheet passes through a filter that is composed of the search criteria. Only if one or more values in the row meets the criteria is the complete row, or desired items from the row, displayed.

All of Excel's relational operators, as listed in Table 7.1, are available for creating search conditions.[5]

Table 7.1 Excel's relational operators

Relational Operator	Meaning	Example
<	less than	<40000
>	greater than	>50000
<=	less than or equal to	<=20
>=	greater than or equal to	>= 15
=	equal to	= 20000
<>	not equal to	<>"Chatham"

As a specific example, consider the spreadsheet shown in Figure 7.29.

	A	B	C	D	E	F
1	**Department**	**Age**	**Gender**	**Degree**	**Years**	**Salary**
2	Finance	42	F	MBA	15	$87,000
3	Management	29	F	MBA	4	$60,000
4	Production	35	M	BA	11	$45,000
5	Research	28	F	BS	5	$44,000
6	Production	39	M	MA	14	$36,000
7	Management	28	F	MBA	5	$48,000
8	Finance	33	M	MBA	7	$55,000
9	Marketing	20	F	MBA	1	$32,000
10	Research	28	M	BS	5	$38,000
11	Production	27	F	MA	8	$37,000
12	Research	24	M	BS	2	$36,000
13	Finance	26	F	MBA	3	$44,000
14	Accounting	32	M	BA	7	$38,000
15	Accounting	28	F	BA	6	$34,000
16	Production	27	M	MA	3	$29,000

Figure 7.29 Salary data

[5] These operators were initially introduced in Section 4.1.

Although the search criteria can be placed anywhere within the spreadsheet (and even on a different sheet, for convenience), by convention the search criteria are typically placed above the data being searched. This is done by inserting at least 5 rows at the top of the data, as shown in Figure 7.30. Initially, the top-most additional row should contain the same headers as those in the worksheet being searched, and the other four are initially left blank. These additional rows are used for creating both simple and more complex searches.

	A	B	C	D	E	F
1	Department	Age	Gender	Degree	Years	Salary
2						
3						
4						
5						
6	Department	Age	Gender	Degree	Years	Salary
7	Finance	42	F	MBA	15	$87,000
8	Management	29	F	MBA	4	$60,000
9	Production	35	M	BA	11	$45,000
10	Research	28	F	BS	5	$44,000
11	Production	39	M	MA	14	$36,000
12	Management	28	F	MBA	5	$48,000
13	Finance	33	M	MBA	7	$55,000
14	Marketing	20	F	MBA	1	$32,000
15	Research	28	M	BS	5	$38,000
16	Production	27	F	MA	8	$37,000
17	Research	24	M	BS	2	$36,000
18	Finance	26	F	MBA	3	$44,000
19	Accounting	32	M	BA	7	$38,000
20	Accounting	28	F	BA	6	$34,000
21	Production	27	M	MA	3	$29,000

Figure 7.30 Additional rows added for the search criteria

This new area which has been created is known as the *criteria range*. Regardless of where this criteria range is placed, it needs to be in the proper format to be used to do an Advanced Filter. Once the additional rows have been added, as illustrated in Figure 7.30, the actual search criteria can be specified. It is important to understand that all criteria entered on a single line are considered by Excel to constitute AND conditions. Initially, we will illustrate a search using only one criteria line. More complex searches using AND and OR conditions are presented at the end of this section. In all cases, both simple and more complex searches are completed using the following three-step search procedure:

Step 1: Fill in the criteria range with the search criteria.

Step 2: Select the Excel ribbon's Advanced Filter option, shown in Figure 7.31.

Figure 7.31 Selecting the Advanced Filter option

Step 3: Complete the Advanced Filter Dialog, shown in Figure 7.32.

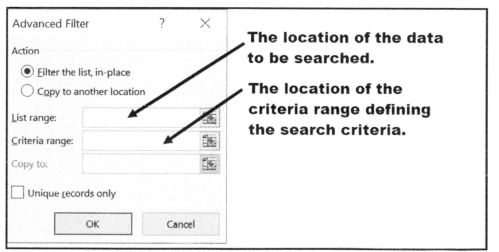

Figure 7.32 The Advanced Filter dialog box

The **Filter the List, In Place** action will display the filtered list superimposed over the original list, with the filter result record numbers listed in blue, indicating that the list is missing records due to the filter being applied. The **Copy to Another Location** action will paste a copy of the filtered results to an indicated location on the spreadsheet, which is indicated in the **Copy to** box (in this example, greyed out, since we are doing a Filter in Place).

The **List Range** is your entire list or table of original data, including the header row. The **Criteria Range** is the entire area listing your filter criteria, including the header row.

To continue our example, we will search the spreadsheet shown in Figure 7.30 for all employees who are over 27 years of age, are female, and have an MBA degree. To

---

Application Note
Copying Selected Record Columns

Clicking the Advanced Filter dialog box's *Copy to another location* (see Figure 7.35) button allows you to display individual records in a specified location, rather than using Filter in Place. However, in some cases, you only need a subset (not all) of the field columns in your result. The following procedure shows you how.

This is accomplished by

Step 1: Setting up your search criteria in the Criteria Range. This will restrict the output only to the records which match your specified criteria.

Step 2: Selecting Data – Sort & Filter – Advanced

Step 3: Checking the *Copy to another location* button in the Advanced Filter dialog.

Step 4: Enter the List Range (Normally, if you use the entire list and data, you will get ALL of the fields from the records which match the specified criteria. However, if you only want SOME of the fields (columns) to be displayed as the output, then only select those headers and fields that you want, and enter these as the List Range.)

Step 5: Enter the Criteria Range

Step 6: Provide the Copy To range

Step 7: Clicking OK to filter the list and paste the result.

This will provide the customized output in a designated location, providing a filtered list and only displaying selected field columns.

---

see how this is accomplished, initially add the data in cells B2 through D2, as shown in Figure 7.33, and entered as indicated.

	A	B	C	D	E	F	G	H	I	J	K
1	Department	Age	Gender	Degree	Years	Salary					
2		>27	F	MBA			Enter as MBA				
3							Enter as F				
4							Enter as >27				
5											
6	Department	Age	Gender	Degree	Years	Salary					
7	Finance	42	F	MBA	15	$87,000	Note: Make sure				
8	Management	29	F	MBA	4	$60,000	criteria cells are				
9	Production	35	M	BA	11	$45,000	formatted as Numeric.				
10	Research	28	F	BS	5	$44,000					
11	Production	39	M	MA	14	$36,000					
12	Management	28	F	MBA	5	$48,000					
13	Finance	33	M	MBA	7	$55,000					
14	Marketing	20	F	MBA	1	$32,000					
15	Research	28	M	BS	5	$38,000					
16	Production	27	F	MA	8	$37,000					
17	Research	24	M	BS	2	$36,000					
18	Finance	26	F	MBA	3	$44,000					
19	Accounting	32	M	BA	7	$38,000					
20	Accounting	28	F	BA	6	$34,000					
21	Production	27	M	MA	3	$29,000					
22											

Figure 7.33 Preparing to Do an Advanced Filter

If you have a text field criteria, simply enter the text string into the appropriate location in the Criteria range. No quotes or equals sign needed. The same applies to comparison expressions, where all you need is the expression. Again, neither an equals sign or a quote is needed.

It is important, however, when using the equality operator that (1) *no spaces be added within the string* (the reason is that as an exact match is being searched for and any additional spaces changes the search value) and (2) *any numeric criteria cells have been formatted using a numeric format.*

Once you have created the spreadsheet shown in Figure 7.33, select the Data Ribbon's Advanced option, as shown in Figure 7.34. This will bring up the Advanced Filter dialog box shown in Figure 7.35.

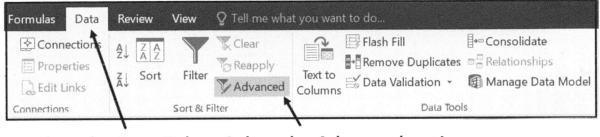

Select the Data Tab   Select the Advanced option

Figure 7.34 Selecting the Advanced option on the Excel Ribbon, Data tab, and Sort & Filter Group

	A	B	C	D	E	F	G	H	I	J	K
1	Department	Age	Gender	Degree	Years	Salary					
2		>27	F	MBA							
3											
4											
5											
6	Department	Age	Gender	Degree	Years	Salary					
7	Finance	42	F	MBA	15	$87,000					
8	Management	29	F	MBA	4	$60,000					
9	Production	35	M	BA	11	$45,000					
10	Research	28	F	BS	5	$44,000					
11	Production	39	M	MA	14	$36,000					
12	Management	28	F	MBA	5	$48,000					
13	Finance	33	M	MBA	7	$55,000					
14	Marketing	20	F	MBA	1	$32,000					
15	Research	28	M	BS	5	$38,000					
16	Production	27	F	MA	8	$37,000					
17	Research	24	M	BS	2	$36,000					
18	Finance	26	F	MBA	3	$44,000					
19	Accounting	32	M	BA	7	$38,000					
20	Accounting	28	F	BA	6	$34,000					
21	Production	27	M	MA	3	$29,000					
22											

Advanced Filter dialog box contents:

Action
- (●) Filter the list, in-place
- ( ) Copy to another location

List range: $A$6:$F$21

Criteria range: $A$1:$F$2

Copy to:

☐ Unique records only

[OK]   [Cancel]

Figure 7.35 The Advanced Filter dialog box

Application Note
Simple Find and Replace Searches

In addition to locating and displaying complete records, Excel also provides for simple Find and Replace searches. This search option is located in the Editing group of the Excel ribbon's Home tab. A Find and Replace search is identical to those found in word processing programs; it locates all occurrences of a specified numeric or text value and permits replacing the value with another, if necessary.

Using the wildcard symbols presented in Section 8.4, a Find and Replace search is a powerful method of easily correcting spelling errors or replacing simple one or two character codes with a longer text values. These techniques are presented in Section 8.4.

Filling in this dialog box, as shown in Figure 7.35, and then clicking the OK button, creates the filtered spreadsheet as a Filter the List, in-place display, which shows the records meeting the given criteria.

	A	B	C	D	E	F
1	**Department**	**Age**	**Gender**	**Degree**	**Years**	**Salary**
2		>27	F	MBA		
3						
4						
5						
6	**Department**	**Age**	**Gender**	**Degree**	**Years**	**Salary**
7	Finance	42	F	MBA	15	$87,000
8	Management	29	F	MBA	4	$60,000
12	Management	28	F	MBA	5	$48,000

Figure 7.36 The spreadsheet data meeting the stated criteria

Pressing the Undo Button on the Quick Access Toolbar at the top of the screen will reset the spreadsheet back to its original form. Alternatively, you can have the filtered data output copied to a different region on the spreadsheet by clicking on the *Copy to another location* button in the dialog shown on Figure 7.35, and then designating where the selected data is to be displayed.

More Complex Searches

In creating OR conditions, it is important to remember that all criteria entered on a single line are considered by Excel to constitute AND conditions (where all stated conditions must evaluate to TRUE), while conditions entered on the following and subsequent lines are considered as a new set of AND conditions within an OR condition (where at least one, but up to all, must evaluate to TRUE). This basic organization for the first three criteria lines is shown in Figure 7.37. If a fourth criteria line is used, the conditions on this line are put together, and then Excel uses OR with the previous lines, and so on for all criteria lines.

1st line - labels ⟶	Labels are located in this line - Add additional labels as needed
2nd line "AND"s ⟶	All conditions in this line are "AND"ed
are "OR"ed with ⟶	All conditions in this line are "AND"ed
3rd line "AND"s	

Figure 7.37 Criteria range organization

The following examples illustrate how more complex searches comprised of ORs, multiple ANDs, and ORs with multiple AND conditions are created using the organizational approach shown in Figure 7.37. For each of the following examples, the data shown in Figure 7.35 is searched.

Example 1

OR condition

Search the spreadsheet shown in Figure 7.35 for all records where

Degree = BS OR Degree = BA

Solution: As the criteria requires an OR condition, two lines of criteria values are required. The first criteria line following the label line specifies the criteria that Degree = BS while the OR condition (Degree = BA) is specified in the next line. Figure 7.38 shows the required criteria and the resulting selected records from those originally displayed in Figure 7.35.

	A	B	C	D	E	F
1	Department	Age	Gender	Degree	Years	Salary
2				BS		
3				BA		
4						
5						
6	Department	Age	Gender	Degree	Years	Salary
9	Production	35	M	BA	11	$45,000
10	Research	28	F	BS	5	$44,000
15	Research	28	M	BS	5	$38,000
17	Research	24	M	BS	2	$36,000
19	Accounting	32	M	BA	7	$38,000
20	Accounting	28	F	BA	6	$34,000

Figure 7.38 Spreadsheet for sample OR search

Note that either ranges $A1:$F3 or $D1:$D3 are valid for specifying the criteria shown in Figure 7.38.

Example 2

Multiple ANDs on the same Criteria Range Row

Search the spreadsheet shown in Figure 7.35 for all records where

Salary > 40000 AND Salary <50000

Solution: Here we have two AND conditions for Salary. Because additional criteria can be added to the first row of the criteria range (row 2), this search criteria is accomplished by adding a second Salary criterion on the same criteria range row, as shown in Figure 7.39. As such, both Salary specifications are specified on Row 2. Figure 7.39 shows the required criteria and the resulting selected records from those originally displayed in Figure 7.35.

	A	B	C	D	E	F	G
1	Department	Age	Gender	Degree	Years	Salary	Salary
2						>40000	<50000
3							
4							
5							
6	Department	Age	Gender	Degree	Years	Salary	
9	Production	35	M	BA	11	$45,000	
10	Research	28	F	BS	5	$44,000	
12	Management	28	F	MBA	5	$48,000	
18	Finance	26	F	MBA	3	$44,000	

Figure 7.39 Spreadsheet for sample AND search

Note that either ranges $A1:$G2 or $F1:$G2 are valid for specifying the criteria shown in Figure 7.39. Also, notice that if you specified the Salary criteria using three rows, as shown in Figure 7.40, the resulting criteria becomes the OR condition Salary >40000 OR Salary <50000, which is incorrect for the specified filter.

	A	B	C	D	E	F
1	Department	Age	Gender	Degree	Years	Salary
2						>40000
3						<50000

Figure 7.40 Advanced Filter Using Salary >40000 OR Salary < 50000

Example 3

Multiple AND Conditions on the same Criteria Range Row

Filter the spreadsheet shown in Figure 7.35 for all records where

Degree = BS AND Salary > 40000 AND Salary <50000

Solution: As this search consists of ANDs only, all of the criteria can be placed on the first criteria range row following the label row. As in Example 2, because the Salary criteria is required twice, a second Salary criterion is added to the same row. Figure 7.41 shows the required criteria and the resulting selected records from those originally displayed in Figure 7.35.

	A	B	C	D	E	F	G
1	Department	Age	Gender	Degree	Years	Salary	Salary
2				BS		>40000	<50000
3							
4							
5							
6	Department	Age	Gender	Degree	Years	Salary	
10	Research	28	F	BS	5	$44,000	

Figure 7.41 Advanced Filter Using Multiple AND conditions

Note that either ranges $A1:$G2 or $D1:$G2 are valid for specifying the criteria shown in Figure 7.40.

Example 4

Criteria employing both AND and OR conditions

Search the spreadsheet shown in Figure 7.35 for all records where

(Salary > 40000 AND Salary <50000) OR (Degree = BS)

Solution: As this search criteria requires an OR condition, two rows of criteria range values are needed. The first line following the header row specifies the first set of ANDs (Salary > 40000 AND Salary <50000), while the OR condition (Degree = BS) is specified in the next line. Figure 7.42 shows the required criteria and the resulting selected records from those originally displayed in Figure 7.35.

	A	B	C	D	E	F	G
1	Department	Age	Gender	Degree	Years	Salary	Salary
2						>40000	<50000
3				BS			
4							
5							
6							
7	Department	Age	Gender	Degree	Years	Salary	
10	Production	35	M	BA	11	$45,000	
11	Research	28	F	BS	5	$44,000	
13	Management	28	F	MBA	5	$48,000	
16	Research	28	M	BS	5	$38,000	
18	Research	24	M	BS	2	$36,000	
19	Finance	26	F	MBA	3	$44,000	

Figure 7.42 Advanced Filter Using AND and OR conditions

Note that either ranges $A1:$G3 or $D1:$G3 are valid for specifying the criteria shown in Figure 7.41.

As you have seen, the Advanced Filter is a very powerful tool for doing filter (search) operations on an Excel list or table. It allows for detailed and complex filters to be done relatively easily. However, for simple searches, it should be pointed out that there is the option to use the **AutoFilter** feature which would allow you to do relatively straightforward filters using drop-down boxes and menus. The determination as to which one to use should be based the complexity of the filters you plan to use. More information is readily available through various online and reference sources as to the operation of the AutoFilter feature.

EXERCISES 7.4

1. Using the data shown in the first spreadsheet, and following the Advanced Filter procedure presented in this section, produce the second spreadsheet shown.

	A	B	C	D	E	F
	Department	**Age**	**Gender**	**Degree**	**Years**	**Salary**
1	Department	Age	Gender	Degree	Years	Salary
2						
3						
4						
5						
6	Department	Age	Gender	Degree	Years	Salary
7	Finance	42	F	MBA	15	$87,000
8	Management	29	F	MBA	4	$60,000
9	Production	35	M	BA	11	$45,000
10	Research	28	F	BS	5	$44,000
11	Production	39	M	MA	14	$36,000
12	Management	28	F	MBA	5	$48,000
13	Finance	33	M	MBA	7	$55,000
14	Marketing	20	F	MBA	1	$32,000
15	Research	28	M	BS	5	$38,000
16	Production	27	F	MA	8	$37,000
17	Research	24	M	BS	2	$36,000
18	Finance	26	F	MBA	3	$44,000
19	Accounting	32	M	BA	7	$38,000
20	Accounting	28	F	BA	6	$34,000
21	Production	27	M	MA	3	$29,000

	A	B	C	D	E	F
1	**Department**	**Age**	**Gender**	**Degree**	**Years**	**Salary**
2		>27	F	MBA		
3						
4						
5						
6	**Department**	**Age**	**Gender**	**Degree**	**Years**	**Salary**
7	Finance	42	F	MBA	15	$87,000
8	Management	29	F	MBA	4	$60,000
12	Management	28	F	MBA	5	$48,000

2. Create a spreadsheet, using the data in Exercise 1 that shows all personnel with a BA degree who have been with the company for more than 2 years. At the bottom of the spreadsheet, use the SUM, AVERAGE, MAX, and MIN functions so that your spreadsheet also lists the total, average, maximum, and minimum salaries for the displayed salary data.

3. Complete parts a-b.

a. For the spreadsheet in Figure 7.43, create a filtered list that displays all Sales values (Column D) greater than $190,000, using the Advanced Filter.

	A	B	C	D
1	**Year Sold**	**Company**	**Type**	**Sale**
2	2018	Berkshire	Lower	$180,000
3	2018	Olney	Lower	$180,000
4	2018	Olney	Middle	$179,000
5	2018	Olney	Middle	$235,000
6	2018	Lenox	Upper	$235,000
7	2019	Lenox	Lower	$195,000
8	2019	Berkshire	Lower	$219,000
9	2019	Berkshire	Lower	$225,000
10	2019	Olney	Middle	$225,000
11	2019	Lenox	Middle	$245,000
12	2019	Berkshire	Upper	$240,000
13	2020	Lenox	Lower	$285,000
14	2020	Lenox	Lower	$216,000
15	2020	Lenox	Middle	$188,000
16	2020	Berkshire	Middle	$198,000
17	2020	Olney	Upper	$224,000

Figure 7.43 Data for Exercise 3

b. Using the spreadsheet given in Exercise 3a, create a filtered list using the Advanced Filter showing all sales for the Lenox company that were greater than $190,000.

4. Complete parts a-b.

   a. Using the spreadsheet given in Exercise 3a and the Advanced Filter, create a spreadsheet showing all sales that were between $190,000 and $230,000.

   b. Using the spreadsheet given in Exercise 3a, create a filtered list using the Advanced Filter showing all sales for the Lenox company that were between $190,000 and $230,000.

5. For the following criteria section, fill in values satisfying the given criteria:

	A	B	C	D	E	F
1	Department	Age	Gender	Degree	Years	Salary
2						
3						
4						

   a. Age > 25 AND Years < 14

   b. Gender = F and Salary > $35,000

   c. Gender = M and Salary > $35,000

   d. Department = Production AND Gender = F

   e. Department = Finance AND Years >= 8 AND Salary > $40,000

6. For each of the criteria used in Exercise 5, provide criteria ranges that can be used in the Advanced Filter dialog box to correctly identify the given criteria. For all parts, use the spreadsheet shown in Exercise1 to do the following:

   a. Using the given criteria, filter to find the following results.

	A	B	C	D	E	F
1	Department	Age	Gender	Degree	Years	Salary
2				BS		
3				BA		
4						
5						
6	Department	Age	Gender	Degree	Years	Salary
9	Production	35	M	BA	11	$45,000
10	Research	28	F	BS	5	$44,000
15	Research	28	M	BS	5	$38,000
17	Research	24	M	BS	2	$36,000
19	Accounting	32	M	BA	7	$38,000
20	Accounting	28	F	BA	6	$34,000

b. Using the given criteria, recreate the following filtered spreadsheet.

	A	B	C	D	E	F	G
1	**Department**	**Age**	**Gender**	**Degree**	**Years**	**Salary**	**Salary**
2						>40000	<50000
3							
4							
5							
6	**Department**	**Age**	**Gender**	**Degree**	**Years**	**Salary**	
9	Production	35	M	BA	11	$45,000	
10	Research	28	F	BS	5	$44,000	
12	Management	28	F	MBA	5	$48,000	
18	Finance	26	F	MBA	3	$44,000	

c. Using the given criteria, recreate the filter below using the Advanced Filter.

	A	B	C	D	E	F
1	**Department**	**Age**	**Gender**	**Degree**	**Years**	**Salary**
2						>40000
3						<50000

d. Using the given criteria, recreate the filter and results using the Advanced Filter.

	A	B	C	D	E	F	G
1	**Department**	**Age**	**Gender**	**Degree**	**Years**	**Salary**	**Salary**
2				BS		>40000	<50000
3							
4							
5							
6	**Department**	**Age**	**Gender**	**Degree**	**Years**	**Salary**	
10	Research	28	F	BS	5	$44,000	

7. For the following criteria range section, fill in values satisfying the criteria provided:

	A	B	C	D	E	F	G	H	I
1	**Department**	**Age**	**Age**	**Gender**	**Degree**	**Years**	**Years**	**Salary**	**Salary**
2									
3									
4									

a. Age > 25 AND Age < 35

b. Years >= 8 AND Years < =14

c. Salary > $40,000 AND <= $60,000

d. Department = Finance OR =Accounting

    e. (Age > 25 AND Age < 35) OR (Years > 8 AND Years < 14)

    f. (Age > 25 AND Age < 35) OR (Years >8 AND Years <14) OR (Salary > $40,000)

  8. For each of the criteria used in Exercise 8, provide two different criteria ranges that can be used in the Advanced Filter dialog to correctly identify the given criteria.

7.5 DATABASE FUNCTIONS

Consider the data shown in Figure 7.44 (originally shown as Figure 7.29). Filtering this data using the criteria (Degree = BA AND Years > 1) provides the record listing shown in Figure 7.45. The shaded sum, average, and maximum and minimum salary figures at the bottom of the figure were created *after* the search was completed, using the respective Excel formulas after the filtered data was determined.

    Frequently, all that is needed in many applications is a numeric summary statistic of selected records, such as the shaded values appearing at the bottom of Figure 7.45, and not a complete list of the filtered records themselves. Using Excel's database functions, the most commonly used of which are listed in Table 7.2, such summaries can be obtained directly. Doing so eliminates the need of first searching and listing selected records, as is done in Figure 7.45.

	A	B	C	D	E	F
1	**Department**	**Age**	**Gender**	**Degree**	**Years**	**Salary**
2	Finance	42	F	MBA	15	$87,000
3	Management	29	F	MBA	4	$60,000
4	Production	35	M	BA	11	$45,000
5	Research	28	F	BS	5	$44,000
6	Production	39	M	MA	14	$36,000
7	Management	28	F	MBA	5	$48,000
8	Finance	33	M	MBA	7	$55,000
9	Marketing	20	F	MBA	1	$32,000
10	Research	28	M	BS	5	$38,000
11	Production	27	F	MA	8	$37,000
12	Research	24	M	BS	2	$36,000
13	Finance	26	F	MBA	3	$44,000
14	Accounting	32	M	BA	7	$38,000
15	Accounting	28	F	BA	6	$34,000
16	Production	27	M	MA	3	$29,000

Figure 7.44 Employee Data records

	A	B	C	D	E	F
1	**Department**	**Age**	**Gender**	**Degree**	**Years**	**Salary**
2				BA	>1	
3						
4						
5						
6	**Department**	**Age**	**Gender**	**Degree**	**Years**	**Salary**
9	Production	35	M	BA	11	$45,000
19	Accounting	32	M	BA	7	$38,000
20	Accounting	28	F	BA	6	$34,000
22					Sum:	$487,000
23					Average:	$71,643
24					Maximum	$55,000
25					Minimum:	$32,000

Figure 7.45 Filtered records after using the Advanced Filter (data from Figure 7.44)

Table 7.2 Commonly-used database functions

Function	Description
DAVERAGE()	Returns the average of the selected database entries
DCOUNT()	Counts the cells that contain numbers in a database
DCOUNTA()	Counts nonblank cells in a database
DMAX()	Returns the maximum value from the selected database entries
DMIN()	Returns the minimum value from the selected database entries
DSUM()	Adds the numbers in the field column of records in the database that match the criteria

All Excel database functions require three pieces of data:

1. The range where the original data is located (list range)

2. The name of the field whose data is being calculated

3. The location of the selection criteria (criteria range)

For example, the following database functions can be used to directly obtain the average and maximum and minimum salaries of the selected records shown in Figure 7.45.

=DAVERAGE(A6:F21,"Salary",D1:E2)
=DSUM(A6:F21,"Salary",D1:E2)
=DMAX(A6:F21,"Salary",D1:E2)
=DMIN(A6:F21,"Salary",D1:E2)

While database functions (DFUNCTIONS) are very useful for generating summary statistics based on a filtered list, they do require the use of an Advanced Filter (and its associated inputs, including the list range, criteria range, and output specifications). An alternate approach to doing this would be to use Conditional =IF functions, which generally work well with list/table data and do not require the use of neither the Advanced Filter, nor a criteria range. By specifying the list to be worked on, the filter criteria, and the field to be summarized, it is possible to use Conditional =IF functions to generate a similar result to that obtained by DFUNCTIONS.

The functions include =SUMIF( ), =COUNTIF( ), and =AVERAGEIF( ) for single criteria, and =SUMIFS( ), =COUNTIFS( ), and =AVERAGEIFS( ) for multiple sets of criteria. Excel 2019 also introduced the =MAXIFS( ) and =MINIFS( ) functions.

These functions can be used both for a wide range of applications. It should be noted that Conditional =IF functions are not the same as the =IF function, in that each type uses a different format and works differently. There are numerous resources which you can consult for more information on Conditional =IF functions.

EXERCISES 7.5

1. List the three arguments that must be provided to an Excel database function.

2. Create the spreadsheet data shown below. Then, using only database functions, produce the summary data values shown in the shaded region of the following figure.

	A	B	C	D	E	F
1	**Department**	**Age**	**Gender**	**Degree**	**Years**	**Salary**
2	Finance	42	F	MBA	15	$87,000
3	Management	29	F	MBA	4	$60,000
4	Production	35	M	BA	11	$45,000
5	Research	28	F	BS	5	$44,000
6	Production	39	M	MA	14	$36,000
7	Management	28	F	MBA	5	$48,000
8	Finance	33	M	MBA	7	$55,000
9	Marketing	20	F	MBA	1	$32,000
10	Research	28	M	BS	5	$38,000
11	Production	27	F	MA	8	$37,000
12	Research	24	M	BS	2	$36,000
13	Finance	26	F	MBA	3	$44,000
14	Accounting	32	M	BA	7	$38,000
15	Accounting	28	F	BA	6	$34,000
16	Production	27	M	MA	3	$29,000

	A	B	C	D	E	F
1	**Department**	**Age**	**Gender**	**Degree**	**Years**	**Salary**
2				BA	>1	
3						
4						
5						
6	**Department**	**Age**	**Gender**	**Degree**	**Years**	**Salary**
9	Production	35	M	BA	11	$45,000
19	Accounting	32	M	BA	7	$38,000
20	Accounting	28	F	BA	6	$34,000
22					Sum:	$487,000
23					Average:	$71,643
24					Maximum	$55,000
25					Minimum:	$32,000

3. For the spreadsheet shown below, and using database functions only,

   a. calculate and display the sum and average of all Berkshire company sales.

   b. calculate and display the sum and average of all Lenox company sales.

   c. calculate and display the sum and average of all Olney company sales.

	A	B	C	D
1	**Year Sold**	**Company**	**Type**	**Sale**
2	2018	Berkshire	Lower	$180,000
3	2018	Olney	Lower	$180,000
4	2018	Olney	Middle	$179,000
5	2018	Olney	Middle	$235,000
6	2018	Lenox	Upper	$235,000
7	2019	Lenox	Lower	$195,000
8	2019	Berkshire	Lower	$219,000
9	2019	Berkshire	Lower	$225,000
10	2019	Olney	Middle	$225,000
11	2019	Lenox	Middle	$245,000
12	2019	Berkshire	Upper	$240,000
13	2020	Lenox	Lower	$285,000
14	2020	Lenox	Lower	$216,000
15	2020	Lenox	Middle	$188,000
16	2020	Berkshire	Middle	$198,000
17	2020	Olney	Upper	$224,000

7.6   COMMON EXCEL ERRORS

The errors common to sorting and searching a spreadsheet are the following:

1. Forgetting to highlight the complete spreadsheet when sorting on values in one or more columns. If the complete spreadsheet is not highlighted, the sort will only be applied to the selected highlighted columns. This has the effect of mixing the sorted column values with the unsorted remaining columns.

2. Forgetting to uncheck the *Replace current subtotals* checkbox (see Figure 7.22) when creating nested subtotals. When this checkbox is not cleared, the most recent subtotals will erase all the preceding ones.

3. Inserting extra spaces within search criteria. Generally, specific values are being searched for, and extra spaces can make exact searches fail, especially when searching for an exact text match.

7.7   CHAPTER APPENDIX: SPREADSHEETS AS DATABASES

By definition, a *database* is any collection of related data, organized and stored as fields and records, usually employing a pre-set structure.[6] Databases are used to store the following:

- Patient data
- Employee data
- Customer data
- Expense data
- Product data
- Sales data

---

[6] Formally, a database is defined as a organized collection of stored information, and it can be organized to show the relationships among the stored items.

An example of a small database is shown in Figure 7.46 (originally shown as Figure 7.1). This information can be entered into an Excel spreadsheet, using its existing structure, including the inclusion of a field header row.

ID	Office	Last Name	First Name	Address	City	State	Zip
10010	HM	Bottle	Bill	614 Tremont Ave.	Hoboken	NJ	07030
10015	HM	Deiter	Alan	892 Freeman St.	Orange	NJ	07050
10020	FLD	Dreskin	Mary	56 Lyons Ave, Apt 12	Bloomfield	NJ	07112
10025	FLD	Farrel	Jayne	78 Barnstable Rd.	Berkeley Hgts.	NJ	07922
10030	HM	Grill	Mellisa	643 Schuller Dr.	Orange	NJ	07050
10035	HM	Jones	Helen	932 Coleridge Rd.	Camden	NJ	08030
10040	HM	Jones	Mark	93 Fairmount Ter.	Maplewood	NJ	07040
10045	FLD	Miller	Scott	745 Skyline Dr.	Chatham	NJ	07928
10050	FLD	O'Neil	Pat	17 Tuney St.	Madison	NJ	07940
10055	HM	Somers	Ann	2 Travers Way	Trenton	NJ	08601
10060	FLD	Swan	Kurt	16 Rollinson Rd.	Orange	NJ	07050
10065	HM	Thomas	Harriet	192 Oakridge St.	Summit	NJ	07901
10070	HM	Timers	John	849 Birchwood Dr.	Hoboken	NJ	07030
10075	FLD	Ward	Kay	2 Pine Ter.	Chatham	NJ	07928
10080	FLD	Williams	Blake	85 Wellforest Ave.	Madison	NJ	07940

Figure 7.46 Employee location data

In Excel terminology, this is called an Excel list or an Excel table. As shown in Figure 7.46, this database is organized as a table consisting of fields and records. When the following conditions hold, the spreadsheet operates similar to a *relational database:*

1. Each location in the table can contain only a single value

2. Each column (field) in the table has a unique identifying name

3. All values in a column are of the same basic data type (text, numeric, etc.)

4. The data in each row is distinct (that is, generally speaking, no two rows should have the same data)

5. No information is lost by reordering rows

6. No information is lost by reordering columns

Each row in a database is referred to as a *record,* and consists of related data items known as *fields.* The data items in a field correspond to the table's columns. In Figure 7.46, for example, there are fifteen records, where each record contains eight fields associated with a specific employee. The column headings describe what each item represents. Although specific data values can be missing (none are in Figure 7.46), each record contains the same number and types of data, one item per column.

As another example, consider the student records shown in Figure 7.47. Here, similar to the last example, the structure of the records as rows and fields as the individual data items conforms to the structure of the rows and columns of a spreadsheet. As such, a spreadsheet can operate in some ways like a database when each row in the spreadsheet is used to store a single record, with the columns conforming to a record's fields. When viewed this way, the sorting and searching of rows becomes the sorting and searching of records within a database.

Student ID Number	Last Name	First Name	Major	Year Entered	Credits Earned	Grade Pt. Average
1st ID						
2nd ID						
3rd ID						
.						
.						
.						
.						
Last ID						

Figure 7.47 A student database

CHAPTER **8**

INTERMEDIATE AND ADVANCED TECHNIQUES

This Chapter Contains

8.1   CREATING DROP-DOWN LISTS

Drop-down lists are used to limit the choices that a user can enter into a cell. As shown in Figure 8.1, the cell providing the list, in this case cell B1, has an arrow on its right-hand side. (This arrow only appears when the cell providing the drop-down list is selected.) Once the drop-down arrow is clicked, the user has the option of either selecting one of the displayed list items, which is automatically entered into the cell, or typing in the desired item.

	A	B	C	D
1	Enter the desired size:	▾		
2		6 ounce		
3		8 ounce		
4		12 ounce		
5		16 ounce		
6		32 ounce		

Figure 8.1 A cell with a drop-down list of choices

Attempting to type in an item not on the list results in the error message shown in Figure 8.2.

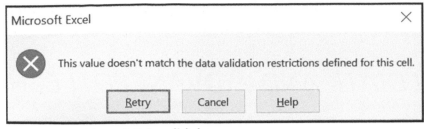

Figure 8.2 Invalid data entry error message

Creating a drop-down list requires the two elements shown in Figure 8.3: a cell to display the list, which is cell B2 in the figure, and the drop-down list, which is stored in cells E1 through E5.

	A	B	C	D	E
1	Enter the desired size:	▾			6 ounce
2					8 ounce
3	This is where the drop-down list will be displayed.				12 ounce
4		This is the list.			16 ounce
5					32 ounce
6					

Figure 8.3 Creating a drop-down list

Drop-down lists are created through setting up the data, and employing the Data Validation feature. The following three steps detail the complete method for creating a drop-down list.

Step 1: Create a list of items, either in a single row or in a single column of cells. In Figure 8.3, the list is located in cells E1 through E5. Generally, the list would be hidden on a second sheet and protected (see Section 8.6) so that it only appears when the receiving cell's arrow is clicked and cannot be tampered with by the user.

Step 2: Click on the cell you want to receive the drop-down list. This cell is referred to as the *data entry* cell. In Figure 8.3, the data entry cell is B1.

Step 3: Select the Excel Data tab's **Data Validation** option, as shown on Figure 8.4.

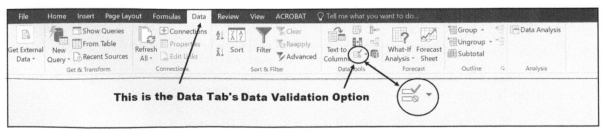

Figure 8.4 Locate and then select the Excel Data Validation option

Selecting the Data Validation option causes the dialog shown in Figure 8.5 to appear. In this dialog, and as shown on the figure, you then click the arrow on the right-hand side of the Allow text box. This will bring up the drop-down menu shown in Figure 8.6.

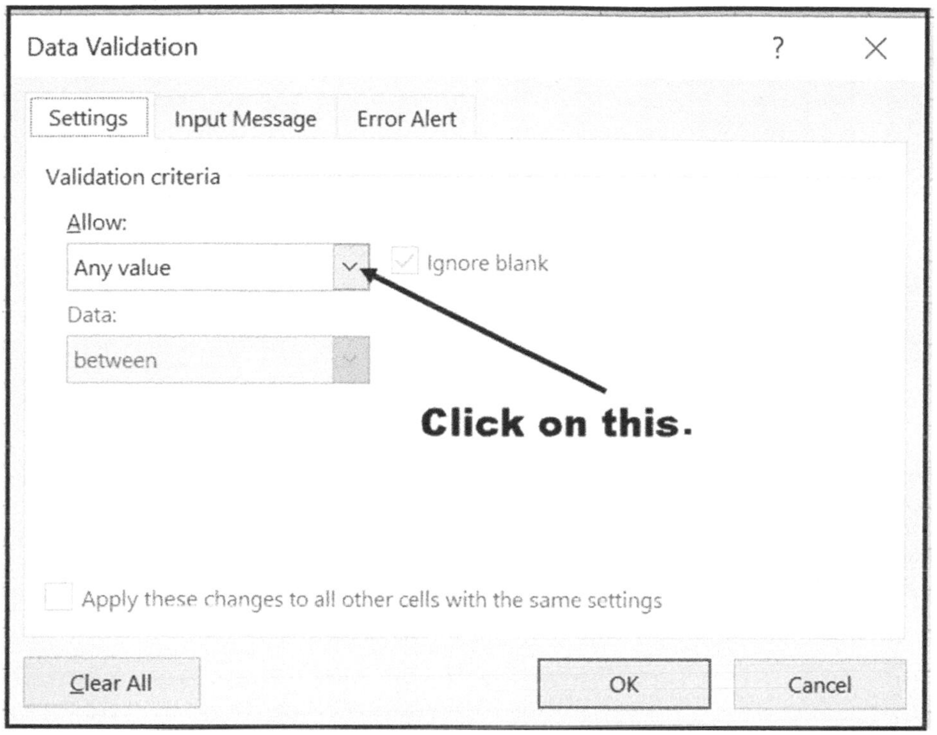

Figure 8.5 The Data Validation dialog box

For a drop-down list, select the List option shown in Figure 8.6. It is worthwhile noticing, however, all of the other cell data validation options that are available.

While the main goal of this section is to explain how to create drop-down lists, Data Validation also has many other uses and options which makes it a highly useful feature. Among the capabilities of this feature include the ability to remind users about the proper data to enter, specifying the correct and proper data type to be entered into a cell, and restricting entry of data into the cell(s) based on specific criteria and varying levels of control. In essence, as the name suggests, there are options to attempt to validate the data being entered, so as to ensure that only the proper type of data is entered into a specified cell. You can consult other resources to explore the many other uses of this feature.

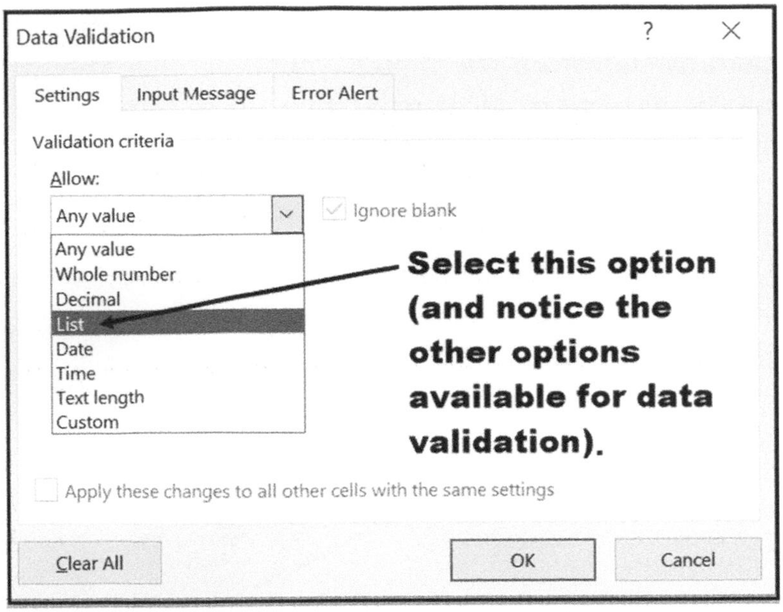

Figure 8.6 Selecting the List option

Once the List option is selected, all that remains is to designate the location of the drop-down choice list, as shown in Figure 8.7. As our example list, previously shown in Figure 8.3, is located in cells E1 through E5, this is the entered cell range. Note the equal sign before the range. This sign is automatically entered if the list is entered by highlighting, but must be typed in when the list range is entered manually.

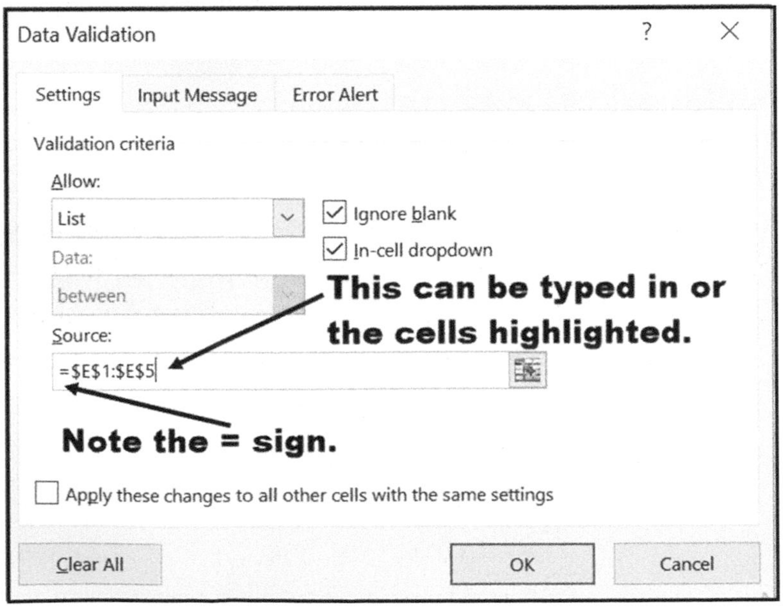

Figure 8.7 Designating the drop-down list location

After the list location is designated in the Data Validation dialog and the OK button pressed, the drop-down list has been activated for the selected data entry cell.

EXERCISES 8.1

1. What is the primary purpose for using a drop-down list?

2. What are the two required elements needed for a drop-down list?

3. Using the three-step procedure presented in this section, create the drop-down list shown below with the following changes: put the label currently in cell A1 in cell A4 and make B4 the data entry cell.

	A	B	C	D
1	Enter the desired size:	▼		
2		6 ounce		
3		8 ounce		
		12 ounce		
4		16 ounce		
5		32 ounce		
6				

4. Add a second drop-down list to the spreadsheet created in Exercise 3 that displays the label *What drink do you want* in cell A1 and creates cell B1 as the data entry cell for a drop-down list containing the seven choices: Water, Coke, Pepsi, 7-Up, Dr. Pepper, Sierra Mist, and Slurpee.

5. Create a spreadsheet that asks for a state and have a data entry cell of your choice select from a list containing the following 10 choices: CA, CT, FL, IL, IN, KY, NJ, NY, MA, and WI.

8.2   CORRECTING ROUNDING ERRORS

Seemingly incorrect results are sometimes displayed when monetary values are displayed to the nearest penny or dollar. For example, consider the display shown in Figure 8.8. The value in cell B5 was correctly calculated using the formula =B3+B4. Clearly, however, the displayed sum is incorrect and should be $58 and not $59.

	A	B
1	**Off by a Dollar**	
2	**Item**	**Price**
3	A101B	$36
4	A101C	$22
5	Total	$59

Figure 8.8 An incorrect total

The problem is that although the values in cells B3 and B4 are displayed to the nearest dollar, the actual cell values are $36.42 and $22.25, and the value stored in cell B5 is

$58.67. When rounded to the nearest dollar amount, however, this value gets rounded up to the next highest dollar amount, which results in $59 being displayed in cell B5. The correct total is displayed in Figure 8.9.

	A	B
1	**Accurate to the Dollar**	
2	**Item**	**Price**
3	A101B	$36
4	A101C	$22
5	Total	$58

Figure 8.9 A correct total

The solution to displaying a correct total is to round the values in the cells B3 and B4 to the nearest dollar amount *before* they are added. This is done using the ROUND( ) function when the total is calculated. The format of the ROUND( ) function is

ROUND*(value, digits)*

where *digits* is the number of decimal digits the *value* is to be rounded. Figure 8.10 shows how this formula is used in cell B5 to produce the display shown in Figure 8.9.

	A	B
1	**Accurate to the Dollar**	
2	**Item**	**Price**
3	A101B	36.42
4	A101C	22.25
5	Total	=ROUND(B3,0)+ROUND(B4,0)

Figure 8.10 The formulas underlying Figure 8.9

In practice, for long lists of numbers, it is easier to either create a new column where each cell in the new column contains the rounded value of the corresponding cells in the original list of values, as shown in Figure 8.11.[1]

	A	B	C
1	**Accurate to the Dollar**		
2	**Item**	**Price**	**Rounded**
3	A101B	36.4	=ROUND(B3,0)
4	A101C	22.2	=ROUND(B4,0)
5	Total	=B3+B4	=C3+C4

Figure 8.11 Adding a column for the rounded values

---

[1] Additionally, a single array formula can be used to calculate the total. Array formulas are introduced in Section 8.4. Briefly, using an array formula, you would leave all cell values as they are and enter the following formula into cell B5: =SUM(**ROUND**(B3:B4,0)). Pressing the Shift + Ctrl + Enter keys creates the array formula. For a longer and different list of numbers, simply replace the range B3:B4 with the data range you want to round and sum.

8.3   CREATING DE-DUPING KEYS FOR REMOVING DUPLICATE RECORDS

Deleting duplicate names and addresses in email and postal mailing lists, informally referred to as *de-duping*, is a major concern for most organizations. The reason is that duplicate entries in postal lists directly affect mailing costs, with generally no offsetting advantages. Similarly, duplicate emails tend to annoy the recipient, which is the opposite of what the sender is trying to achieve.

As an example, consider the list of names illustrated in Figure 8.12.

As shown, all of the entries represent the same person, but have different representation of the names and street addresses. The general problem is that names are frequently misspelled or nicknames used, such as Jack for John and Bob for Robert. These all result in the same person having multiple entries in the list. Interestingly, city and state names generally are not a problem, because they are generally entered automatically from a look-up table based on the address zip code.

Although there is no removal method that is 100% fool-proof, a number of de-duping methods can be used. One of the simplest and extremely effective methods is to create a text string, referred to as a *de-dup key*, that extracts pertinent information for each list item.

As an example, consider Figure 8.12 that contains five names, all of which refer to the same person. A de-dup key for this list is displayed in column G. This de-dup key consists of the first letter in a person's first and last names, the first four letters of the street address, and the zip code. This particular key relies heavily on numbers, which typically are not mis-typed on entry, and the first letter of a name, which typically is accurate (It will not, of course, catch a name that starts with a different letter.) The majority of de-dup keys use this type of scheme, with specific changes in the key to account for specifics of the list being maintained.

	A	B	C	D	E	F	G
1	First name	Last Name	Street Address	City	State	Zip	De-Dup Key
2	Jack	Simpson	285 Freeman St.	Lenox	MA	01240	JS285 01240
3	John	Simpson	285 Freemont St.	Lenox	MA	01240	JS285 01240
4	J.	Simpson	285 Freeman St.	Lenox	MA	01240	JS285 01240
5	John	Simpsan	285 Fremon St.	Lenox	MA	01240	JS285 01240
6	J.	Sampson	285 Freeman St.	Lenox	MA	01240	JS285 01240

Figure 8.12 Duplicate data for the same person

8.4   ARRAY FUNCTIONS - THE SUMPRODUCT( ) FUNCTION

We have been using Excel's functions to operate on individual cells and values, one data item at a time. Additionally, many Excel functions can manipulate complete arrays, one array with another. Such array formulas require ranges of cells as individual arguments and are entered by pressing the Ctrl-Shift-Enter keys together. Doing so places the formula in curly braces, {*formula in here*}, which indicates that the formula will be applied to each cell in the range listed in the formula. An array can be either a single row, column, or a table consisting of rows and columns.

Although the mechanics of array processing is beyond the scope of this text, the SUMPRODUCT( ) array function can be employed by simply entered by simply writing the function and pressing the Enter key. As such, it operates in much the same fashion as the functions described in the prior sections. The reason that this function is so useful is that it can be used to multiply the corresponding values of two or more rows or columns (arrays) and sum the resulting products to find a total. The syntax for this function is

SUMPRODUCT(range-1, range-2, ... range-n)

The only requirement in using this function is that the range sizes of each argument must be the same. If only one range is supplied, the function will sum the values in the range; if two or more ranges are supplied, the first range values in each array will be multiplied together, and the result then added to the total. Then, this process would continue through all elements of the array until the end is reached, with the total being updated after the multiplication of each corresponding set of values. The final total would be the sum of all of the multiplications done with the arrays provided. Up to 255 arrays(ranges) can be included as function arguments and any non-numeric array is treated as a zero.

Example

Consider Figure 8.13, which includes the number of individual items sold and their prices, in columns A and C, respectively. The individual revenue values in column D are generated by multiplying the corresponding values in columns B and C, and the total displayed in cell D8 uses the formula =SUM(D2:D7)

	A	B	C	D
1	**Item ID**	**Sales**	**Price**	**Revenue**
2	5A62	100	$15.00	$1,500.00
3	7B45	64	$27.00	$1,728.00
4	7B47	45	$37.00	$1,665.00
5	10A55	175	$22.00	$3,850.00
6	14C24	210	$17.00	$3,570.00
7	26Z82	83	$35.00	$2,905.00
8				$15,218.00
9	**Total Revenue:**		$15,218.00	

Figure 8.13 Calculating Total revenue

If, however, all that is required is the total revenue, this can be calculated directly without the necessity of column D at all, as shown in cell C9. The formula in cell C9 computes this total using the formula =SUMPRODUCT(B2:B7,C2:C7).

The first function argument is the range B2:B7, and the second function argument is the range C2:C7. The SUMPRODUCT( ) function multiplies each corresponding element in these arrays; that is B2*C2, B3*C3, and so on, stores them temporarily in an internal array, and then sums the values to provide the final result.

Although the SUMPRODUCT( ) function may be of limited use in basic spreadsheets, it is extremely valuable in advanced applications containing hundreds of entries. In these applications where total revenue, time, and other business metrics are needed without the creation of an extra column, such as column D in Figure 8.13, it is invaluable. Additionally, it has useful applications in Conditional Formatting, as presented in the next section.

EXERCISES 8.4

1. Create the following spreadsheet on your computer.

	A	B	C	D
1	**Item ID**	**Sales**	**Price**	**Revenue**
2	5A62	100	$15.00	$1,500.00
3	7B45	64	$27.00	$1,728.00
4	7B47	45	$37.00	$1,665.00
5	10A55	175	$22.00	$3,850.00
6	14C24	210	$17.00	$3,570.00
7	26Z82	83	$35.00	$2,905.00
8				$15,218.00
9	**Total Revenue:**		$15,218.00	

2. Eliminate Column D in Figure 8.14 below and calculate the Total Paid using a SUMPRODUCT( ) function. The formula containing this function should be placed in cell C8 and the text **Total Paid:** placed in cell B8.

	A	B	C	D
1	**Name**	**Hourly Rate ($/Hr)**	**Hrs. Worked**	**Net Pay**
2	Bill Biggins	20	40	=B2*C2
3	Jane Cousins	22.5	40	=B3*C3
4	Laura Demaio	16.8	35	=B4*C4
5	John Farnsworth	16.8	35	=B5*C5
6	Rachel Smith	25	38	=B6*C6
7	Douglas Timinsky	22.7	38	=B7*C7
8			**Total Paid:**	=SUM(D2:D7)

Figure 8.14 Spreadsheet for Exercise 2

8.5 USER-ENTERED CONDITIONAL FORMATTING FORMULAS

Once a spreadsheet cell is highlighted, most applications also require either highlighting the complete row or another item in the row containing the initially highlighted quantity. For example, in a spreadsheet highlighting sales exceeding a given amount, the sales person achieving this sales goal would also be highlighted.

Highlighting a complete row, or individual row items, depending on one cell's value in the row requires a user-entered conditional formatting rule. To see how this is accomplished, consider that each row in Figure 8.15 with a final grade average greater than 90 is to be highlighted.

	A	B	C	D	E	F
1						
2						
3	Name	Test 1	Test 2	Test 3	Test 4	Final Grade (Average)
4	Andrew	50	90	58	70	67
5	Anthony	90	70	65	72	74
6	Charles	95	85	90	95	91
7	Danielle	95	70	82	83	83
8	Denise	90	95	87	95	92
9	Jane	75	85	60	74	74
10	Jeffrey	50	55	70	58	58
11	Joseph	93	87	95	88	91
12	Mary	85	85	65	69	76
13	Matthew	80	85	85	82	83

Figure 8.15 The original grade sheet

To accomplish the task of highlighting a complete row based on one cell's value in the row requires the following steps:

Step 1: Highlight all of the columns or rows that will be subject to the conditional formatting. For Figure 8.15 this means highlighting the range A4 through F13.

Step 2: Activate Conditional Formatting by clicking on the Home tab, Styles Group Conditional Formatting Icon, as shown in Figure 8.16

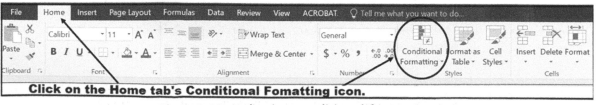

Figure 8.16 Activating conditional formatting

Step 3: Select the *New Rule* option from the displayed drop-down menu, as shown in Figure 8.18, once the Conditional Formatting has been activated.

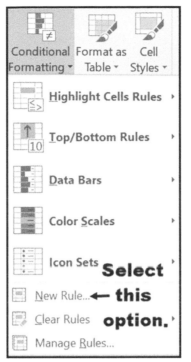

Figure 8.17 Creating a user-entered rule

Clicking the New Rule option brings up the New Formatting Rule dialog box shown in Figure 8.18. As shown in this figure, enter the formula =$F4 > 90, and then click the Format button to set the specifics of the conditional cell format. Once the format has been set, click "OK" to set the conditional format.

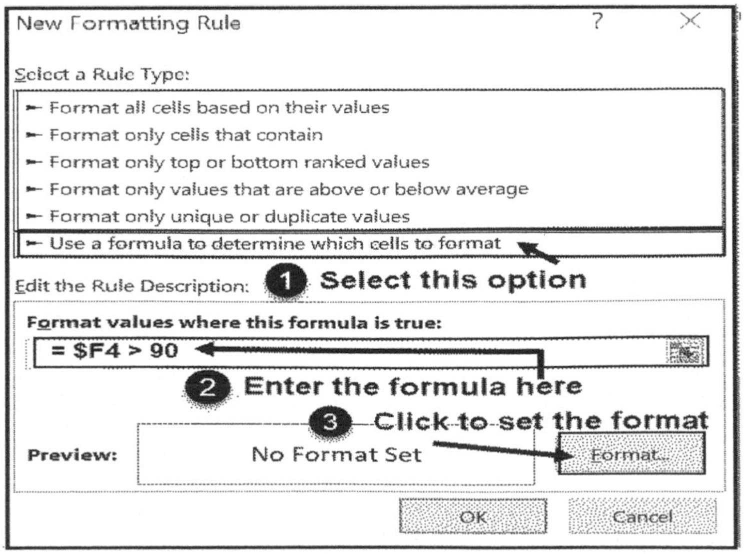

Figure 8.18 Entering Conditional Formatting (using a formula)

Figure 8.19 illustrates the effect of entering the conditional formatting formula = $F4 > 90 in the Dialog Box shown in Figure 8.17 and pressing the OK button.

	A	B	C	D	E	F
1						
2						
3	**Name**	**Test 1**	**Test 2**	**Test 3**	**Test 4**	**Final Grade (Average)**
4	Andrew	50	90	58	70	67
5	Anthony	90	70	65	72	74
6	Charles	95	85	90	95	91
7	Danielle	95	70	82	83	83
8	Denise	90	95	87	95	92
9	Jane	75	85	60	74	74
10	Jeffrey	50	55	70	58	58
11	Joseph	93	87	95	88	91
12	Mary	85	85	65	69	76
13	Matthew	80	85	85	82	83

Figure 8.19 The display produced by the user-entered Conditional Format

To understand how the condition was applied, it is easier to visualize the formula as being copied to each cell in the designated range, as is shown in Figure 8.20. The $F designation ensures that the column letter will not be changed as the formula is copied (mixed cell referencing). However, as the formula is copied down to each row, the row number is changed because the row number has not been locked with a $ sign. Thus, each cell in a row will use the value in that row's column F to determine if the final grade for each row is greater than 90. When this condition is met, every cell in the row has its conditional criteria met, and the cell is highlighted. Because each cell is highlighted, it appears to make the complete row highlighted, which is the desired effect.

This is a good example of the value of mixed cell referencing, when only one, but not both of the components of a cell reference, is prevented from changing, and the other can change. In this case, we wanted to ensure that the reference would continue to be in Column F, but the row number could change.

	A	B	C	D	E	F
1	This is the only condition that is entered.					
2	Note: The $F4 stays the same for all cells in row 4 but					
3	changes to $F5 for row 5, $F6 for row 6, and so on...					
4	$F4 > 90	$F4 > 90	$F4 > 90	$F4 > 90	$F4 > 90	$F4 > 90
5	$F5 > 90	$F5 > 90	$F5 > 90	$F5 > 90	$F5 > 90	$F5 > 90
6	$F6 > 90	$F6 >90	$F6 > 90	$F6 > 90	$F6 > 90	$F6 > 90
7	$F7 > 90	$F7 > 90	$F7 > 90	$F7 > 90	$F7 > 90	$F7 > 90
8	$F8 > 90	$F8 > 90	$F8 > 90	$F8 > 90	$F8 > 90	$F8 > 90
9	$F9 > 90	$F9 > 90	$F9 > 90	$F9 > 90	$F9 > 90	$F9 > 90
10	$F10 > 90	$F10 > 90	$F10 > 90	$F10 > 90	$F10 > 90	$F10 > 90
11	$F11 > 90	$F11 > 90	$F11 > 90	$F11 > 90	$F11 > 90	$F11 > 90
12	$F12 > 90	$F12 > 90	$F12 > 90	$F12 > 90	$F12 > 90	$F12 > 90
13	$F13 > 90	$F13 > 90	$F13 > 90	$F13 > 90	$F13 > 90	$F13 > 90

Figure 8.20 Conditional Formatting Using Mixed Cell Referencing

Conditional formatting is a very powerful and useful feature for varying the format of cells based on the meeting of certain conditions. The use of a formula to specify conditional formatting rules can allow increased power and capability when using this feature. As an example, consider the case where you want to test the value in one cell or range of cells (or maybe multiple cells or ranges of cells) as a condition for formatting a third cell (or range of cells). The way to do this would be to specify the condition using a formula employing AND and OR functions to check the values in certain cells, while specifying that other cells would be formatted based on the evaluation of the conditions.

EXERCISES 8.5

1. Enter the following grade spreadsheet, and conditionally format it to produce the spreadsheet shown in the second figure, using the condition of FINAL GRADE(AVERAGE) being greater than 90 (gray highlighting).

	A	B	C	D	E	F
1						
2						
3	Name	Test 1	Test 2	Test 3	Test 4	Final Grade (Average)
4	Andrew	50	90	58	70	67
5	Anthony	90	70	65	72	74
6	Charles	95	85	90	95	91
7	Danielle	95	70	82	83	83
8	Denise	90	95	87	95	92
9	Jane	75	85	60	74	74
10	Jeffrey	50	55	70	58	58
11	Joseph	93	87	95	88	91
12	Mary	85	85	65	69	76
13	Matthew	80	85	85	82	83

	A	B	C	D	E	F
1						
2						
3	Name	Test 1	Test 2	Test 3	Test 4	Final Grade (Average)
4	Andrew	50	90	58	70	67
5	Anthony	90	70	65	72	74
6	Charles	95	85	90	95	91
7	Danielle	95	70	82	83	83
8	Denise	90	95	87	95	92
9	Jane	75	85	60	74	74
10	Jeffrey	50	55	70	58	58
11	Joseph	93	87	95	88	91
12	Mary	85	85	65	69	76
13	Matthew	80	85	85	82	83

2. Remove the first two rows from the original spreadsheet shown in Exercise 1 and then highlight all the rows with a final grade average equal to or greater than 90. Select the format of your choice.

3. Conditionally format the original Exercise 1 grade spreadsheet so that all rows having a final grade average lower than 75 are highlighted. Select the format of your choice.

8.6   CHAPTER APPENDIX: RESTRICTING CELL ACCESS

In most professionally constructed spreadsheets, the end-user is permitted access only to those cells that require user-input data, and is prevented from accessing any other cells. This restriction prevents the user from accidentally or deliberately modifying, deleting, or formatting any cells in the worksheet except for those that require user input.

Two conditions must be fulfilled for a cell to be in a restricted mode (that is, it cannot be accessed by a user): the cell itself must be formatted as locked and the spreadsheet itself, as a whole, must be put into protected mode. When a new spreadsheet is activated, all the cells in the worksheet are, by default, formatted as locked, but the spreadsheet is in an unprotected mode. Thus, initially only one of the two conditions is fulfilled and all cells in the worksheet can be accessed. To restrict user access from one or more cells, one of the following two procedures can be used. The details of implementing each procedure are presented in the following pages.

Procedure 1:

Step 1: Verify and/or set the entire spreadsheet into an ***unprotected*** mode.

Step 2: Verify and/or check that all cells are formatted as ***locked.*** (A locked state is the default for a new sheet).

Step 3: Format those cells that you want a user to have access to as ***unlocked***.

Step 4: Set the entire spreadsheet into ***protected*** mode.

Procedure 2:

Step 1: Verify and/or set the entire spreadsheet into an ***unprotected*** mode.

Step 2: Format all of the cells in the worksheet as ***unlocked.***

Step 3: Format only those cells that you specifically want *to prevent* a user from accessing as ***locked***.

Step 4: Set the entire spreadsheet into ***protected*** mode.

In the first procedure, you are initially preventing access to all the cells in the complete worksheet and then opening access only to those cells that you ***do want*** the user to access. In the second procedure, you are first opening user access to all the cells in the worksheet and then preventing access to those cells that you *do not want* the user to access.

The first procedure is more generally used because in a practical application the user is only given access to a small number of input cells, with the remaining cells in the worksheet (which form the majority of cells in the worksheet) effectively being placed off-limits. Thus, it makes sense to first put all cells off-limits and then provide open access to the few cells that you do want users to access. For completeness, the second approach is also presented.

Procedure 1

Step 1: To ensure that the spreadsheet, as a whole, is in its *unprotected mode*, click on the Excel ribbon Review tab, Protect Group, and check that the Protect Sheet Option is as shown in Figure 8.21a. This option is a toggle switch, so if you clicked on it as it is shown, it will protect the entire sheet and the icon will appear as shown in Figure 8.21b. Thus, if the ribbon does appear as shown in Figure 8.21b, click on the icon to unprotect the spreadsheet so that the ribbon appears as illustrated in Figure 8.21a.

Figure 8.21a The entire worksheet is in unprotected mode

Figure 8.21b The entire worksheet is in protected mode

Step 2: To make sure that all the cells in the worksheet are Formatted as *locked*, select all of the cells by left clicking the left, upper hand corner icon in the table, as shown in Figure 8.22. Then right click the mouse to bring up the submenu shown in Figure 8.23. From this menu, select the Format option. Because all of the cells in the table have been selected, the format that you select will apply to all of the cells in the worksheet.

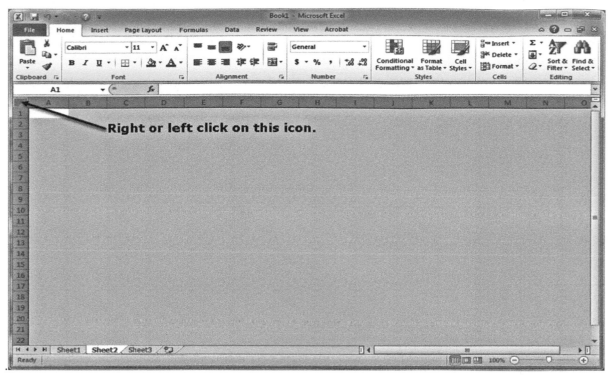

Figure 8.22 Selecting all of the cells in a worksheet

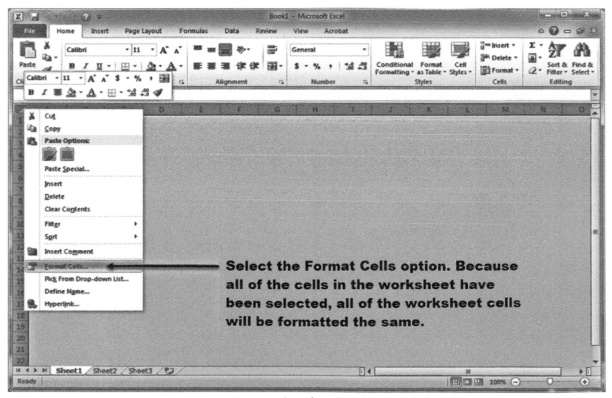

Figure 8.23 Formatting the complete worksheet

Once you have selected the Format option, the dialog shown in Figure 8.24 will appear. On this dialog, click on the Protection Tab; this will bring up the dialog shown in Figure 8.25. Once this dialog appears, make sure the **Locked** box is checked (If it isn't, check it). Doing this will place all of the cells into a locked format. Note that this locked cell format only becomes activated and into play when the worksheet itself is placed in a **protected** mode.

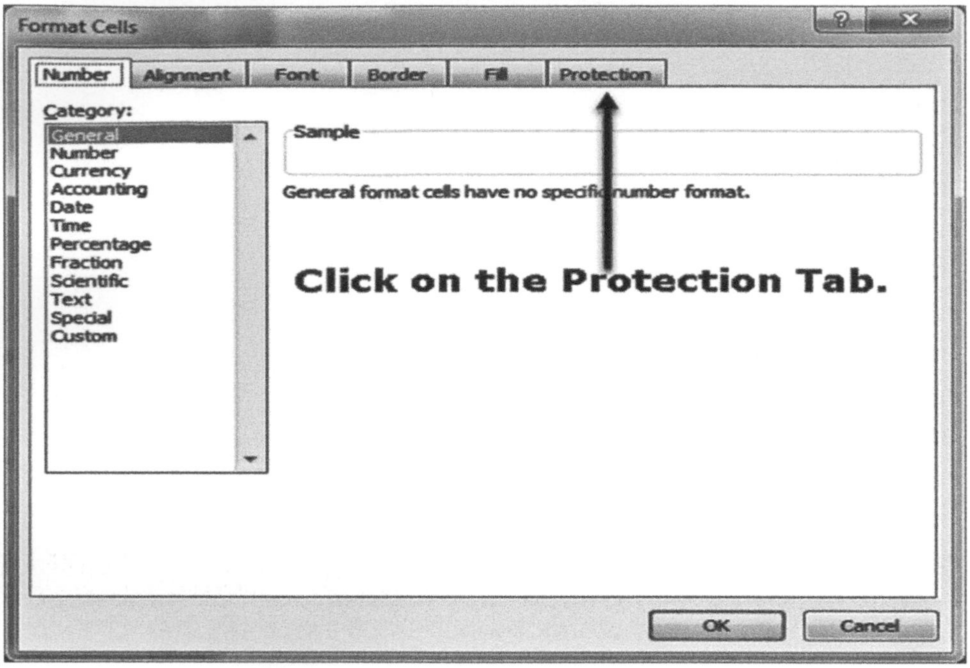

Figure 8.24 Selecting the Protection tab

Step 3: Once all of the cells in the worksheet have been formatted as locked (see Figure 8.25), you must now unlock only those cells that you want the user to have access to. Generally, these are the input cells where you want the user to input data.

To do this, select an individual cell or a range of cells that you want to permit the user access. Then, format these cells as unlocked by right clicking the mouse or selecting the Home tab's Number Group, Format Cells menu, and Protection tab. Because all of the cells were locked in Step 2, you will find a check mark in the Locked box option for the cell or range of cells that you highlighted in your spreadsheet. De-select this format by clicking on the box, so that it appears as shown in Figure 8.26. Doing this unlocks these cells.

Repeat Step 3 for every cell or range of cells that you want the user to access. When this process is complete, proceed to Step 4 to activate all of the locks that remain from Step 2.

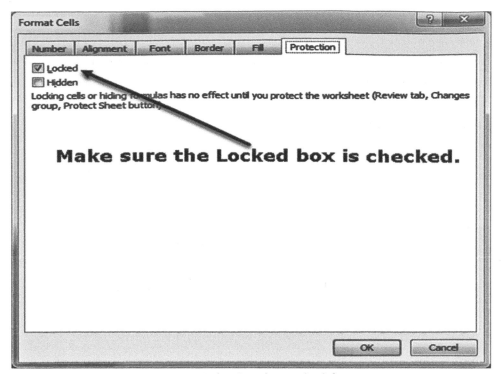

Figure 8.25 Selecting the Locked format

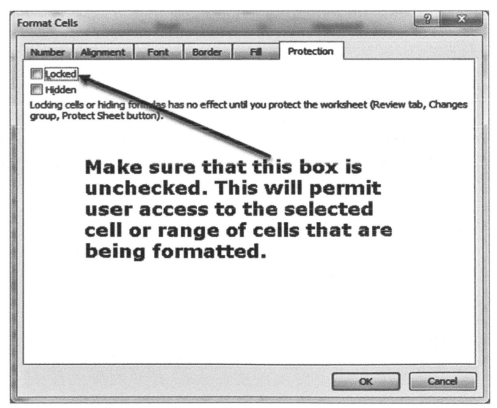

Figure 8.26 Unlocking the selected cell or range of cells

Step 4: To activate all of the locks that have been put in place and leave access open only to those cells that have been formatted as unlocked, click on the Review Tab and check the Protect Sheet Option, as shown in Figure 8.27. You will be asked to supply a password, and then reconfirm this password. If you do not supply a password, any user can use the Review tab's Protect Sheet option to unprotect the sheet by toggling the option shown in Figure 8.21b. If you do supply a password, make sure to secure it in a safe place, as there is no method of retrieving it if it is lost.

Figure 8.27 Activating all of the cell locks

NOTE

1. *The same procedure used to lock or unlock a cell can be used to hide the formula in a cell. That is, by clicking the hidden option in the Protection dialog, formulas in cells designated as hidden will not appear when using the Ctrl and (`) shortcut keys. This can be set up using the Excel ribbon Home Tab, Number Group, Format Cells menu, Protection, and checking the box for the "Hidden" cell format.*
2. *To undo any of the locks you have put in place, or to lock additional cells, you first have to set the status of the complete worksheet to an unprotected state (Step 1). If you have used a password in Step 4, you will be asked to entire this password before being allowed to unprotect the spreadsheet.*

Procedure 2

The only difference in procedure 2, as opposed to procedure 1, is that in procedure 2 every cell in the worksheet is first formatted as unlocked. Then, in Step 3, the formats of those cells that you **do not want** the user to have access to are formatted as locked. Steps 1 and 4 remain the same.

No matter which procedure you select to restrict user access to cells within your spreadsheet, the combination of individually formatting a cell as locked or not, along with the protection status of the spreadsheet as a whole remains the same. The effects of the various combinations are summarized in Table 8.1.

Table 8.1 Effect of spreadsheet protection status and individual cell protection formats

Entire Spreadsheet Status	Individual Cell Format	Result
Unprotected	Locked or Unlocked	Data can be entered, changed, or formatted in *every* worksheet cell.
Protected	Locked	Data cannot be entered, changed, or formatted in the locked cell.
Protected	Unlocked	Data can be entered or changed, but not formatted in the unlocked cell. This prevents a user from locking the cell.

CHARACTER CODE STORAGE

Prior to 1987, the ASCII (American Standard Code for Information Interchange) code was used to store characters. This code was limited to representing 256 unique English language characters. To accommodate international applications using non-English character sets, Unicode was introduced in 1987. This code is now universally used and can represent 65,536 unique character codes. The first 256 Unicodes have the same numerical values as the original 256 ASCII codes. TableA.1 lists the numeric code values and their corresponding characters.

An individual character's Unicode can be seen using Table A.1 last listed Unicode function. Thus, the formula =UNICODE("A") returns the number 65. Correspondingly, the formula =CHAR(65) and =UNICHAR(65) both return the letter A.

Table A.1 ASCII and first 128 UNICODE Codes

Code	Key	Code	Key	Code	Key	Code	Key
0	Ctrl 1	32	Space	64	@	96	'
1	Ctrl A	33	!	65	A	97	a
2	Ctrl B	34	"	66	B	98	b
3	Ctrl C	35	#	67	C	99	c
4	Ctrl D	36	$	68	D	100	d
5	Ctrl E	37	%	69	E	101	e
6	Ctrl F	38	&	70	F	102	f
7	Ctrl G	39		71	G	103	g
8	Ctrl H	40	(	72	H	104	h
9	Ctrl I	41	)	73	I	105	i
10	Ctrl J	42	*	74	J	106	j
11	Ctrl K	43	+	75	K	107	k
12	Ctrl L	44	,	76	L	108	l
13	Ctrl M	45	-	77	M	109	m
14	Ctrl N	46	.	78	N	110	n
15	Ctrl O	47	/	79	O	111	o
16	Ctrl P	48	0	80	P	112	p
17	Ctrl Q	49	1	81	Q	113	q
18	Ctrl R	50	2	82	R	114	r
19	Ctrl S	51	3	83	S	115	s
20	Ctrl T	52	4	84	T	116	t
21	Ctrl U	53	5	85	U	117	u
22	Ctrl V	54	6	86	V	118	v
23	Ctrl W	55	7	87	W	119	w
24	Ctrl X	56	8	88	X	120	x
25	Ctrl Y	57	9	89	Y	121	y
26	Ctrl Z	58	:	90	Z	122	z
27	Esc	59	;	91	[	123	{
28	Ctrl <	60	<	92	\	124		
29	Ctrl /	61	=	93	]	125	}
30	Ctrl =	62	>	94	^	126	~
31	Ctrl ~	63	?	95	_	127	Delete

INSTALLING THE ANALYSIS TOOLPAK

You will need the Analysis ToolPak to create histograms and perform more extensive statistical analyses than computing simple averages and standard deviations. Before attempting to install the package, however, first check that it is not already installed. This is done by seeing if the Data Analysis option, shown as item B in Figure B is present on the Excel ribbon Data tab, Analysis Group, Data Analysis option, shown as item A on the figure.

If the Data Analysis option is displayed, the Analysis ToolPak has already been installed; if not, the installation is begun by first clicking on the File menu option, shown as item 1 on Figure B.1.

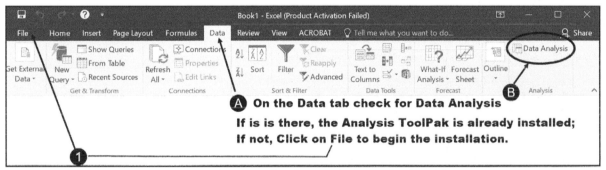

Figure B.1 Checking for the Analysis ToolPak Add-In

Clicking on the File menu option brings up the File submenu, shown in Figure B.2. Clicking on the options button, shown as item 2 in this figure brings up the first Excel Options dialog, which is shown in Figure B.3

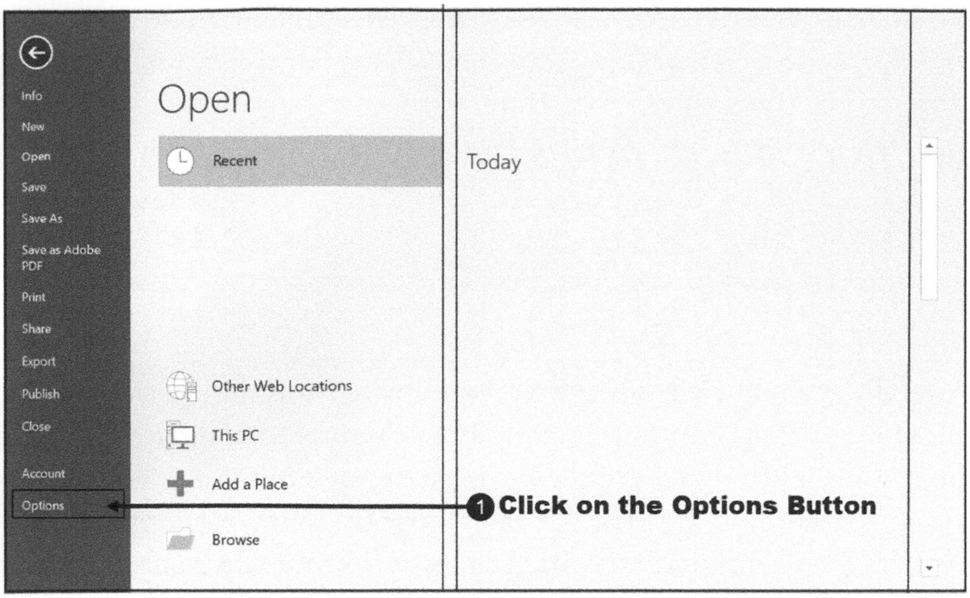

Figure B.2 Use File Options to Load an Add-In

Once the Excel Options dialog box is displayed (see Figure B.3), select the Add-Ins choice (item 3 and press the OK button (item 4). This will cause the next Excel Options dialog box, shown in Figure B.4, to appear.

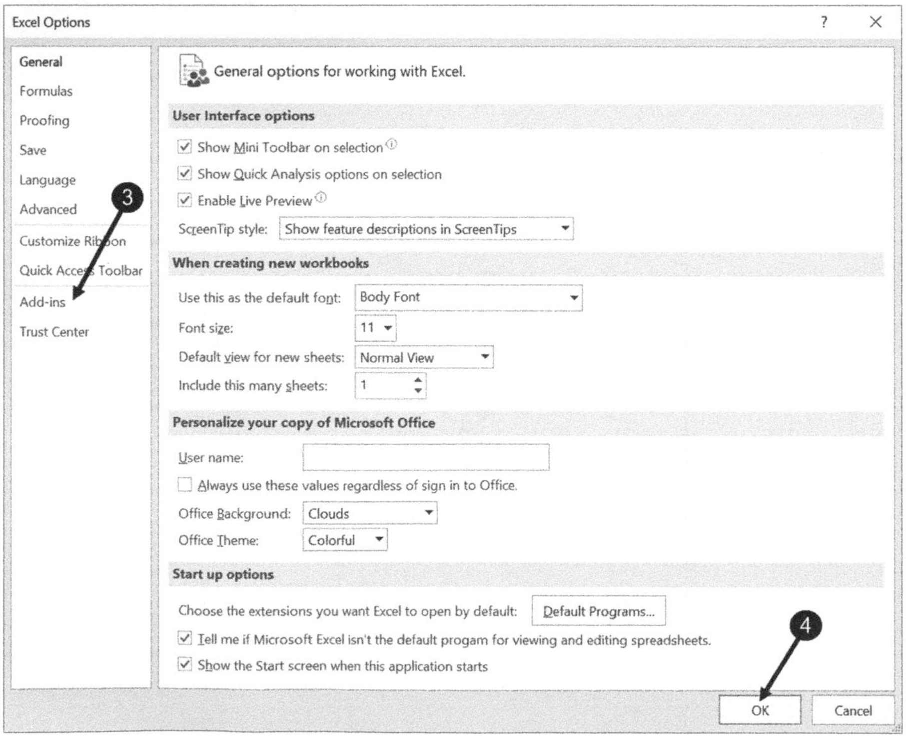

Figure B.3 The first Excel options dialog box

When the dialog shown as Figure B.4 is displayed, click on the Analysis ToolPak (item 5) and then press the Go button (item 6) as shown in the figure. This brings up the Add-ins dialog box shown in Figure B.5.

The final installation step is to check the Analysis ToolPak checkbox, shown as item 7 on Figure B.4, and then press the OK button (item 8). When this is completed, you should check that the installation has been completed by rechecking that the Data Analysis option is available, as shown in Figure B.1.

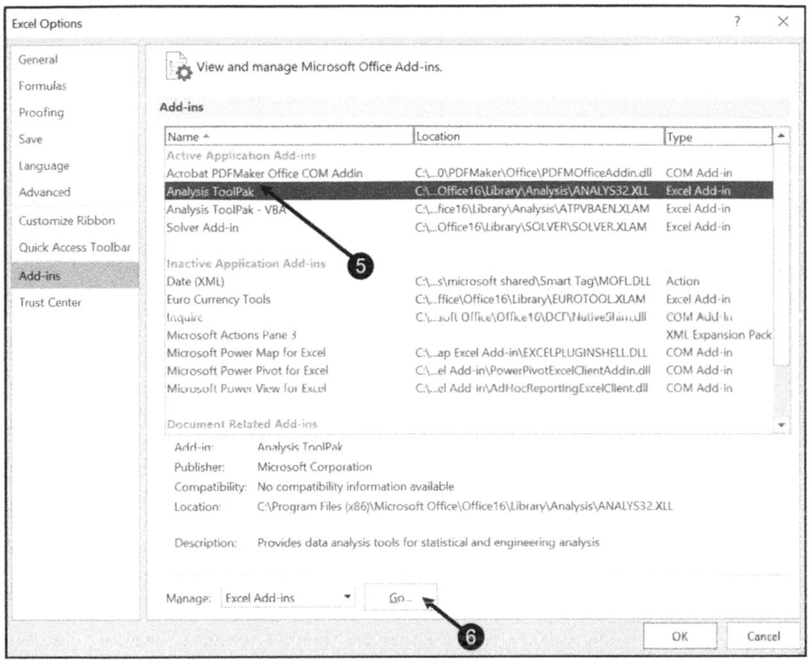

Figure B.4 The second Excel options dialog box

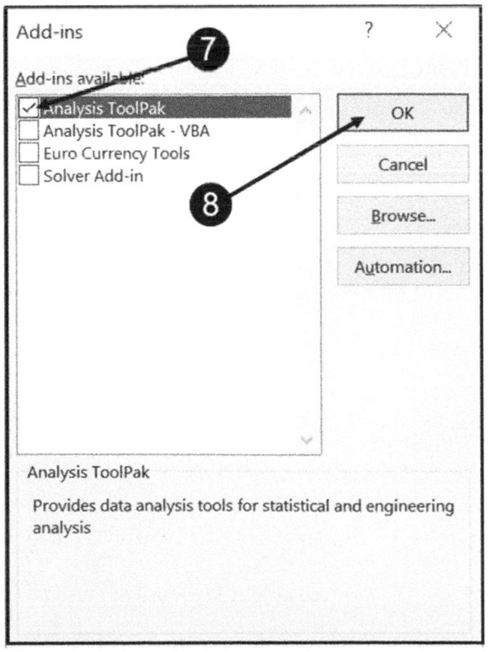

Figure B.5 The Excel Add-ins dialog box

INDEX